FRANCE

TRINIDAD

JAPAN

ITALY

MEXICO

AUSTRIA

GREECE

BRITAIN

GERMANY

CHILE

SOUTH AFRICA

INDIA

PERU

PAKISTAN

CHINA

BRAZIL

TURKEY

THAILAND

AUSTRALIA

D1529202

The
Embassy Cookbook

with drawings by Betty Fraser

The Embassy Cookbook

by Allison Williams

Little, Brown and Company · Boston · Toronto

COPYRIGHT © 1966 BY LITTLE, BROWN AND COMPANY (INC.)

ALL RIGHTS RESERVED. NO PART OF THIS BOOK MAY BE REPRO-
DUCED IN ANY FORM WITHOUT PERMISSION IN WRITING FROM THE
PUBLISHER, EXCEPT BY A REVIEWER WHO MAY QUOTE BRIEF PAS-
SAGES IN A REVIEW TO BE PRINTED IN A MAGAZINE OR NEWSPAPER.
LIBRARY OF CONGRESS CATALOG CARD NO. 66–21000

FIRST EDITION

Published simultaneously in Canada
by Little, Brown & Company (Canada) Limited

PRINTED IN THE UNITED STATES OF AMERICA

Introduction

THE embassies of foreign governments located in Washington are deservedly famous for their food. Most ambassadors, gourmets to a man, bring their own chefs along when appointed as their countries' representatives to the United States. These chefs are usually among the finest the particular country has. In some cases, however, the chef remains at the embassy even though a new ambassador replaces the former diplomat.

At formal dinners, in many cases, French cooking is served despite the nationality of the country, as France is considered to have the finest cuisine of the world. Great Britain, for example, has French menus, except for family dinners. Some countries mix their menus, serving some of their own national specialties and some French or international dishes. Service at state dinners is usually very elegant, but family meals are less formal.

Every menu in this book was actually provided by the particular embassy. Wines and liquors of the country are usually served at both formal and family dinners, except where none are produced, or where liquor is not the custom.

We are all more or less familiar with the Western-style menu, generally consisting of appetizer, soup, main course, vegetables, salad and dessert, but the multiple courses of the Orient are quite different. Course after course is served — perhaps in smaller quantities, but with greater variety.

Dining at an embassy is an experience very few people are privileged to enjoy, but *The Embassy Cookbook* makes it possible for you to re-create the dishes they serve and experience the great pleasures of dining upon the finest food specialties of the entire world.

Contents

The
Embassy Cookbook

Australia

THE front entrance to the Australian Embassy is in the Grecian style with tall imposing columns topped by a triangular pediment in the classical fashion. The embassy's exterior, although it makes some architectural compromises between authentic design and modern needs, comes off successfully. From a distance, the impression it gives is much like that of a plantation manor in the Southern United States in antebellum days.

The entrance hall is cheery and homelike. The library is paneled in California redwood, lending a slightly country-style air; its walls

are decorated with paintings by modern Australian artists. The drawing room is well proportioned, gracefully decorated and furnished. On
the walls are more Australian modern paintings.

The embassy's dining room is bright and gay. Very light colors reminiscent of spring — yellow and pale green — create a fresh, young
atmosphere, much like that of Australia itself. The woodwork is finished in white, which sets off the colors very well. The country's
unique animal, the kangaroo, appears in several panels of a screen
which is placed in one corner of the dining room.

[3]

Australian Embassy

Consommé Julienne
DRY SHERRY

Lobster Mornay
RIESLING

Crown of Lamb Cutlets
with Creamed Potatoes
CABERNET OR CLARET

Green Peas

Strawberry Mousse
CHAMPAGNE

Fresh Fruits in Season

CONSOMMÉ JULIENNE

2 carrots	2 leeks, white part only
1 parsnip	1 white turnip
2 hearts of celery	2 quarts beef consommé

Cut the vegetables into matchlike strips 1 inch long. Bring 2 cups of the consommé to a boil, and cook each vegetable separately until tender, but still crisp. Serve the consommé very hot, in heated bouillon cups, with some mixed vegetables in each.

Serves 8.

LOBSTER MORNAY

4 1¼-pound live lobsters	½ cup dry white wine
2 teaspoons salt	1 teaspoon dry mustard
½ teaspoon white pepper	4 tablespoons flour
¼ pound butter	1 cup chicken broth
2 tablespoons olive oil	1 cup light cream
¼ cup chopped shallots or	¾ cup grated Swiss cheese
onions	¼ cup grated Parmesan cheese

Have the live lobsters split in half lengthwise, and the claws removed and cracked. Remove the black vein and green soft parts of the lobsters. Sprinkle the lobster halves with half the salt and pepper and dot with 2 tablespoons of the butter.

Put the olive oil in a shallow baking pan, and in it arrange the lobster halves and claws. Bake in a 425° oven 18 minutes.

Melt 2 tablespoons butter in a saucepan. Add the shallots and wine. Cook over high heat until liquid is reduced to about 3 tablespoons. Remove from the heat and blend in the mustard.

Melt the remaining butter in a saucepan; blend in the flour and the remaining salt and pepper. Add the broth and cream, stirring steadily to the boiling point, then cook over low heat for 5 minutes. Add the Swiss cheese, stirring until melted. Stir in the reduced wine mixture.

Remove the meat of the lobster bodies and claws and dice it. Add about ¾ of the sauce. Fill the lobster bodies with the mixture, and cover with the remaining sauce. Sprinkle with the Parmesan cheese. Place under a hot broiler until golden brown and glazed.

Serves 8.

CROWN OF LAMB CUTLETS

16 loin lamb chops, cut 1½ inches thick	Salt
16 slices bacon	Black pepper

Have the chops boned, rolled and wrapped in the bacon. Arrange the chops on a broiling pan and broil close to the source of heat 5 minutes on each side for medium, or to desired degree of rareness. Season with salt and pepper, and arrange the chops on a hot platter in the shape of a crown. Fill the center with creamed potatoes.

Serves 8.

CREAMED POTATOES

3 pounds medium-sized potatoes	¼ teaspoon white pepper
2 cups light cream	⅛ teaspoon nutmeg
1 teaspoon salt	2 tablespoons buttter
	2 tablespoons minced parsley

Wash the unpeeled potatoes and cook in boiling salted water about 18 minutes, or until tender but still firm. Drain, and when cool enough to handle, peel them and cut in ¼-inch slices.

Put the potatoes, cream, salt, pepper and nutmeg in a skillet. Cook over high heat until cream is reduced to half. Break the butter into small pieces and add to the potatoes, swirling it in gently. Taste for seasoning and sprinkle with the parsley.

Serves 8.

STRAWBERRY MOUSSE

1 quart strawberries	1 envelope (1 tablespoon)
½ cup sugar	gelatin
1½ cups water	3 egg whites
	1 cup heavy cream

Hull and wash the berries. Select 2 cups of the choicest ones and reserve them for garnishing.

Combine the sugar and 1 cup of the water in a saucepan. Bring to a boil, stirring until the sugar dissolves, then cook until a syrup is formed. Add the remaining 2 cups of the berries and cook over low heat until berries are soft. Force through a sieve and return to the saucepan.

Soften the gelatin in the remaining water, then stir it into the strawberry purée until dissolved. Cool. Beat the egg whites until stiff but not dry. Fold into the strawberry purée. Whip the cream until it begins to hold its shape and fold it into the previous mixture. Turn into a 1½-quart mold and chill for 4 hours, or until set. Garnish with the reserved berries, and whipped cream if desired.

Serves 8.

Austria

UNLIKE the vast majority of foreign embassies, that of Austria is not located in the District of Columbia. Instead, the Austrians have chosen the former Ourisman estate, handsomely situated on a lovely tract of land in Maryland which is a short ride from downtown Washington. The embassy building itself, quite modern in design, is hidden from the road by a wooded area and reached by a long driveway.

However contemporary the exterior may be, the embassy's interior is that of the Old World. Although rooms have picture windows in the American suburban manner, the decor is Viennese, with richly colored, handwoven tapestries, deep-piled rugs, elaborate furniture and oil

paintings of the European school. The drawing room is very pleasing in appearance, and although the lines of the room are clean-cut and modern, the furnishings are stylized Viennese, and the contrast is refreshing to the eye. The dining room, in the classic European style, is the scene of numerous formal dinners during the course of a year. When the weather is fine, the Ambassador prefers to serve his guests at small tables in the garden. When the weather is not cooperative, and large numbers of guests are expected, small tables are placed throughout the embassy, including the drawing and reception rooms, and some are even placed on the staircase or in other open areas.

Austrian Embassy

FORMAL MENU

Balkanische Chlodnik
Paprikahühnchen
Butternudeln
GUMPOLDSKIRCHNER

Grüner Salat

Schneeballen   Coffee
mit
Himbeersauce

INFORMAL MENU

Polnischer Blumenkohl
Erbsensuppe
Polnischer Karpfen
Kartoffel in der Schale
Krautsalad
Rigo Torte   Coffee

BALKANISCHE CHLODNIK
Cold Balkan Soup

8 large beets and leaves
6 cups water
1½ teaspoons salt
1½ pounds cooked cleaned
    shrimp
3 hard-cooked eggs, sieved

1 cucumber, peeled, seeded
    and chopped
¼ cup minced fresh dill
3 tablespoons chopped chives
1 lemon, thinly sliced
2 cups beer
4 cups sour cream

Wash and scrub the beets. Wash the leaves. Combine the beets, leaves, water and salt in a saucepan. Bring to a boil and cook over medium heat 45 minutes, or until tender. Drain the beets and leaves; reserve the beet water. Finely chop the beets and leaves and return to the beet water. Chop half the shrimp and add to the beets with the eggs, cucumber, dill, chives and lemon. Mix the beer very slowly into the sour cream to keep it smooth, then stir into the soup. Taste for seasoning, adding salt and pepper if necessary. Chill. Serve very cold, garnished with the whole shrimp and an ice cube in each plate.

Serves 10 to 12.

PAPRIKAHÜHNCHEN
Squab Chickens with Paprika Sauce

8 1-pound squab chickens
2 teaspoons salt
½ teaspoon pepper
8 slices bacon
1½ cups minced onions

2 tablespoons sweet Hungarian
    paprika
2 cups chicken stock
2 cups sour cream

Wash and clean the squabs, then dry. Rub the squabs with the salt and pepper. Chop, mash and reserve the livers.

Cover the bacon with water, bring to a boil and cook 3 minutes. Drain and dice. Put the bacon in a Dutch oven, skillet or casserole large enough to hold the birds. Cook until fat runs out, then mix in the onions and paprika. Add the birds and cook, turning them frequently with two spoons (to prevent pricking) until browned. Add the broth. Cover and cook over low heat 30 minutes, turning them a few times. Mix in the livers. Re-cover and cook 10 minutes longer, or until squabs are tender. Blend the sour cream into the pan juices, taste for seasoning and heat.

Arrange the birds in a circle on a round platter. Sprinkle with paprika. Heap noodles in the center, pour a little sauce around them, and serve the rest in a sauceboat.

Serves 8.

BUTTERNUDELN
Buttered Noodles

2 cups flour	¾ cup warm water (about)
1 egg, beaten	6 tablespoons hot melted butter
¼ teaspoon salt	

Sift the flour onto a board. Make a well in the center, and into it put the egg, salt and 2 tablespoons of the water. Mix the ingredients in the well, then work in the flour, gradually adding enough of the remaining water to make a workable dough. Knead until smooth and elastic. Cover the dough with a bowl and let stand 30 minutes.

Divide the dough into two pieces and roll out each piece as thin as possible. Let the rolled out dough dry for 1 hour, then cut into ½-inch-wide strips. Cook the noodles in a large quantity of boiling salted water for 10 minutes or until tender. Drain well, rinse under cold water, drain again and toss with the melted butter.

Serves 8 to 10.

SCHNEEBALLEN
Snow Balls

2½ cups flour
⅛ teaspoon salt
¼ pound butter
1 whole egg

4 egg yolks
½ cup white wine
Vegetable oil for deep frying
Vanilla sugar

Sift the flour and salt into a bowl. Cut in the butter until the mixture looks like cornmeal. Make a well in the center. Beat together the egg, egg yolks and wine; pour into the well. Work the ingredients into a smooth dough, cover with a cloth, and let stand in a cool place for 1 hour.

Roll out the dough less than ⅛ inch thick and cut into rectangles 4 by 5 inches. With a pastry wheel, make six parallel cuts lengthwise through each piece of dough, separating and opening the strips. Form each rectangle loosely into a ball and place in a strainer large enough to hold it.

Heat deep-frying oil to 370° and lower the strainer into it. Fry balls until golden. Drain on paper towels and let cool. Continue frying one ball at a time. Sprinkle with vanilla sugar and serve with raspberry sauce. To make the vanilla sugar, put a vanilla bean in fine granulated sugar in a tightly closed jar and let stand 24 hours or longer.

Makes about 20 balls.

HIMBEERSAUCE
Raspberry Sauce

1 quart raspberries
¾ cup red currants

2½ cups water
Sugar

Combine the raspberries, currants and water in a saucepan. Bring to a boil, stirring constantly, then cook over low heat until the fruit is completely disintegrated. Pour into a jelly bag and let the juice drip for 12 hours.

Measure the juice, and for each cup, add 1 cup sugar. Bring to a boil, stirring until sugar dissolves, then cook until clear and syrupy. Pour into a jar, cover tightly and refrigerate until needed.

POLNISCHER BLUMENKOHL
Cauliflower Polonaise

1 large cauliflower	½ cup fresh toasted fine bread
½ pound cooked ham, cut into	crumbs
julienne strips	¼ cup chopped parsley
2 teaspoons lemon juice	¼ cup hot browned melted
1 hard-cooked egg	butter
	2 teaspoons grated lemon rind

Remove the leaves of the cauliflower and wash the cauliflower carefully. Cook over low heat in boiling salted water to cover for 15 minutes, or until barely tender. Drain well and place in a buttered casserole or baking dish just large enough to hold it. Sprinkle with the ham and lemon juice. Cover and bake in a 350° oven 10 minutes.

Put the white and yolk of the egg through a sieve separately. Stir together the egg white, bread crumbs and parsley. Spread gently over the cauliflower, then slowly pour the butter over all. Sprinkle with the sieved yolk and lemon rind.

Serves 8 to 10.

ERBSENSUPPE
Cream of Green Pea Soup

4 pounds green peas, shelled, or	½ cup sliced onion
3 packages, frozen	1 cup shredded lettuce
2 cups water	2 sprigs parsley
4 tablespoons butter	2 egg yolks
4 tablespoons flour	1 cup light cream
6 cups chicken broth	

Cook the peas in the 2 cups water for 25 minutes. Drain, reserving ½ cup water.

Melt the butter in a large saucepan; blend in the flour until golden. Add the reserved water and chicken broth, stirring steadily to the boiling point. Add the onion, lettuce and parsley. Cook over low heat 20 minutes. Purée the soup and peas in an electric blender or force through a sieve.

Beat the egg yolks and cream; gradually add a little hot soup, stirring steadily to prevent curdling. Stir into all the soup, taste for seasoning and heat, but do not let boil.

Serves 8 to 10.

POLNISCHER KARPFEN
Carp in Sweet-Sour Sauce

1 5 to 6 pound carp	3 slices lemon
3 teaspoons salt	3 sprigs parsley
1 cup rye bread crumbs	½ teapoon thyme
1 cup chopped mushrooms	3 peppercorns
3 tablespoons chopped parsley	¼ cup sugar
1½ cups chopped onions	2 tablespoons vinegar
¼ pound butter	¼ cup sliced blanched almonds
½ teaspoon black pepper	2 tablespoons slivered orange
½ cup chopped shallots	rind
6 cups dry red wine	1 tablespoon slivered lemon
1 cup bottled clam juice	rind
½ cup gingersnap crumbs	Paprika
1 bay leaf	6 green onions, sliced (white
3 slices orange	part only)

Have the carp split for stuffing. (If carp is not available, sea bass, blue fish or similar fish can be substituted.) Rinse and dry the fish and rub with 2 teaspoons salt.

Mix together the bread crumbs, chopped mushrooms, chopped parsley and ½ cup of the onions. Melt the butter until it browns and blend in with the pepper. Stuff the fish and sew or skewer the opening.

In a roasting pan or skillet large enough to hold the fish, make a bed of the remaining onions and the shallots. Lay the fish over it and add the wine, clam juice, crumbs, bay leaf, orange and lemon slices, parsley sprigs, thyme, peppercorns and remaining salt. Cover the pan and bake in a 350° oven 1 hour, or until the fish flakes easily when tested with a fork. Carefully transfer fish to a serving dish and keep hot.

Strain the sauce into a saucepan and cook over high heat until reduced to 2 cups. Cook the sugar and vinegar until light brown and add to the sauce with the almonds and the orange and lemon rind. Sprinkle the fish with paprika and pour the sauce around it. Sprinkle the sauce with sliced green onions. Garnish the fish with sliced oranges and lemons, if desired.

Serves 8 to 10.

KARTOFFEL IN DER SCHALE
Glazed New Potatoes

3 pounds small new potatoes	½ teaspoon white pepper
¼ pound butter	3 tablespoons sugar
¾ cup minced onions	2 tablespoons minced chives
1½ teaspoons salt	

Buy potatoes of uniform size. Wash the unpeeled potatoes and cook over low heat in boiling salted water for 15 minutes, or until just tender. Drain well.

Melt the butter in a skillet; sauté the onions until golden. Add the potatoes, salt, pepper and sugar. Cook, shaking the pan frequently, until the sugar browns and the potatoes are glossy and glazed. Serve sprinkled with the chives.

Serves 8 to 10.

KRAUTSALAD
Cabbage Salad

6 cups shredded cabbage	1 teaspoon salt
1 cup mayonnaise	¼ teaspoon white pepper
3 tablespoons ketchup	2 tablespoons grated fresh
1 orange	horseradish (optional)
½ cup chopped walnuts	

Soak the shredded cabbage in ice water for 2 hours. Drain well and dry in a towel. Mix together the mayonnaise and ketchup. Toss with the cabbage.

Grate the orange rind. Separate the orange into sections, removing the pits and white membranes. Add the rind, sections, the walnuts, salt and pepper to the cabbage. Toss again. Sprinkle with the horse-radish.

Serves 8 to 10.

RIGO TORTE
Chocolate Torte

Pastry:

2⅔ cups flour	2 teaspoons grated lemon rind
½ cup sugar	½ pound butter
2 egg yolks	

Sift the flour onto a board. Make a well in the center and into it put the sugar, egg yolks and lemon rind; blend together the ingredients in the well. Cut the butter into small pieces and add to the well. Work in the flour, gradually but quickly, until a smooth dough is formed. Chill 4 hours, then roll out ¼ inch thick and fit on the bottom of a 10-inch springform pan. Prick the pastry in several places and bake in a preheated 375° oven 25 minutes or until delicately browned. Cool. Brush the exposed sides of the pan with oil.

Praline:

1 cup sugar	¾ cup toasted chopped filberts
1 tablespoon lemon juice	

Combine the sugar and lemon juice in a heavy skillet. Cook over low heat, stirring constantly with a wooden spoon until a dark gold color. Stir in the nuts and pour out onto a well-oiled pan. When cold and hard, break into pieces and pulverize in an electric blender or put through a nut grinder. Reserve.

Filling:

1 pound butter	1 teaspoon vanilla extract
2 cups sugar	1 teaspoon rum
1 pound semi-sweet chocolate, grated	1 cup toasted finely chopped filberts

Cream the butter, gradually beating in the sugar. Beat until light and fluffy, then beat in the chocolate, vanilla and rum. Spread over the baked pastry and chill until set. Mix the praline with the chopped filberts and spread over the chocolate filling.

Icing:

½ pound semi-sweet chocolate	2 teaspoons butter
1 cup strong-brewed coffee	

Break the chocolate into small pieces. Place over low heat until melted. Gradually stir in the coffee, then the butter. Cook, stirring steadily, until thickened and smooth, about 6 minutes. Cool 5 minutes, then very slowly pour evenly over the nut mixture. Chill until icing sets.

Serves 8 to 10.

Belgium

THE Belgian Embassy is situated in a house patterned after a renowned old structure, the Hôtel Mademoiselle de la Charolais, the original of which is just outside Paris. The charming house is located in a sweep of woods, and has a delightful, secluded atmosphere.

The entrance hall is paneled, somewhat elaborately. To the left is a large grand staircase with an ornately carved oak rail. The main drawing room is large and cheerful, decorated in light, pleasing colors; the upholstered furniture is covered with petit point. The room's furniture is arranged in several areas, permitting numerous conversational groups to gather when a large party is in progress.

The dining room is quite impressive in size and general appearance.

It is rectangular, with a fireplace at one end; a tremendous built-in buffet is positioned on the right-hand side. The walls are of a light-colored boiserie (paneled wainscoting), into which are placed a pair of antique French landscape paintings. At each end of the dining room, placed in an arched recess, a biscuit (unglazed pottery) shepherdess may be found. At formal dinners the table is laid with exquisite individual mats, handwoven by the famed lacemakers of Bruges. Candelabra decorate the table and lend a soft, shimmering light. The flat silver is elaborate in design, and the crystal tableware has been produced by the finest Belgian glassmakers.

Ambassade de Belgique

DINNER MENU

La Crème d'Asperges
Les Anguilles au Vert
L'Oie à l'Instar de Visé
La Glace aux Fraises

LUNCHEON MENU

Les Chicorées au Jambon Gratinées
Le Rognon de Veau à la Liégeoise
Le Fromage
La Dame Blanche

LA CRÈME D'ASPERGES
Cream of Asparagus Soup

1½ pounds asparagus	1 cup light cream
1½ quarts chicken broth	3 tablespoons minced parsley
3 egg yolks	

If possible, buy white asparagus, the type used in Belgium. If only the green type is available, peel off the outer green portions. Cut off about 16 tips and reserve. Cut the remaining asparagus into small pieces and combine with the broth. Bring to a boil and cook over low heat 30 minutes. Purée in an electric blender, then strain, or force through a sieve. Cook the asparagus tips 10 minutes, then drain.

Beat the egg yolks in a bowl; mix in the cream. Gradually add the hot soup, stirring steadily to prevent curdling. Return to the saucepan. Taste for seasoning. Sprinkle with parsley. Heat, but do not let boil.
Serves 6 to 8.

LES ANGUILLES AU VERT
Eels in Green Sauce

3 pounds small eels	⅛ teaspoon tarragon
2 teaspoons salt	⅛ teaspoon sage
½ teaspoon black pepper	⅛ teaspoon chervil
6 tablespoons butter	2 shallots, chopped
1 cup finely chopped sorrel	1½ cup dry white wine
1 cup finely chopped spinach	3 egg yolks
¼ cup chopped parsley	¼ teaspoon lemon juice

Have the skin removed and the eels cleaned. Wash, dry and cut crosswise into 2-inch pieces. Season with the salt and pepper.

Melt the butter in a skillet; lightly brown the eels in it. Add the sorrel, spinach, parsley, tarragon, sage, chervil, shallots and wine. Bring to a boil and cook over low heat 10 minutes.

Beat the egg yolks and lemon juice in a bowl. Gradually beat in the liquid from the skillet. Return to skillet and cook, stirring gently until thickened, but do not let boil. Taste for seasoning. Serve hot or cold.

Serves 8 to 10.

L'OIE A L'INSTAR DE VISÉ
Goose in Garlic Sauce

10-pound goose, disjointed	6 tablespoons flour
1½ teaspoons salt	3 egg yolks
½ teaspoon white pepper	¼ cup cream
1½ quarts chicken broth	1 tablespoon minced mashed
2 cloves garlic, sliced	garlic

Wash the goose and remove as much fat as possible. Rub with the salt and pepper. Combine the goose, broth and sliced garlic in a saucepan. Bring to a boil and cook over medium heat 1¼ hours. Drain the goose well and put in a Dutch oven. Skim the fat from the broth and pour about 6 tablespoons of it over the goose pieces. If there isn't enough, dice the fat previously removed from the goose and add it. Cover the pan and cook the goose until browned, turning the pieces frequently.

Heat or melt 6 tablespoons goose fat in a saucepan. Blend in the flour, then add 3 cups of the broth, stirring steadily to the boiling point. Cook over low heat 10 minutes. Beat the egg yolks in a bowl, gradually add the hot broth, stirring steadily to prevent curdling. Return to the saucepan and cook over low heat, stirring constantly until thickened, but do not let boil. Strain into another pan, stir in the cream and garlic. Drain the goose pieces and add to the sauce. Serve with braised celery and fried potatoes.

Serves 6 to 8.

LA GLACE AUX FRAISES
Ice Cream with Strawberries

1 quart strawberries	1½ quarts vanilla ice cream
¾ cup Grand Marnier or orange liqueur	

Wash and hull the berries. Drain and dry. Pour the liqueur over the berries and chill for 1 hour.

Divide the ice cream among individual serving dishes and arrange the berries around and over them.

Serves 6 to 8.

LES CHICORÉES AU JAMBON GRATINÉES
Endive with Cheese

24 endive	2 cups milk
3 tablespoons lemon juice	⅛ teaspoon white pepper
⅓ cup water	24 thin slices cooked ham
1⅛ teaspoons salt	1 cup grated Gruyère or Swiss cheese
4 tablespoons butter	
4 tablespoons flour	

Wash the endive, cut off the tips of the stem ends and any brown leaves. Combine in a large skillet with the lemon juice, water and ⅛ teaspoon of the salt. Bring to a boil, cover and cook 15 minutes. Drain, cool and press out all the water.

Melt the butter in a saucepan; blend in the flour. Add the milk, stirring steadily to the boiling point. Add the pepper and remaining salt. Cook over low heat 10 minutes.

Wrap each endive in a slice of ham and arrange side by side in a buttered baking dish. Pour the sauce over the ham-wrapped endive and sprinkle with cheese. Bake in a preheated 400° oven on the upper level 10 minutes. Serve hot.

Serves 6 to 8.

LE ROGNON DE VEAU À LA LIÉGEOISE
Braised Kidneys

8 veal kidneys	3 juniper berries, crushed
2 tablespoons butter	1 tablespoon meat glaze or
1 teaspoon salt	broth
¼ teaspoon black pepper	¼ cup warm gin

Wash the kidneys very well, cut out the cores and trim, leaving only a thin layer of fat around them.

Melt the butter in a skillet. Add the kidneys, salt and pepper. Cook over low heat 10 minutes, turning the kidneys frequently to brown all sides. Add the juniper berries and meat glaze or broth. Set the gin aflame and pour over the kidneys. Serve with parsley potatoes and peas.

Serves 6 to 8.

LA DAME BLANCHE
Vanilla Ice Cream with Chocolate Sauce

4 squares (ounces) unsweet-	2 tablespoons white corn syrup
ened chocolate	Dash salt
2 tablespoons butter	¾ cup light cream
½ cup sugar	1½ quarts vanilla ice cream

Break the chocolate into small pieces and combine in the top of a double boiler with the butter. Place over hot water until melted and smooth. Blend in the sugar, corn syrup and salt until smooth, then gradually add the cream, stirring steadily. Cook, stirring very frequently, for 10 minutes.

Put scoops of ice cream in glass dishes or sherbet glasses and pour the hot sauce over them.

Serves 6 to 8.

Brazil

THE Embassy of Brazil was once a notable private home; the architect was John Russell Pope, who was also the designer of the National Gallery of Art in Washington. The house, built of Indiana limestone, is generally in the Italian Renaissance style.

The entrance hall has interesting antiques; there is a pair of carved rosewood altar rails of the Brazilian Colonial period from Bahia, also two old rosewood chests which came from the vestry of a church in Paracatu. To the left of the entrance hall, there is the Rugandas Room, the dining room, which has a wall decorated with hand-printed paper depicting Brazilian life of several centuries ago, albeit somewhat fanci-

fully. The china service is mostly Minton, the glassware is Baccarat, and the flatware is English silver, of the King's Pattern, made by Mappin & Webb.

Of special interest is the embassy's ballroom on the second floor. It has a remarkable silver candelabrum, a massive seven-light antique of the Portuguese rococo period, usually kept upon the piano. When the room is not in use as a ballroom, a magnificent Aubusson rug is placed upon the floor. Adjacent to it, there is the so-called Middle Room, used for receptions, which is an excellent example of Empire design.

Brazilian Embassy

FORMAL MENU

Soupe à l'Oignon
Darne de Saumon Grillée au Sauce Béarnaise
Pigeons Rôtis au Sauce Périgueux
Riz Sauvage
Salada de Palmito
Mousse au Grand Marnier
Café

INFORMAL MENU

Sopa de Abobora
Frango ao Môlho Pardo
Arroz   Angú de Milho
Pudim de Côco

SOUPE À L'OIGNON
Onion Soup

2½ pounds yellow onions	3 quarts boiling beef broth
4 tablespoons butter	¾ cup dry white wine
1 tablespoon vegetable oil	Dried French bread rounds
½ teaspoon sugar	Grated Parmesan or Swiss
2 teaspoons salt	cheese
4 tablespoons flour	

Peel the onions and slice very thin. Heat the butter and oil in a heavy saucepan. Add the onions, cover and cook over low heat 15 minutes, stirring occasionally. Sprinkle with the sugar and salt and cook uncovered until onions are brown; stir frequently. Stir in the flour for 3 minutes.

Remove from the heat and mix in the boiling broth, then the wine. Cover loosely, and cook over low heat 45 minutes. Taste for seasoning. Serve with a bread round in each bowl, and pass the cheese.

Serves 8 to 10.

DARNE DE SAUMON GRILLÉE AU SAUCE BÉARNAISE
Broiled Salmon with Béarnaise Sauce

Fish:

8 small salmon steaks	½ teaspoon black pepper
1½ teaspoons salt	½ cup melted butter

Sprinkle both sides of the salmon with salt and pepper and let stand 20 minutes.

Heat a broiling pan and brush heavily with melted butter. Arrange the steaks on the pan and brush with melted butter. Broil about 2 inches from the source of heat for 7 minutes, or until delicately browned. Turn over and pour the remaining butter over the salmon. Broil 7 minutes longer, or until fish flakes easily when tested with a fork. Arrange on a hot serving dish and garnish with parsley and lemon wedges. Pass the sauce separately.

Sauce:

2 teaspoons chopped fresh tarragon or ½ teaspoon dried	⅛ teaspoon salt
	¼ cup tarragon vinegar
	5 egg yolks
3 teaspoons chopped shallots or onions	¾ cup melted butter
	Dash cayenne pepper
2 teaspoons chopped fresh chervil or ½ teaspoon dried	1 teaspoon chopped fresh tarragon, chervil, chives or parsley
2 peppercorns	

Combine the tarragon, shallots, chervil, peppercorns, salt and vinegar in a saucepan. Cook over low heat until only about 1 tablespoon vinegar remains. Cool.

Beat the egg yolks with a whisk in a saucepan; strain the vinegar mixture into it. Place over low heat, and gradually beat in the butter. Beat with the whisk until thickened, but do not let sauce boil. Mix in the cayenne pepper and, if fresh herbs are available, the tarragon, chervil, chives or parsley, a teaspoon of any or a mixture.

Makes about 1 ½ cups.

PIGEONS RÔTIS AU SAUCE PÉRIGUEUX
Roast Squabs with Truffle Sauce

Pigeons:

8 pigeons or squabs, trussed	½ teaspoon tarragon
3 teaspoons salt	⅜ pound butter
½ teaspoon black pepper	8 strips bacon
4 tablespoons minced shallots or green onions	2 tablespoons olive oil

Wash the birds and season inside and out with the salt and pepper. Divide the shallots, tarragon and 4 tablespoons butter among the cavities of the birds. Turn and rub the outsides with butter, reserving

4 tablespoons. Cover the bacon with water, bring to a boil, and cook 10 minutes. Drain, rinse under cold water and dry. Cut the strips in half and place a piece on each breast and leg, running them under the trussing strings.

Heat the oil and the remaining butter in a shallow roasting pan. Arrange the birds in it. Roast in a preheated 400° oven 40 minutes, or until tender and browned. Baste and turn frequently. Remove the strings. Reserve 6 tablespoons of pan juices.

Sauce:

2 tablespoons vegetable oil	3 sprigs parsley
4 tablespoons butter	1 small bay leaf
3 tablespoons flour	¼ teaspoon thyme
4 cups boiling beef broth	¾ cup Madeira or port
1 tablespoon tomato paste	4 truffles, diced
½ cup dry red wine	

Heat the oil and 1 tablespoon butter in a saucepan. Blend in the flour, and cook, stirring steadily over low heat until browned. Remove from heat and stir in the broth. Return to low heat, stir in the reserved pan juices, the tomato paste and red wine. Add the parsley, bay leaf and thyme. Bring to a boil and cook over low heat 1½ hours. Taste for seasoning.

In a separate saucepan, cook the Madeira until reduced to half its original quantity. Strain the brown sauce into it. Bring to a boil and taste for seasoning. Mix in the remaining butter in small pieces, then the truffles.

Serves 8.

RIZ SAUVAGE
Wild Rice

2 cups wild rice	1½ cups boiling beef broth
4 teaspoons salt	1 teaspoon Worcestershire
6 cups boiling water	sauce
6 tablespoons butter	½ teaspoon black pepper
½ cup minced onions	

Wash the rice until the water runs clean. Add the salt to the boiling water, then add the rice. Cook over medium heat 10 minutes. Drain thoroughly.

While the rice is cooking, melt the butter in a casserole; sauté the onions 5 minutes. Stir in the rice until coated with the butter. Add the broth, Worcestershire sauce and pepper. Cover and bake in a 350° oven 25 minutes, or until rice is tender and liquid absorbed. Taste for seasoning and mix lightly with two forks.

Serves 8.

SALADA DE PALMITO
Heart of Palm Salad

Hearts of palm are available in cans in fine food shops. Arrange chilled hearts of palm on salad plates and pour over them a spicy French dressing. Garnish with pimientos and sieved hard-cooked egg yolks.

MOUSSE AU GRAND MARNIER
Mousse with Orange Liqueur

6 egg yolks	1½ cups light cream, scalded
⅛ teaspoon salt	½ cup Grand Marnier
1½ cups sugar	3 cups heavy cream, whipped
1¼ cups milk, scalded	

Beat the egg yolks and salt in the top of a double boiler until thickened. Gradually beat in the sugar, then very gradually add the scalded milk and cream, stirring steadily to prevent curdling. Place over hot, not boiling, water and cook, stirring constantly, until thick and mixture coats a metal spoon. Remove from heat and mix in the Grand

Marnier. Cool. Fold in the whipped cream and pour into a 2-quart mold or serving dish. Cover and chill, then freeze for 3 hours.

Serves 8 to 10.

⊶⊶

SOPA DE ABOBORA
Pumpkin Soup

3 tablespoons butter	1 teaspoon salt
½ cup minced onions	Dash cayenne pepper
4 cups cooked or canned	2 cups light cream
puréed pumpkin	Dash nutmeg
6 cups chicken broth	

Melt the butter in a saucepan; sauté the onions 5 minutes. Mix in the pumpkin, broth, salt and cayenne pepper. Bring to a boil and cook over low heat 30 minutes. Mix in the cream; heat and taste for seasoning. Sprinkle with nutmeg.

Serves 8 to 10.

⊶⊶

FRANGO AO MÔLHO PARDO
Chicken with Brown Gravy

2 4-pound roasting chickens, disjointed	1 bay leaf
¼ pound chicken livers	1 stalk celery and leaves chopped small
2½ teaspoons salt	2½ cups chicken broth
½ teaspoon black pepper	16 very small white onions
2 tablespoons olive oil	1 tablespoon flour
2 tablespoons butter	2 teaspoons Kitchen Bouquet
1 cup chopped onions	3 tablespoons water

Wash and dry the chicken pieces. Purée all the livers in an electric blender or chop to a paste. Refrigerate until needed. Season the chicken pieces with the salt and pepper.

Heat the oil and butter in a Dutch oven; brown the chicken in it very well. Add the chopped onions and let brown. Add the bay leaf, celery and broth. Cover and cook over low heat 1 hour. Add the white onions and cook 30 minutes longer.

Mix the flour, Kitchen Bouquet and water to a smooth paste. Stir into the gravy. Cook 5 minutes and taste for seasoning. Just before serving, stir the livers into the gravy. Heat, but do not let boil. Serve with rice and cornmeal mush.

Serves 8.

ANGÚ DE MILHO
Cornmeal Mush

2 tablespoons lard or butter	2 teaspoons salt
¾ cup chopped onions	5 cups water
¼ teaspoon minced garlic	2 cups yellow cornmeal
1 tablespoon chopped parsley	

Melt the lard or butter in a saucepan; sauté the onions, garlic and parsley 5 minutes. Add the salt and 3 cups of the water. Bring to a boil.

Mix the cornmeal with the remaining water and gradually stir into the boiling liquid. Keep stirring until mixture begins to thicken, then cook over low heat 25 minutes, or until thick and tender.

Serves 8 to 10.

PUDIM DE CÔCO
Coconut Pudding

2 cups milk	⅓ cup sugar
1½ cups flaked coconut	¼ teaspoon salt
6 egg yolks	1 cup light cream

Combine the milk and 1¼ cups coconut in a saucepan; bring to a boil and let stand 30 minutes. Run in an electric blender or strain, pressing through all the liquid.

Beat the egg yolks with the sugar and salt; stir in the cream and coconut milk. Strain into 8 custard cups. Place the cups in a pan. Add enough water to reach 2 inches up the cups. Bake in a preheated 375° oven 20 minutes. Quickly sprinkle the remaining coconut over the tops and bake 10 minutes longer, or until a knife inserted in the center comes out clean. Cool, then chill.

Serves 8.

Britain

THE British Embassy, executed on a grand scale, is surrounded by spacious, sloping gardens; there is an excellent view of Washington from much of the embassy.

The magnificence of the structure may be first noted at the great entrance doors. The entrance hall is extremely large, and flanked by two broad staircases which converge at the landing. The floor is covered with large squares of alternating black and white marble, lined with columns of bright yellow. The walls are decorated with a series of portraits of the various regents of England.

At a slightly higher level than the main hall, there is a very spacious

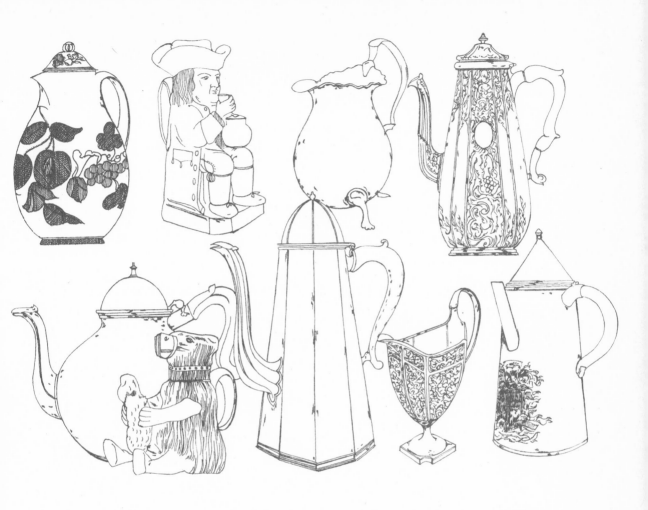

drawing room; when required, it also serves as a ballroom. The regular drawing room is in the southeast corner of the embassy building. It is a charming room, of very good proportions, with high ceilings, and has a fireplace as its focal point. The marble mantel is quite simple; over it hangs an exquisite Chinese painting. Flowers in profusion tend to make the room homelike in spite of its large size.

The dining room is quite attractive and very spacious, permitting large numbers of guests to be served at seated meals. Embassy dinners are served in an atmosphere of Old World formality combined with British hospitality.

British Embassy

FORMAL DINNER

Consommé Madrilène
Crabe au Vin Blanc
CHABLIS

Noix de Veau Braisée
Fonds d'Artichauts Farcis
Haricots Verts au Beurre
CHEVAL BLANC

Charlotte Russe Pralinée
Sauce Framboise
CHAMPAGNE

Le Café

Cognac

FORMAL LUNCHEON

Avocado Vinaigrette
Poulet Sauté au Citron
Courgettes Braisées
Pommes de Terre Noisette
Fromages, Biscuits et Salade
Cerises Jubilee
Le Café

CONSOMMÉ MADRILÈNE

3 pounds stewing beef, cut up
3 pounds cracked beef and veal
    bones
1 pound veal knuckle
5 quarts cold water
2 teaspoons salt
2 carrots
2 onions

2 stalks celery
1 bay leaf
2 cloves
¼ teaspoon thyme
2 egg whites
⅓ cup Madeira or port
1½ cups tomato sauce

Wash the meat, bones and knuckle and place in a large kettle with the cold water. Bring to a boil over medium heat, skimming the scum as it forms. Add the salt, carrots, onions, celery, bay leaf, cloves and thyme. Cook over low heat 5 hours, adding water if necessary to keep ingredients barely covered. Strain into a bowl, cool, chill and remove all the fat.

Beat 1 cup of the cold stock with the egg whites. Bring the remaining stock to a boil, add to the egg white mixture slowly, beating steadily. Return to saucepan and, mixing steadily with a wire whisk, bring to a boil. Remove from heat and let stand 15 minutes.

Line a colander with damp cheesecloth, and pour the stock through it. Mix in the wine and tomato sauce and chill until jellied. The soup may also be served hot.

Serves 8 to 10.

CRABE AU VIN BLANC
Crab Meat in Wine Sauce

1½ cups dry white wine
1 small bay leaf
3 tablespoons minced shallots
1 teaspoon salt
¼ teaspoon pepper
½ pound mushrooms, sliced

6 tablespoons butter
4 tablespoons flour
1 cup milk
2 egg yolks
½ cup heavy cream
1½ pounds lump crab meat

Bring the wine, bay leaf, shallots and half the salt and pepper to a boil; simmer 5 minutes. Add the mushrooms, simmer 5 minutes. Remove the mushrooms with a slotted spoon and set aside. Boil the liquid until reduced to 1 cup.

Melt 4 tablespoons butter in a saucepan; stir in the flour. Add the wine mixture, then the milk. Simmer and stir 5 minutes. Beat the egg yolks and cream in a bowl; gradually add a little hot sauce, stirring constantly. Return to balance of sauce and cook 1 minute, stirring. Add the remaining salt and pepper. Strain. Gently mix the crab meat and mushrooms into the sauce. Taste for seasoning. Spoon into 8 scallop shells or baking dishes. Dot with the remaining butter and bake on the upper level of a preheated 400° oven 10 minutes or until heated through and lightly browned on top.

Serves 8.

NOIX DE VEAU BRAISÉE
Braised Veal

5 pounds rump or veal	2 onions, chopped
4 slices bacon	½ cup chopped celery
½ teaspoon thyme	2 cups broth
¾ teaspoon pepper	2 cups dry white wine
2 tablespoons oil	2 teaspoons salt
6 tablespoons butter	1 bay leaf.
½ cup grated carrots	2 teaspoons arrowroot
2 tablespoons chopped parsley	

Have the veal tied into a nice firm shape. Pour boiling water over the bacon and simmer 10 minutes. Drain and dry. Cut each slice of bacon into 4 long strips. Season the strips with the thyme and ½ teaspoon pepper. With a larding needle pull the strips through the meat.

Heat the oil and 4 tablespoons butter in a Dutch oven. Add the carrots, parsley, onions and celery. Cover and simmer 10 minutes. Add the veal and brown lightly on all sides. Add the broth, wine, salt, bay leaf and remaining pepper. Bring to a boil and simmer 3 hours, or until the veal is tender.

Transfer the veal to a hot serving platter and keep warm. Strain the gravy, pressing through the vegetables. Mix arrowroot to a paste with a little water and stir into gravy over low heat, then swirl in the remaining butter. Carve the veal and serve the gravy in a sauceboat.

Serves 8 to 10.

◦⟨⟩◦

FONDS D'ARTICHAUTS FARCIS
Stuffed Artichoke Hearts

8 cooked or canned artichoke hearts	¼ cup minced onions
1½ teaspoons salt	¼ cup minced celery
½ teapoon pepper	¼ cup minced carrots
6 tablespoons butter	1 cup chopped mushrooms

Scoop out the choke (prickly center) of the artichoke hearts and sprinkle the hearts with half the salt and pepper. Melt half the butter in a casserole. Add the artichokes and simmer 5 minutes, basting frequently.

Melt the remaining butter in a skillet; sauté the onions, celery, carrots and mushrooms 8 minutes. Season with the remaining salt and pepper. Stuff the hearts. Cover with a piece of buttered waxed paper and bake in a preheated 325° oven 20 minutes.

Serves 8.

◦⟨⟩◦

HARICOTS VERTS AU BEURRE
Green Beans in Butter

2 pounds green beans	2 tablespoons chopped parsley
5 tablespoons butter	

Prepare the beans. Cut them lengthwise in strips, French-style, or, if they are small, they may be left whole. Cook in boiling salted water until the beans are tender but still crisp. Drain well.

Melt the butter in a skillet; add the beans, parsley and salt and pepper to taste. Cook over low heat 3 minutes tossing all the while. *Serves 8.*

CHARLOTTE RUSSE PRALINÉE

Praline:

¾ cup sugar	½ cup sliced blanched almonds
¼ cup water	¼ cup chopped blanched hazel
¼ teaspoon cream of tartar	nuts

Bring the sugar, water and cream of tartar to a boil, stirring until the sugar dissolves. Add the nuts and simmer without stirring until the syrup turns a rich dark brown. Pour into a buttered shallow pan and cool until it turns brittle. Crush fine in a mortar with pestle or put a little at a time in an electric blender.

Charlotte Russe:

24 ladyfingers	1 envelope (1 tablespoon)
¼ cup sugar	gelatin
4 egg yolks	½ cup cold water
2 cups hot milk	Praline
	2 cups heavy cream, whipped

Separate the ladyfingers into halves. Cut a round out of one and place in the center of the bottom of a buttered charlotte mold or other 1½-quart round dish, then cover the bottom, arranging the fingers like spokes. Now cover the sides with the ladyfingers in an upright position. Chill while preparing the cream.

Beat the sugar and egg yolks in a saucepan; gradually add the milk, stirring. Cook, stirring all the while, until thickened. Soften the gelatin in the water, then stir into the hot milk until dissolved. Cool. Stir in the praline, then fold in the whipped cream. Slowly pour into the lined mold. Chill until firm, then unmold carefully onto a serving dish. Serve with raspberry sauce.

Serves 8 to 10.

◐⟨⟩◑

AVOCADO VINAIGRETTE
Avocado with Herb Sauce

⅔ cup olive oil
3 tablespoons wine vinegar
¼ teaspoon salt
¼ teaspoon pepper
½ teaspoon dry mustard

⅛ teaspoon basil
⅛ teaspoon tarragon
1 tablespoon minced parsley
3 avocados

Combine all the ingredients but the avocados in a jar or blender bowl. Shake or blend until thoroughly mixed.

Cut the avocados in half lengthwise and remove the pits. Prick each half in several places with a fork, and put some sauce in each half. (The avocados may also be peeled and sliced and served with the sauce poured over the slices.) Arrange on plates, surrounded with shredded lettuce.

Serves 6.

◐⟨⟩◑

POULET SAUTÉ AU CITRON
Chicken in Lemon Sauce

2 3½-pound pullets, disjointed
2 teaspoons salt
½ teaspoon pepper
2 tablespoons olive oil
6 tablespoons butter

¼ cup dry white wine
3 shallots, chopped
1 tablespoon chopped parsley
2 tablespoons lemon juice
Lemon wedges

Wash and dry the chicken pieces; season with the salt and pepper.

Heat the oil and 3 tablespoons of the butter in a large skillet. Place the chicken pieces in it in a single layer and brown on all sides. Cover and cook over low heat until tender, about 45 minutes. Arrange the chicken on a hot serving platter and keep warm.

To the pan juices, add the wine, shallots and parsley. Bring to a boil, scraping the bottom of browned particles. Remove from the heat and stir in the remaining butter until melted, then the lemon juice. Pour over the chicken and garnish with the lemon wedges.

Serves 6 to 8.

COURGETTES BRAISÉES
Braised Zucchini

3 pounds zucchini	3 tablespoons butter
2 teaspoons salt	½ cup broth
⅓ cup flour	¼ teaspoon pepper
3 tablespoons olive oil	

Scrub the zucchini with a vegetable brush, wash and dry. Slice the zucchini thin, then sprinkle with the salt and let stand 30 minutes, mixing a few times. Drain well and dry on paper towels. Toss the slices in the flour.

Heat the oil and butter in a large skillet. Lightly brown the zucchini in it. Add the broth and pepper; cover and simmer 15 minutes, or until tender but still crisp.

Serves 6 to 8.

POMMES DE TERRE NOISETTE
Sautéed Potato Balls

3 pounds potatoes	1 teaspoon salt
3 tablespoons oil	1 tablespoon minced parsley
6 tablespoons butter	

Peel and wash the potatoes. With the small end of a melon ball cutter, scoop out balls.

Heat the oil and half the butter in a skillet until the foam dies. Add the potato balls and cook over medium heat until light gold in color, shaking the pan frequently. Add the salt, cover and cook over low heat 10 minutes, or until tender, shaking the pan a few times. Add the parsley and remaining butter, shaking the pan until butter melts.

Serves 6 to 8.

CERISES JUBILEE
Cherries in Flaming Sauce

2 pounds Bing cherries (see note)	1 cup sugar
1½ cups water	2 teaspoons cornstarch
	½ cup kirsch (cherry liqueur)

Wash, stem and pit the cherries. Cook the water and sugar until syrupy. Add the cherries; simmer until tender but still firm. Drain the cherries and divide among silver or heat-proof glass serving dishes. Cook the syrup over high heat 5 minutes. Mix the cornstarch with a little cold water and add to the syrup, cooking and stirring until thickened. Spoon over the cherries, pour a little kirsch over each serving and set aflame at the moment of serving.

Serves 6 to 8.

NOTE: Two large cans of Bing cherries may be used when cherries are out of season. Heat the cherries in their juice, drain and divide among the dishes. Then proceed as above to thicken.

Canada

IN 1947 the Canadian government purchased a Georgian structure, designed by architect Nathan Wyeth, for its embassy. The house is constructed principally of red brick, and has a pleasing entrance doorway flanked by Ionic columns.

The main entrance hall is graceful in proportions, and has a winding staircase leading to the second floor. On the left-hand side there is a dining room reached through double doors. The mahogany Chippendale table seats sixteen, but can accommodate twenty-two if necessary. The chairs are covered with a rust-colored fabric, and a large oriental rug is spread over the floor. An interesting twelve-light chandelier, probably Victorian in origin, hangs over the dining table. The china is English Crescent in green and gold, and features the Canadian crest.

The glassware is Val St. Lambert with the Canadian maple-leaf design, and the flatware is English.

On the right-hand side of the entrance hall, the drawing room may be reached. It features high ceilings and floor-length French windows, which add to a general feeling of spaciousness. Doors from the drawing room open into a small sitting room, one of the most popular rooms in the embassy; from this sitting room doors lead into a walnut-paneled library.

The embassy conveys a bright and attractive feeling, no doubt influenced by the extensive use of paintings, mostly by contemporary Canadian artists.

Ambassade du Canada

FORMAL MENU

Velouté d' Huîtres
Filet Mignon au Sauce Béarnaise
Pommes de Terre Château   Courgettes Meunière
Salade d' Endive
Mandarin Délice
Café

LUNCHEON

Hors d' Oeuvres
Halibut Steaks Maître d' Hôtel Butter
Potato Balls
Green Beans
Lemon Tarts

VELOUTÉ D'HUÎTRES
Cream of Oyster Soup

⅓ pound butter
¾ cup chopped onions
6 tablespoons flour
6 cups hot milk
1½ teaspoons salt

½ teaspoon white pepper
Dash nutmeg
24 shucked oysters and their
    juice
1 cup light cream

Melt 6 tablespoons of the butter in a saucepan; add the onions and let cook without browning for 5 minutes. Blend in the flour, then add the milk, stirring steadily to the boiling point. Cook over low heat 10 minutes. Add the salt, pepper and nutmeg.

Cook the oysters in their juice for 3 minutes. Remove the oysters and chop. Pour the oyster juice into the white sauce. Cook 5 minutes. Strain into a clean saucepan. Add the cream and remaining butter. Taste for seasoning, thin with a little milk if necessary, then add the oysters. Heat for 2 minutes.

Serves 8.

FILET MIGNON AU SAUCE BÉARNAISE
Fillet of Beef with Béarnaise Sauce

Fillet:

4-pound fillet of beef
2 teaspoons salt
½ teaspoon black pepper
3 tablespoons butter
¼ cup chopped onions
¼ cup grated carrots
¼ cup diced celery

⅛ teaspoon thyme
1 teaspoon crushed bay leaf
2 sprigs parsley
⅓ cup Madeira
2 tablespoons vegetable oil
½ cup beef broth

Season the meat with 1½ teaspoons salt and ¼ teaspoon pepper.

Melt the butter in a saucepan; add the onions, carrots, celery, thyme, bay leaf, parsley and remaining salt and pepper. Sauté 10 minutes. Add the Madeira and cook over high heat until almost all the wine is evaporated.

[51]

Heat the oil in a deep skillet or shallow roasting pan. Brown the meat in it on all sides. Pour off all the fat. Spread the vegetable mixture over the fillet and add the broth. Roast in a preheated 350° oven 35 minutes, basting frequently. Transfer the meat to a serving platter. Prepare the sauce while the meat is cooking.

Sauce:

¼ cup dry white wine	⅛ teaspoon white pepper
¼ cup white wine vinegar	3 egg yolks
1 tablespoon minced green onions	¾ cup hot melted butter
1½ teaspoons tarragon	2 tablespoons minced fresh tarragon or parsley
Dash salt	

Combine the wine, vinegar, green onions, tarragon, salt and pepper in a saucepan. Bring to a boil and cook until reduced to about 2 tablespoons. Strain and cool.

Beat the egg yolks in the top of a double boiler. Beat in the vinegar mixture. Place over hot water and, drop by drop, beat in the melted butter. As the mixture thickens, add the butter in a slow steady stream. Taste for seasoning. Add the tarragon or parsley.

Carve the meat and serve with the sauce.

Serves 8.

POMMES DE TERRE CHÂTEAU
Potatoes Sautéed in Butter

3 pounds potatoes	6 tablespoons butter
3 tablespoons vegetable oil	½ teaspoon salt

Scrub and peel the potatoes, but do not wash them. Cut each potato into olive or oblong shapes about 2 inches long and 1 inch wide. Pat the pieces dry in a towel.

Heat the oil and butter in a large skillet until the foam begins to settle down. Add the potatoes in a single layer. Sauté 2 minutes, keeping the heat low enough so that the fat doesn't brown. Shake the skillet to turn potatoes to other side, then cook 5 minutes, or until all sides are golden in color. Sprinkle with the salt, shake skillet again and cover. Cook over low heat 10 minutes, shaking the pan frequently to prevent sticking. Test potatoes for doneness by pricking with a sharp knife.

Serves 8.

COURGETTES MEUNIÈRE
Zucchini in Butter

3 pounds small zucchini	¼ pound butter
2 teaspoons salt	2 tablespoons chopped parsley
¼ cup flour	

Scrub the zucchini, peel and slice thin. Sprinkle with the salt and let stand 15 minutes. Drain off the liquid and dry the zucchini slices. Toss in the flour.

Melt half the butter in a skillet; add the zucchini and cook until delicately browned. Transfer to a serving dish. Quickly melt the remaining butter and pour over the zucchini. Sprinkle with the parsley.

Serves 8.

SALADE D'ENDIVE
Endive Salad

2 pounds endive	⅛ teaspoon pepper
¾ cup olive oil	⅛ teaspoon minced garlic
¾ teaspoon salt	¼ cup wine vinegar

Wash the endive, remove any tough outer leaves and cut away the bottoms. Cut the endive in quarters lengthwise. Soak in ice water for 10 minutes, drain and wrap in a towel. Chill until ready to serve. Shake all the dressing ingredients together vigorously.

Arrange the endive in a salad bowl and pour the dressing over it.

Serves 8.

MANDARIN DÉLICE
Tangerine Ice

8 tangerines	½ cup water
¾ cup sugar	¼ cup tangerine liqueur

Wash and dry the tangerines. Cut a circular piece about the size of a quarter from the stem end of each fruit. Reserve. Carefully scoop out the pulp without breaking the shells. Discard the seeds and purée the pulp in a blender or force through a sieve.

Combine the sugar and water in a saucepan. Bring to a boil, stirring until the sugar melts, then cook until thickened and syrupy. Cool slightly, then mix in the tangerine purée and liqueur. Fill the shells and replace the tops. Place in the freezing compartment until frozen. Decorate with a leaf.

Serves 8.

HALIBUT STEAKS WITH MAÎTRE D'HÔTEL BUTTER

Maître d'Hôtel Butter:

¼ pound softened butter	2 tablespoons minced parsley
2 tablespoons minced chives	2 tablespoons lemon juice

Cream the butter, then blend in the chives and parsley, adding the lemon juice a little at a time. Shape into a roll, wrap tightly in foil or waxed paper and chill until firm.

Fish:

3 or 6 halibut steaks, cut 1¼ inches thick	Salt and pepper
	2 tablespoons butter

For six people, buy 3 or 6 halibut steaks, depending on the size of the fish. Rinse and dry the fish. Season with salt and pepper and arrange in a shallow buttered baking pan. Put small lumps of the butter on each steak. Bake in a preheated 350° oven 30 minutes, or until the fish flakes easily when tested with a fork and is delicately browned. Place a slice of Maître d'Hôtel butter on each. Serve with potato balls and buttered green beans.

Serves 6.

◖◯◗

LEMON TARTS

Pastry:

1½ cups sifted flour	3 tablespoons chilled vegetable
¼ teaspoon salt	shortening
4 teaspoons sugar	5 tablespoons ice water
5 tablespoons chilled butter	

Sift the flour, salt and sugar into a bowl. Cut in the butter and shortening until mixture looks like coarse cornmeal. Toss in just enough of the water to make the particles hold together, then form into a ball and chill 30 minutes.

Roll out the dough and fit into six tart shells. Prick the bottoms, fit a piece of waxed paper in each and then fit an empty tart pan on top, or fill with rice or beans; this keeps the shells from shrinking and puffing. Bake in a preheated 400° oven 10 minutes. Remove the weights, prick the bottoms again and bake 3 minutes longer, or until delicately browned. Cool on a cake rack and remove from pans.

Lemon Filling:

5 egg yolks	2 teaspoons grated lemon rind
½ cup sugar	4 tablespoons butter
⅓ cup lemon juice	1 cup whipped cream

In the top of a double boiler, beat the egg yolks and sugar until thickened. Add the lemon juice and rind. Place over hot water and, stirring steadily, add the butter, a small piece at a time. Still stirring steadily, cook until thick. Cool and fill the shells. Pipe the whipped cream around the edges.

Serves 6.

Chile

THE Embassy of Chile is housed in a large, handsome structure, offering an overall impression of solidity and substance. It is an impressive three stories in height, with a rounded façade.

The interior is quite formal, and the decor is French. At the front entrance, there is an imposing grand staircase with an intricately carved railing running its entire length. The staircase, gracious and attractive, lends an air of elegance to the embassy. The floors throughout are inlaid parquet and partly covered with Oriental rugs of a dull finish.

The dining room has a large fireplace, lighted on formal occasions

during the winter months. The walls are covered with damask, and the furniture is similarly upholstered. Elaborate drapes reach from the ceiling to the floor. On one side of the room, there is a large buffet table with mirrored panels. On the walls are Chilean paintings, especially of pastoral scenes. There is a lovely ancient Beauvais screen from the collection of Prince Talleyrand.

Meals are served very formally, with elaborate service. There are usually many courses, served upon fine French china, with Peruvian silverware and Baccarat stemware.

Embajada de Chile

INFORMAL DINNER MENU

Empanadas   *Cocktails*

Aguacates Rellenos con Camarones
DRY WHITE CHILEAN WINE

Chupe de Mariscos
DRY WHITE CHILEAN WINE

Ensalada de Tomates y Cebollas

Bizcocho Relleno de Crema Española
Demi-Tasse

Liqueurs

EMPANADAS
Hors d'Oeuvre Pastries

1 pound ground chuck steak	1½ teaspoons baking powder
2 tablespoons vegetable oil	½ cup shortening
2 cups chopped onions	1 egg, beaten
½ cup boiling water	½ cup ice water
1 tablespoon Spanish paprika	½ cup seedless raisins
1 teaspoon ground cumin	½ cup pitted black olives
2 teaspoons salt	3 hard-cooked eggs, chopped
3 cups sifted flour	Fat for deep frying

Have the meat ground through a coarse blade. Heat the oil in a skillet; add the onions and meat. Cook over medium heat, stirring frequently, until browned. Mix in the boiling water, paprika, cumin and 1½ teaspoons of the salt. Cook 10 minutes. Taste for seasoning. Chill.

Sift the flour, baking powder and remaining salt into a bowl. Cut in the shortening with a pastry blender or two knives. Add the egg and water, tossing until a ball of dough is formed.

Add the raisins, olives and chopped eggs to the chilled filling. Roll out the dough very thin and cut into 3-inch circles. Put a teaspoonful of the meat mixture on each and fold over into a half-moon, sealing the edges with a little water or egg white. Flute the edges.

Heat the fat to 370° and fry a few empanadas at a time until browned. Drain and serve hot.

Makes about 40.

AGUACATES RELLENOS CON CAMARONES
Shrimp-Stuffed Avocados

2 pounds cooked, cleaned shrimp	1 hard-cooked egg, chopped
1 cup olive oil	2 tablespoons chopped onion
⅓ cup white wine vinegar	2 tablespoons minced parsley
1¼ teaspoons salt	2 tablespoons minced pimientos
⅛ teaspoon Tabasco	4 avocados
2 tablespoons chopped capers	Shredded lettuce

Cut each shrimp in four pieces. Mix together the oil, vinegar, salt, Tabasco, capers, egg, onion, parsley and pimientos. Pour over the shrimp and mix well. Let stand 15 minutes.

Cut the avocados in half lengthwise. Discard the pits, and with a sharp knife, cut the flesh away from the shells, but leave in place. Fill with the shrimp mixture and serve each half on shredded lettuce. *Serves 8.*

CHUPE DE MARISCOS
Seafood Casserole

3 1½-pound live lobsters	¾ cup chopped onions
1½ quarts water	2 cups soft bread crumbs
2 teaspoons salt	1½ cups milk
2 pounds raw shrimp	½ cup cottage cheese
24 clams	3 egg yolks
24 mussels	⅛ teaspoon cayenne pepper
6 tablespoons butter	4 hard-cooked eggs, cut in half
1 tablespoon Spanish paprika	

Wash the lobsters. Bring the water and salt to a boil. Drop the lobsters into it and cook 20 minutes. Drain the lobsters. Drop the shrimp into the boiling liquid and cook 5 minutes. Drain, reserving the liquid.

Scrub the clams and mussels. Put in a pan with ½ cup of the reserved liquid. Cover and steam until the shells open. Drain and discard the shells.

Remove the meat of the lobsters and cut into 2-inch pieces. Shell and devein the shrimp. Put all the seafood in a 3-quart casserole.

Melt the butter in a saucepan; stir in the paprika and onions. Cook over low heat 5 minutes. Add the bread crumbs, milk and 1½ cups of the reserved liquid. Bring to a boil and cook over low heat 10 minutes.

In a bowl, mix together the cottage cheese, egg yolks and cayenne

pepper. Add the hot sauce, stirring steadily to prevent curdling. Taste for seasoning. Pour over the seafood. Cover and bake in a 350° oven 40 minutes. Remove cover and place under the broiler until top browns. Garnish with the eggs. Serve with French bread and rice.
Serves 8.

ENSALADA DE TOMATES Y CEBOLLAS
Tomato and Onion Salad

1 pound yellow onions	¾ teaspoon salt
3 tomatoes, peeled and sliced	¼ teaspoon black pepper
¾ cup olive oil	⅛ teaspoon minced garlic
¼ cup red wine vinegar	

Peel the onions and cut into very thin slices lengthwise. Cover with boiling water and let stand 10 minutes. Drain, dry and chill.

Arrange the tomatoes and onions on individual salad plates. Make a dressing of the oil, vinegar, salt, pepper and garlic. Pour over the salad.
Serves 8.

BIZCOCHO RELLENO DE CREMA ESPAÑOLA
Cake Roll

Cake:

4 egg yolks	⅛ teaspoon salt
⅓ cup sugar	¼ cup flour
2 teaspoons grated lemon rind	¼ cup cornstarch
4 egg whites	Cinnamon

Beat the egg yolks until thick. Gradually add half the sugar, beating until very light in color. Mix in the lemon rind. In another bowl beat the egg whites and salt until soft peaks form, then gradually beat in the remaining sugar until stiff. Fold ¼ of the egg whites into the yolk, then pour this mixture over the remaining whites. Sift the flour and cornstarch over the top and fold all together gently.

Grease an 11- by 16-inch jelly roll pan, line with wax paper and grease the paper. Pour the batter into the lined pan evenly. Bake in a preheated 400° oven 12 minutes, or until very lightly browned. Run a spatula under the paper and immediately turn out onto a towel covered rack, paper side down. Cover with a moist towel until cool. Peel the paper off when cake cools and sprinkle with cinnamon.

Filling:

1 cup milk	⅛ teaspoon salt
1-inch piece cinnamon stick	4 egg yolks
1 teaspoon grated lemon rind	2 tablespoons butter
2 tablespoons cornstarch	Confectioners' sugar
¾ cup sugar	

Combine the milk, cinnamon stick and lemon rind in a saucepan. Bring to a boil, remove from heat and let stand 10 minutes. Strain.

Mix the cornstarch, sugar and salt in the top of a double boiler. Stir in the milk mixture. Cook over low heat, stirring steadily, until mixture boils. Place over hot water and cook, stirring frequently, for 10 minutes.

Beat the egg yolks in a bowl; gradually add a little of the hot sauce, stirring steadily to prevent curdling. Return to double boiler, add the butter and cook, stirring steadily for 2 minutes. Cool. Spread the cake roll with the filling and roll up. Sprinkle the top with confectioners' sugar.

Serves 8.

China

THE Chinese Embassy, often called "Twin Oaks," was once of the estate of Alexander Graham Bell. It occupies a lovely wooded hill in the heart of Washington with extensive grounds of over nineteen sprawling acres. The building itself is charming, reminiscent of a less hectic period, offering an air of tranquillity befitting its occupants.

The reception and sitting rooms are all pleasant and attractive, decorated with furniture of several different styles, which somehow intermix with ease. Perhaps of more interest is the embassy's main dining room. It is a good-sized area with a sun porch at one end through which

can be seen the rolling grounds and wooded areas surrounding the embassy. There is a fireplace fronted by a Chinese lacquer screen inlaid with mother-of-pearl. The floor is carpeted in crimson; the wallpaper was made in France and consists of a light beige background with bamboo patterns executed in gold. The flatware and crystal are from Taiwan (Formosa). The dining table is round, in the traditional Chinese style, and seats from ten to fourteen people comfortably. It is customary on informal occasions to place a sort of lazy Susan in the center of the table, and the guests can help themselves as they wish.

[65]

Embassy of the Republic of China

MENU FOR THE STATE DINNER IN HONOR
OF PRESIDENT KENNEDY

Chicken Consommé with Shredded Mushrooms
Sea Bass, Hangchow Style
Spiced Crisp Fried Duck, Szechuan Style
Braised Assorted Vegetables
Diced Chicken Sauté with Green Peppers
Fried Rice, Yangchow Style
Almond Jelly in Fruit Syrup
Pastry with Mashed Bean Stuffing
Green Tea   Coffee

FORMAL MENU

Shark's Fin Soup
Shrimp, Shanghai Style
Crispy-Skin Duck
Fried Bamboo Shoots with Mustard Greens
Almond Chicken
Buddhist's Feast
Shredded Beef with Green Peppers
Eight Jewel Rice

CHICKEN CONSOMMÉ WITH SHREDDED MUSHROOMS

8 Chinese dried mushrooms	2 tablespoons dry sherry
2 quarts chicken broth	2 tablespoons soy sauce

Wash the mushrooms and soak in hot water for 20 minutes. Drain and cut in matchlike strips.

Bring the broth to a boil; add the sherry, soy sauce and mushrooms. Cook over low heat 10 minutes, or until mushrooms are tender. Taste for seasoning.

Serves 10 to 12.

SEA BASS, HANGCHOW STYLE

4-pound sea bass	6 tablespoons Chinese dark or
2 teaspoons salt	cider vinegar
Peanut oil for deep frying	1½ cups water
⅔ cup sugar	12 green onions, chopped
2 tablespoons cornstarch	6 slices ginger root, chopped
2 tablespoons soy sauce	

Have the fish cleaned, and the head removed or not, as you prefer. (The Chinese leave it on.) Cut four gashes on the fish, and rub inside and out with the salt. Let stand 20 minutes.

Heat deep oil to 365° and fry the fish in it until browned. Drain and keep hot.

Mix together until smooth the sugar, cornstarch, soy sauce and vinegar, then gradually add the water.

Heat 2 tablespoons oil in a saucepan; sauté the green onions and ginger for 1 minute, then add the cornstarch mixture. Cook over low

[67]

heat, stirring steadily until dark and thickened. Pour over the fish and serve hot. In China, the fish is put on the table with the head facing the guest of honor.

Serves 10 to 12.

SPICED CRISP FRIED DUCK, SZECHUAN STYLE

5-pound duck
3 tablespoons dry sherry
2 teaspoons crushed dried red
    peppers, or ½ teaspoon
    cayenne pepper
1½ teaspoons sugar
6 teaspoons salt
1 leek, sliced

6 slices ginger root, cut julienne
4 anise seeds
2 eggs, beaten
6 tablespoons flour
Vegetable oil for deep frying
2 teaspoons coarsely ground
    black pepper

Clean, wash and dry the duck. Rub inside and out with the sherry and let stand 30 minutes.

Roll the red peppers into a powder with a rolling pin (or use ½ teaspoon cayenne pepper). Mix together the red peppers, sugar and half the salt. Rub into the duck. Put the duck in a heat-proof bowl or pan with the leek, ginger and anise seeds. Place on a rack in a kettle containing enough water to reach halfway up the bowl. Cover the kettle, and cook over medium heat 1½ hours, or until duck is tender. Watch water level, adding more if it boils out.

Cool the duck. Mix the eggs with the flour and brush on the duck, coating it well. Heat enough oil to cover the duck to 365° and fry the duck in it until browned and crisp. Drain, and cut into small pieces through the bone, trying to retain the shape of the duck.

While the duck is cooking, put the remaining salt in a dry skillet, and cook until it begins to turn color. Mix it with the black pepper. This mixture is used as a dip for the duck, and is customarily served in tiny dishes.

Serves 10 to 12.

BRAISED ASSORTED VEGETABLES

8 Chinese dried mushrooms	3 tablespoons dry sherry
1 can bamboo shoots	6 tablespoons soy sauce
5 tablespoons peanut or vege- table oil	2 tablespoons sugar ½ teaspoon monosodium
3 cups shredded Chinese or green cabbage	glutamate ⅓ cup water
1 cup julienne-cut green peppers	1 cucumber, peeled and sliced 6 green onions, sliced
1 pound snow peas, strings removed	

Wash the mushrooms well, cover with hot water and let soak 30 minutes. Drain and cut in quarters. Drain the bamboo shoots and cut in cubes.

Heat the oil in a skillet; sauté the mushrooms 5 minutes. Add the cabbage and green peppers; sauté 3 minutes, stirring frequently. Add the snow peas and bamboo shoots; sauté 2 minutes. Mix in the sherry, soy sauce, sugar, monosodium glutamate and water. Cook over medium heat 3 minutes. Add the cucumber and green onions; cook 3 minutes.

Serves 10 to 12.

DICED CHICKEN SAUTÉ WITH GREEN PEPPERS

4 whole chicken breasts	1 clove garlic, minced
5 tablespoons dry sherry	4 slices ginger root, julienne
6 tablespoons soy sauce	6 green peppers, cut in eighths
7 tablespoons cornstarch	2 teaspoons sugar
2⅓ cups peanut or vegetable oil	2 tablespoons water

Remove the skin and bones of the breasts and dice the chicken. Sprinkle with 2 tablespoons of the sherry, then 2 tablespoons soy sauce. Toss. Sprinkle with 6 tablespoons cornstarch. Toss again.

Heat 2 cups of the oil until it bubbles; fry the chicken pieces in it until delicately browned. Drain and keep hot.

Heat the remaining oil in a skillet; add the garlic, ginger and green peppers; sauté 5 minutes. Mix in the chicken; sauté 2 minutes. Add the remaining sherry and soy sauce. Mix together the sugar, water and remaining cornstarch; add to the chicken mixture, stirring until thickened.

Serves 10 to 12.

◦⊂⊃◦

FRIED RICE, YANGCHOW STYLE

½ pound pork	2 eggs
5 tablespoons soy sauce	6 tablespoons lard or vegetable
1 teaspoon cornstarch	oil
⅛ pound cooked smoked ham	1 carrot, grated coarsely
2 slices ginger root	¼ cup cooked or canned green
¼ pound raw shrimp, shelled	peas
and deveined	¼ cup canned sliced mushrooms
¾ teaspoon salt	2 green onions, sliced
¼ teaspoon black pepper	4 cups cooked rice

Cut the pork in matchlike strips; add 2 tablespoons soy sauce and the cornstarch, and toss.

Dice the ham into tiny pieces. Cut the ginger into slivers. Cut the shrimp in quarters and sprinkle with ½ teaspoon salt and ⅛ teaspoon pepper.

Beat the eggs. Heat 1 tablespoon lard in a 7-inch skillet. Pour in half the eggs, turning the pan quickly to coat the bottom. Cook until underside browns, roll up and turn out. Cut into narrow strips. Repeat with remaining eggs and reserve.

Heat 2 tablespoons lard in the skillet; sauté the ginger for a few seconds, then add the pork. Sauté 5 minutes, stirring frequently. Add the carrot, green peas, mushrooms, ham and green onions; sauté 2 minutes, stirring steadily. Add the shrimp, 2 tablespoons soy sauce and remaining salt. Cook and stir for 3 minutes. Keep hot.

Heat the remaining lard in a large skillet; add the rice. Cook, stirring almost steadily, until very lightly browned, about 5 minutes. Mix in the remaining pepper and soy sauce, then the meat mixture, and half the egg strips. Fry for 1 minute, stirring steadily. Heap on a serving dish and sprinkle the remaining egg strips on top.

Serves 10 to 12.

ALMOND JELLY IN FRUIT SYRUP

½ cup raw rice	1 cup sugar
¾ cup blanched almonds	½ teaspoon almond extract
6 cups water	2 17-ounce cans fruit cocktail
2 envelopes (2 tablespoons) gelatin	

Soak the rice in cold water for 30 minutes. Drain. Combine the rice, almonds and 1 cup water in an electric blender, and blend until no pieces remain. Or grind the rice and almonds through the fine blade of a food chopper, adding the 1 cup water as you grind. Pour the mixture into a muslin bag, or several layers of fine cheesecloth, and squeeze out all the liquid. There should be about 1 cup. Soften the gelatin in 1 cup of the remaining water.

Combine the sugar and remaining water in a saucepan; bring to a boil, stirring until sugar dissolves. Stir in the gelatin until dissolved. Add the almond-rice water and cool. Stir in the almond extract. Pour into a large dish, about 12 by 12 inches, and chill until set. Cut into 1-inch diamond shapes.

Drain the fruit, reserving the juice. Dice the fruit and return to the syrup. Add the almond jelly. Serve in Chinese soup cups or other small cups.

Serves 10 to 12.

PASTRY WITH MASHED BEAN STUFFING

½ pound Chinese sweet bean
    paste (tou sa) or
    1 can kidney beans and
    ½ cup sugar

2 cups flour
1 cup boiling water (about)

The sweet bean paste is available in Oriental food shops. If you can't get it, cook a can of kidney beans until soft. Drain, purée and mix in the sugar.

Sift the flour into a bowl. Add just enough of the water to make a soft dough. Knead until smooth, cover with a damp cloth and let stand 30 minutes.

Form the dough into a roll, about 1 inch in diameter, and cut into 1-inch pieces. On a lightly floured surface, roll out each piece into a 3-inch circle. Leave the center a little thicker than the edges. Place a heaping teaspoon of the bean mixture in the center of each, flute the edges and bring edges together, then twist center.

Use a rack in a pan of boiling water, or a special Chinese steamer. Place a wet napkin on the rack, and arrange the pastries on it in a single layer, making sure they don't touch the water. Cover the pan, and steam 20 minutes. Repeat with remaining pastries. Serve hot.

Makes about 36.

SHARK'S FIN SOUP

½ pound shark's fin
2 onions
10 slices ginger root
3 pounds chicken wings and
    backs
2½ quarts water
2 teaspoons sesame or
    vegetable oil

4 green onions, sliced
1 tablespoon dry sherry
1 cup julienne-cut bamboo
    shoots
1 tablespoon soy sauce
1 teaspoon salt
2 tablespoons cornstarch

Wash the shark's fin, cover with water and let soak overnight. Drain and rinse under cold running water for a few minutes. Cover the shark's fin with water, add 1 onion and half the ginger, bring to a boil and cook 2 hours. Drain. Cut the shark's fin into strips.

Cook the chicken wings and backs in the 2½ quarts water with the remaining onion and 2 slices ginger for 1½ hours. Strain and reserve broth. Shred the meat off the wings and backs.

Mince the remaining ginger. Heat the oil in a saucepan; sauté the remaining ginger and the green onions for 3 minutes. Add the sherry, shark's fin, chicken, bamboo shoots and all but ½ cup broth. Bring to a boil. Mix the soy sauce, salt and cornstarch with the ½ cup broth and stir into the soup until thickened.

Serves 10 to 12.

SHRIMP, SHANGHAI STYLE

½ cup lard or peanut oil
2 pounds raw shrimp, shelled and deveined
1 tablespoon minced ginger root
½ cup chopped onions
2 tablespoons soy sauce
2 tablespoons dry sherry
¾ cup chicken broth
2 teaspoons salt
1 cup julienne-cut Smithfield ham
12 water chestnuts, sliced
1 8-ounce can mushrooms, drained and cut into pieces
1 8-ounce can tiny peas, drained
2 teaspoons cornstarch
2 tablespoons cold water

Heat the lard in a skillet; add the shrimp, ginger and onions. Cook over medium heat, stirring almost constantly, for 3 minutes. Add the soy sauce, sherry, broth, salt, ham, water chestnuts, mushrooms and peas. Bring to a boil. Mix the cornstarch with the water; stir into the mixture, then cook 4 minutes.

Serves 10 to 12.

CRISPY-SKIN DUCK

5-pound duck
2 cups soy sauce
1 onion, sliced
2 cloves garlic

2 slices ginger root
4 anise seeds
Vegetable oil for deep frying

Wash and clean the duck. Combine in a deep pan with the soy sauce, onion, garlic, ginger root and anise seeds. Add enough water to cover. Bring to a boil, cover and cook over low heat 1½ hours. Drain and cool. Dry the duck thoroughly.

Heat enough oil to cover the duck to 370°. Fry the duck in it until browned and crisp, about 10 minutes. Baste if necessary to cover all parts. Drain and cut into small pieces through the bone.

Serves 10 to 12.

ALMOND CHICKEN

½ cup white bean paste or ½
    cup canned white beans
    and 2 teaspoons each
    beer and vinegar
8 Chinese dried mushrooms
2 cups peanut or vegetable oil
1 cup blanched almonds

4 whole chicken breasts
2 teaspoons cornstarch
6 tablespoons lard or oil
1 cup diced onions
1 can bamboo shoots, cut in
    strips
½ teaspoon salt

The bean paste is available in Oriental food shops, and is called miso in Japanese. If you can't get it, purée the canned white beans and mix in the beer and vinegar.

Wash the mushrooms and soak in hot water to cover for 30 minutes. Drain and cut into squares.

Heat the oil in a skillet; brown the almonds in it. Drain and reserve.

Remove the skin and bones of the chicken and cut the meat into small squares. Mix together half the bean paste with the cornstarch and 1 tablespoon lard. Rub into the chicken pieces.

Heat 2 tablespoons lard in a skillet; lightly brown the onions in it. Add the bamboo shoots, mushrooms, and salt. Cook, stirring constantly, for 3 minutes. Remove from the skillet. Heat the remaining lard in the skillet; add the chicken and cook, stirring steadily for 5 minutes. Return the vegetable mixture and cook, stirring for 3 more minutes. Mix in the remaining bean paste, then the almonds.

Serves 10 to 12.

FRIED BAMBOO SHOOTS WITH MUSTARD GREENS

1 pound mustard greens (leaves)	Vegetable oil for deep frying
2 cans bamboo shoots	2 teaspoons sugar
	1½ teaspoons salt

Wash the mustard greens thoroughly; drain well and dry very well on towels.

Drain and dry the bamboo shoots; cut in diagonal strips. Heat the oil to 370° and fry the strips until golden brown. Drain and sprinkle with 1 teaspoon sugar and ½ teaspoon salt. Keep hot.

Heat the same oil again to 370°. Fry the mustard greens until very crisp. Drain, place in a serving dish and sprinkle with the remaining sugar and salt. Place the bamboo shoots on top.

Serves 10 to 12.

BUDDHIST'S FEAST

½ pound raw shrimp, shelled and deveined	¼ cup cooked ham, shredded
½ pound scallops	¾ cup cooked julienne-cut chicken
2 tablespoons soy sauce	1 tablespoon salt
1½ cups raw long grain rice	¼ cup dry sherry
6 cups chicken broth	

Wash the shrimp and cut in small pieces. Wash the scallops, and tear apart into shreds; mix in the soy sauce and let stand.

Wash the rice until the water runs clear. Bring the broth to a boil; add the rice and cook over low heat 20 minutes. Add the shrimp, scallops, ham, chicken and salt; cook 20 minutes. Mix in the sherry and cook 5 minutes longer. Serve in Chinese soup or other small cups.
Serves 10 to 12.

SHREDDED BEEF WITH GREEN PEPPERS

2 pounds fillet of beef	1 teaspoon sugar
6 green peppers	2 teaspoons ketchup
¼ cup cornstarch	½ cup lard or vegetable oil
3 tablespoons soy sauce	1 teaspoon salt
1 egg, beaten	

Cut the meat into paper-thin slices and then into strips. Wash and seed the peppers. Cut into strips slightly longer than the beef.

Toss the beef with the cornstarch, then add a mixture of the soy sauce, egg, sugar and ketchup.

Heat 2 tablespoons lard in a skillet; add the peppers and salt. Cook, stirring almost constantly, for 5 minutes. Remove the peppers. Heat the remaining lard in the skillet over high heat. Add the meat; cook, stirring, for 1 minute. Reduce the heat, add the peppers and cook, stirring, for 2 minutes.
Serves 10 to 12.

EIGHT JEWEL RICE

Pudding:

2 cups glutinous rice	1 cup diced candied fruit
3 cups water	¼ cup blanched almonds
¼ cup sugar	10 cooked or preserved
¾ pound dried dates	(marrons) chestnuts
4 tablespoons lard or vegetable oil	¼ cup seedless raisins

Wash the rice, cover with hot water and let stand 30 minutes. Drain, combine with the 3 cups water, bring to a boil, cover, and cook over very low heat 30 minutes. Watch carefully so rice doesn't burn. Drain if any water remains. Mix in the sugar.

Cover the dates with water, bring to a boil and cook 10 minutes. Drain, cool slightly, rub off the skins and remove the pits. Mash the dates. Melt the lard in a skillet, add the date paste and cook, stirring steadily, for 5 minutes.

Grease a 9-inch heatproof bowl or baking dish. Arrange half the candied fruits in the center of the dish, then, in an attractive design, arrange the almonds, chestnuts, raisins and remaining candied fruits over the rest of the bowl. Press half the rice over the arrangement, making a depression in the center. Fill with the date paste, then spread the remaining rice over the top. Place the dish on a rack in a pan; add hot water to pan, cover pan and steam the pudding for 25 minutes. Run a spatula around the edge of the dish and turn pudding out onto a serving dish. Serve hot with the following sauce over it.

Sauce:

1 tablespoon cornstarch	1¼ cups water
2 tablespoons sugar	¼ cup sweet sherry

Mix the cornstarch and sugar in a saucepan; gradually mix in the water and sherry. Cook over low heat, stirring steadily until thickened.

Serves 10 to 12.

Colombia

THIS South American embassy is housed in a massive red brick building, decorated with white stone trim. The grounds which surround the
embassy are pleasant and attractive.

The interior of the broad entrance hall is decorated with fine walnut
paneling; the dining room also has walnut paneling, and its beamed
ceilings are inlaid with designs executed in mother-of-pearl. The formal
drawing room is decorated with pale walls, light-colored drapes, delicate
French furniture and a fine Aubusson rug.

The embassy has its own ballroom, spacious and imposing. The decor is light and pleasant with soft colors prevailing, all of which makes it look even larger. There are high, arched French windows, and a small balcony enclosed with grillwork for the orchestra. When large numbers of guests are expected, the ballroom is filled with small tables, and dinner is served from a long buffet. On lesser occasions, the regular dining room is used.

Embajada de Colombia

FORMAL MENU

Coctel de Caranguejos

Sopa de Lentejas

Codillo Asado

Soufflé de Calabaza

Ensalada de Aguacates

Flan

COCTEL DE CARANGUEJOS
Crab Cocktail

2 tablespoons grated onion
2 tablespoons minced parsley
½ cup olive oil
¼ cup white wine vinegar

¾ teaspoon salt
¼ teaspoon pepper
Pinch sugar
1½ pounds lump crab meat

Make a dressing of all the ingredients but the crab meat. Let stand 2 hours. Beat or shake well just before using.

Pick over the crab meat and divide among eight individual shells or other individual serving dishes. Pour the dressing over each, and chill 2 hours.

Serves 8.

SOPA DE LENTEJAS
Lentil Soup

2 cups lentils
12 cups water
¼ pound salt pork, minced
2 tablespoons butter
½ cup minced onions

1 cup peeled chopped tomatoes
½ teaspoon black pepper
2 teaspoons lemon juice
3 hard-cooked eggs, sliced

Wash the lentils, cover with water and bring to a boil. Let soak 30 minutes. Drain and add the 12 cups water. Bring to a boil, and cook over low heat 30 minutes. Add the salt pork; cook 1 hour.

Melt the butter in a skillet; add the onions, tomatoes, pepper and lemon juice. Cook over low heat 10 minutes, stirring frequently. Add to the soup; cook 30 minutes longer, or until the lentils are tender. Taste for seasoning. Pour the soup into individual bowls and garnish with the egg slices.

Serves 8.

CODILLO ASADO
Roast Marinated Leg of Pork

6-8 pound leg of pork	1½ cups grated onions
1 cup wine vinegar	2 cloves garlic, minced
1 cup ketchup	2 whole allspice
½ cup Worcestershire sauce	2 cups muscatel or sweet
2 teaspoons salt	sherry
½ teaspoon black pepper	

Prick the leg of pork all over with the point of a knife. Combine all the remaining ingredients but the wine and marinate the pork in the mixture in the refrigerator for 3 days, basting and turning twice each day.

Put the drained pork in a roasting pan and roast in a 300° oven 30 minutes a pound. Add the wine after 1 hour, and baste frequently. *Serves 8 to 10.*

SOUFFLÉ DE CALABAZA
Squash Soufflé

2 pounds yellow squash	½ teaspoon white pepper
4 tablespoons butter	⅛ teaspoon nutmeg
3 tablespoons flour	6 egg yolks
1 cup milk	6 egg whites, stiffly beaten
2 teaspoons salt	

Wash and peel the squash. Cut into pieces and cook in a little boiling salted water 15 minutes. Drain well and mash smooth.

Melt the butter in a saucepan; blend in the flour. Add the milk, stirring over low heat until smooth and thickened. Mix in the salt, pepper and nutmeg.

Beat the egg yolks in a bowl; gradually add the white sauce, stirring steadily. Mix in the squash. Taste for seasoning and cool. Fold in the egg whites. Turn into a buttered 2-quart soufflé or baking dish. Bake in a preheated 350° oven 35 minutes, or until puffed and browned. Serve immediately.

Serves 8.

○⊂▭▷○

ENSALADA DE AGUACATES
Avocado Salad

1 cup olive oil	¼ teaspoon dry mustard
3 tablespoons lemon juice	⅛ teaspoon powdered thyme
1 tablespoon grated onion	Lettuce
¾ teaspoon salt	4 avocados, peeled and sliced
Dash cayenne pepper	3 hard-cooked eggs, sliced

Beat together the oil, lemon juice, onion, salt, cayenne pepper, mustard and thyme.

Put some lettuce on eight individual salad plates. Over it arrange the avocado slices and eggs. Pour the dressing over the top.

Serves 8.

○⊂▭▷○

FLAN
Caramel Custard

1 cup milk	3 eggs
1 cup heavy cream	2 egg yolks
2-inch piece vanilla bean or	1½ cups sugar
¾ teaspoon vanilla extract	½ cup water

Combine the milk, cream and vanilla bean in a saucepan. (If vanilla extract is used, don't add until after milk mixture is cooled.) Bring just to a boil. Cool 10 minutes and discard vanilla bean.

Beat together the eggs, egg yolks and ½ cup of the sugar. Gradually beat in the milk mixture.

Put the remaining sugar in a heavy skillet. Keep over medium heat, stirring steadily until melted. Slowly and carefully mix in the water. Cook until browned. Pour into a 9-inch ring mold, turning the pan around until it is well coated with the caramel. Let stand until set. Strain the custard into the mold, and place mold in a pan of hot water. Bake in a preheated 350° oven 45 minutes, or until a knife inserted in the center comes out clean. Cool, chill, run a knife around the edges and turn out onto a chilled serving dish.

Serves 8.

Denmark

THE *newly constructed Danish Embassy overlooks an almost wild gorge of Dunbarton Oaks Park, in a setting of considerable natural grandeur. The split-level building uses a good deal of glass, and features terraces and balconies.*

The embassy is furnished with restrained elegance, resulting in a feeling of informality, typical of what decorators call Danish Modern. The entrance area and reception halls are on the lowest level, and immediately indicate the decorative trend and style of the embassy. The intermediate level contains the sitting room, dining room and library; there is also a conference room on this floor especially designed and equipped for film projection. The dining and sitting rooms feature large

ceiling fixtures, circular in shape, with gold-colored tubes spiked by hundreds of small lights with reflectors of tissue-thin glass in the shape of inverted wine glasses. Throughout these various rooms, basically modern in design and color, are examples of seventeenth-century art, reminders that Denmark is an ancient kingdom.

The dining room is striking indeed. The furniture was designed by Jinn Juhl, the porcelain is Royal Copenhagen and has the initials of King Frederik IX. The silverware was created by Kaj Bojesen, and the candlesticks by Georg Jensen. The stemware, especially made, is from Holmegaard Glasvaerk in Denmark.

[87]

Embassy of Denmark

FORMAL MENU

Gratin
Gaasesteg med Aebler og Svesker
Rødkaal
Risengrød med Mandeldejg
Café

INFORMAL MENU

Gule Aerter
Dyreryg
Kransekage
Café

INFORMAL MENU

Kødsuppe med Boller
Honsesteg
Agurkesalat
Pandekager

GRATIN
Cheese Soufflé

½ cup flour
1 cup light cream
2 tablespoons butter
½ cup grated Samsø or Parmesan
cheese

4 egg yolks
½ teaspoon salt
⅛ teaspoon white pepper
4 egg whites

In a saucepan, mix the flour with the cream until very smooth. Add the butter and cook over low heat stirring constantly until the mixture reaches boiling point. Cook 5 minutes longer, stirring occasionally. Mix in the cheese until melted. Cool, then beat in 1 egg yolk at a time. Stir in salt and pepper. Beat the egg whites until stiff but not dry, and fold into the cheese mixture. Turn into a 1½-quart buttered soufflé dish. Place the dish in a pan containing 2 inches of water and bake in a preheated 375° oven 45 minutes. Serve immediately.

Serves 4.

GAASESTEG MED AEBLER OG SVESKER
Roast Goose with Apples and Prunes

9-pound goose
1 tablespoon salt
½ teaspoon black pepper
1 pound prunes, soaked overnight

2 apples, peeled and sliced
1 tablespoon sugar
2 cups boiling chicken broth
3 tablespoons flour

Wash and dry the goose; remove as much fat as possible and rub the goose inside and out with the salt and pepper. Toss the drained prunes and the apples with the sugar and stuff the goose with them. Close the opening with skewers or sew. Put the goose in a roasting pan, breast side down.

Roast in a 375° oven on the lowest rack 30 minutes. Pour off all the fat. Pour the broth into the pan. Reduce the heat to 325°. Cover the pan and roast 1 hour. Turn the goose breast side up, cover and roast 1¼ hours. Remove the cover and pour off the pan juices into a saucepan. Raise the heat to 375° and roast 30 minutes longer.

Measure the pan juices; you should have about 2 cups. Skim the fat. Mix the flour to a smooth thin paste with a little water. Add to the pan juices, stirring over low heat until thickened, then cook 10 minutes. Taste for seasoning.

Transfer the goose to a platter and carefully take out the prune-apple stuffing. Arrange around the goose. Serve with browned potatoes and red cabbage.

(To brown potatoes in the Danish manner, use cooked small new potatoes or potato balls. Brown in butter and sprinkle with a little sugar.)

Serves 6 to 8.

RØDKAAL
Red Cabbage

4 pounds red cabbage	1 cup red currant juice or ½
¼ pound butter	cup currant jelly mixed
1 apple, peeled and sliced	with ½ cup water
⅓ cup vinegar	1½ teaspoons salt
	¼ cup sugar

Wash the cabbage, discarding any tough outer leaves. Shred the cabbage fine.

Melt the butter in a heavy large saucepan. Add the cabbage and apple. Cover and cook 5 minutes, shaking the pan frequently. Add the vinegar, currant juice, salt and sugar. Recover and cook over low heat 2 hours, stirring frequently and adding a little water if necessary. Taste for seasoning—the cabbage should be sweet and sour.

Serves 6 to 8.

RISENGRØD MED MANDELDEJG
Almond-Rice Pudding

½ cup long grain rice
1 quart milk
½ vanilla bean, or 1 teaspoon
    vanilla extract
½ teaspoon salt

½ cup ground blanched almonds
¼ cup sugar
2 cups heavy cream
2 tablespoons sweet sherry

Wash the rice under cold running water. Rinse a heavy saucepan with cold water, then pour the milk into it and bring to a boil. Add the rice, stirring constantly, then add the vanilla and salt. Cook over medium heat for 5 minutes, stirring steadily. Cover and cook over very low heat on an asbestos pad for 45 minutes, stirring occasionally. Discard the vanilla. Mix in the almonds and sugar and let stand until cold. Whip the cream and fold into the rice mixture with the sherry. Chill and serve with a fruit sauce, if desired.

Serves 8 to 10.

GULE AERTER
Split Pea Soup

1 pound yellow split peas
3½ quarts water
3 pounds pork
¼ pound salt pork
1 parsley root
1 celery root
1 parsnip

4 leeks
2 onions
3 carrots
3 sprigs parsley
½ teaspoon thyme
1 pound potatoes
Salt

Wash the split peas well, then soak in 1½ quarts cold water for 2 hours. Bring to a boil in the same water, then cook over low heat 1¼ hours or until tender.

While the peas are soaking, in a large pan combine the pork, salt pork, parsley root, celery root, parsnip, leeks, onions, carrots, parsley, thyme and potatoes with the remaining water. Bring to a boil. Cover and cook over low heat 3 hours. Strain the stock and add enough to the peas to make it the consistency you like. Cut the vegetables into small pieces and add them to the peas. Add salt to taste. The meat can be served as a separate course with mustard sauce.

Serves 8 to 10.

DYRERYG
Roast Venison

6 pounds venison, rib or saddle	3 tablespoons flour
2 teaspoons salt	2 cups hot milk
¼ teaspoon pepper	1 cup red currant jelly
8 slices bacon	½ cup light cream
3 tablespoons butter	

Have the venison tied up; rub with the salt and pepper, then cover with the bacon. Place the meat in a roasting pan and roast in a 375° oven for 30 minutes.

Melt the butter in a saucepan; blend in the flour, then add the milk, stirring steadily to the boiling point. Add the pan juices and cook over low heat 5 minutes. Taste for seasoning. Pour the sauce over the meat and roast in a 325° oven 1½ hours, basting frequently.

Transfer the meat to a platter and keep warm. Pour the gravy into a saucepan. Skim the fat. Stir the jelly into the gravy, then the cream. Cook 5 minutes. Serve with browned potatoes (see goose recipe, page 90) and small baked apples filled with currant jelly.

Serves 8 to 10.

KRANSEKAGE
Almond Cake

Cake:

10 tablespoons (1 stick plus 2 tablespoons) butter	1⅜ cups sugar
1½ tablespoons heavy cream	1¾ cups sifted flour
4 eggs	2 teaspoons baking powder

Melt the butter, remove from the heat and stir in the cream. Cool. Beat the eggs, gradually adding the sugar. Continue beating until thick. Sift together the flour and baking powder. Add to the egg mixture alternately with the melted butter, stirring gently. Turn into a greased 8-inch springform pan.

Place on the center rack of a preheated 375° oven for 35 minutes. Meanwhile prepare the almond topping.

Almond Topping:

¼ pound butter	2 tablespoons heavy cream
½ cup sugar	1 cup coarsely chopped
2 tablespoons flour	blanched almonds

Combine all the ingredients in a saucepan. Stir over low heat until butter melts and mixture boils. At the end of the 35 minutes baking time, spread it (hot) over the cake. (Test cake first by putting a tablespoon of the almond mixture in the center. If it doesn't sink, continue spreading the almond mixture. If it does, bake cake 5 minutes longer before continuing.) Bake 10 minutes longer, or until the top is golden. Cool.

Serves 8.

KØDSUPPE MED BOLLER
Beef Soup with Meat Balls

Soup:

3 pounds rib, breast or shoulder of beef	1 parsnip
	2 leeks
2½ quarts water	2 stalks celery and leaves
2 teaspoons salt	3 sprigs parsley
½ teaspoon white pepper	1 bay leaf
3 carrots	¼ teaspoon thyme
1 celery root	

Wash the meat and place in a kettle with the water. Bring to a boil, skim the top, add the salt, bring to a boil again and skim the top. Add the pepper, cover and cook over low heat 1½ hours. Add the carrots, celery root, parsnip, leeks, celery, parsley, bay leaf and thyme. Cook 30 minutes longer. Strain, skim the fat and return some of the vegetables, cut up in small pieces. Add salt and pepper to taste. Prepare the meat balls while the soup is cooking.

Meat Balls:

½ pound pork	3 tablespoons flour
1 small onion	¾ cup milk
1 teaspoon salt	1 egg white, lightly beaten
⅛ teaspoon pepper	

Grind the pork 6 times, adding the onion the last time. Mix in the salt and pepper. Mix the flour to a paste with a little milk, then combine with all the milk. Add to the meat gradually, alternating with the egg white. Form teaspoons of the mixture into balls, and drop into boiling salted water. Bring to a boil. Add a little cold water to stop the boiling, then bring to a boil again. Repeat this step four more times, then drain, rinse the meat balls under cold water and drain well. Serve in the hot soup.

Serves 8 to 10.

HONSESTEG
Roast Chicken

3 1¼-pound whole broilers	1 cup chicken broth
3 teaspoons salt	2 tablespoons flour
½ teaspoon pepper	1 cup heavy cream
2 bunches parsley	½ cup red currant jelly
¼ pound butter	

Clean, wash and dry the whole chickens. Rub inside and out with the salt and pepper. Cut away the stems of the parsley, then coarsely chop the parsley. Mix with half the butter, and place one third in the cavity of each chicken. Close the opening with skewers.

Melt the remaining butter in a Dutch oven or heavy casserole. Brown the chickens in it on all sides. Turn the chickens on their sides and add the broth. Cover and roast in a 350° oven 1 hour, turning them on the other side after 30 minutes. Transfer the chickens to a platter. Place the pan over direct heat. Mix the flour with a little cream and stir it into the pan juices, then add all the cream and the jelly. Cook, stirring steadily to the boiling point, then cook over low heat 10 minutes longer. Taste for seasoning. Cut the chickens into halves or quarters, pour sauce over the pieces and surround with parsley potatoes.

Serves 6 to 8.

AGURKESALAT
Cucumber Salad

3 cucumbers	1 cup vinegar
Salt	4 tablespoons sugar
1 cup water	½ teaspoon black pepper

Wash and peel the cucumbers. Cut into very thin slices, sprinkle lightly with salt and let stand for 15 minutes. Pour off all the liquid. Mix together the water, vinegar, sugar and pepper; pour over the cucumbers and place in the refrigerator for 1 hour. Drain.

Serves 6 to 8.

PANDEKAGER
Pancakes

¼ pound butter	½ teaspoon ground cardamon
1½ cups flour	1½ cups milk
1 teaspoon sugar	4 eggs, beaten

Melt half the butter and let it cool. Mix the flour, sugar and cardamon in a bowl; add the milk gradually, mixing until smooth. Beat in the eggs, then the cooled butter. Let the batter stand for 1 hour.

Melt a little butter in a 5-inch skillet. Pour in about a tablespoon of batter, turning the pan quickly to cover the bottom thinly. When the edges of the pancake begin to brown, lift the pancake, put a little more butter on the pan and turn pancake to brown other side. Serve rolled up, or folded into quarters, with jam, or lemon juice and sugar.

Makes about 24.

Ecuador

THE Ecuadorian Embassy, although moderate in size, is exceptionally attractive in appearance. Throughout the building, there is a certain continuity of design and decor which creates an overall harmony of color and style.

The rooms are generally spacious, and decorated in pleasing colors. Often, Ecuador's national colors — red, blue and yellow — are used as a theme. The floors are almost all parquet, some of which is inlaid, and partly covered with rugs of solid hues. There are two receiving rooms, chiefly used when large numbers of guests are expected, and both are warm and friendly. The drawing room is of generous size, and attractively furnished.

The dining salon is a gem of a room, of good proportions and pleasingly furnished. It contains furniture of Spanish influence and Ecuadorian design. Off the dining room is a most attractive garden, arranged in terraces, which has a fountain as its focal point. In the springtime, the view is magnificent, for then the white dogwood blooms, and the garden seems an extension of the dining room itself. When guests come for dinner, meals are formally served with appropriate wines, in an elegant fashion.

Embajada de Ecuador

Locro de Queso
Escabeche de Pescado
Llapingachos
Pavo Relleno
Pudín de Maíz
Dulce de Piña

LOCRO DE QUESO
Cheese Soup

3 tablespoons vegetable oil
4 grains achiote (yellow color-
    ing), or 2 drops yellow
    food coloring
2 pounds potatoes, peeled and
    diced
4 cups water
2 teaspoons salt

⅛ teaspoon cayenne pepper
1 cup shredded Chinese or
    white cabbage
½ cup fresh, canned or frozen
    corn kernels
¾ cup grated Gruyère or
    American cheese
1 quart milk

Heat the oil in a saucepan, stir in the achiote (available in Spanish food stores) and brown the onions in it. Add the potatoes and cook until they change color. Add the water, bring to a boil, then add the salt, cayenne pepper, cabbage and corn. Cook over low heat 20 minutes. Mix in the cheese until melted. Just before serving, add the milk, taste for seasoning and heat.

Serves 8.

ESCABECHE DE PESCADO
Fish in Pickle Sauce

3 pounds fillet of sole or
    mackerel
3 teaspoons salt
1 teaspoon black pepper
Flour
1¾ cups olive oil
1½ cups thinly sliced red onions

½ cup lemon juice
1½ cups white vinegar
1 tablespoon prepared mustard
1 tablespoon Worcestershire
    sauce
½ teaspoon Tabasco
⅓ cup chopped mustard pickles

Cut each fillet of fish in thirds, rinse and dry. Sprinkle the fish with 2 teaspoons of the salt and ½ teaspoon pepper; dip in the flour.

Heat ¼ cup of the oil in a skillet; brown the fish in it. Drain and cool. Mix the onions with the lemon juice; let stand 30 minutes. Drain, reserving the lemon juice.

Mix the remaining oil with the remaining salt and pepper; gradually beat in the vinegar, then the mustard, Worcestershire sauce, Tabasco and reserved lemon juice. Mix the pickles with the onions. Add to the dressing and pour over the fish. Cover and refrigerate overnight or for at least several hours. The fish will keep for a week.

Serves 8 to 10.

LLAPINGACHOS
Potato Pancakes with Fried Eggs and Peanut Sauce

Pancakes:

2½ pounds potatoes, peeled	½ cup minced onions
¾ teaspoon salt	¼ pound cream cheese
¼ teaspoon white pepper	8 fried eggs
6 tablespoons butter	Sliced avocados

Cook the potatoes until tender. Drain and mash smooth with the salt, pepper and 2 tablespoons of the butter.

Melt 1 tablespoon of the remaining butter in a skillet; sauté the onions until browned.

Make eight pancakes of the potatoes, pressing some onions and a piece of cheese into the center of each. Cover the filling. Melt the remaining butter in a skillet and brown the pancakes in it. Put a fried egg on each and cover with the peanut sauce. Garnish with avocado slices.

Peanut Sauce:

2 tablespoons butter	½ teaspoon salt
½ cup chopped onions	¼ teaspoon black pepper
½ cup diced tomatoes	½ cup ground peanuts
2 tablespoons minced green peppers	½ cup water

Melt the butter in a skillet; sauté the onions until browned. Add the tomato, green peppers, salt and pepper. Cook over low heat 5 minutes. Add the peanuts and then gradually mix in the water. Cook 5 minutes.

Serves 8.

PAVO RELLENO
Stuffed Turkey

12-pound turkey	1½ cups chopped onions
4½ teaspoons salt	¾ cup chopped green peppers
1½ teaspoons black pepper	½ pound ground pork
¾ cup grated onions	½ teaspoon thyme
2 cloves garlic, minced	3 cups ground almonds
3 cups dry red wine	3 tablespoons minced parsley
2 cups fresh bread crumbs	1 cup seedless raisins
¾ cup milk	1 cup sliced green olives
¼ pound bacon	3 hard-cooked eggs, diced

Clean and wash the turkey. Rub the turkey with 3 teaspoons of the salt, 1 teaspoon pepper, the grated onions and garlic. Pour the wine over it and let marinate in the refrigerator overnight; turn and baste a few times.

Soak the bread crumbs in the milk when ready to prepare the stuffing.

Fry the bacon until crisp; drain and crumble. Pour off all but 3 tablespoons fat. Add the onions and green peppers; sauté 5 minutes. Add the pork, thyme and remaining salt and pepper; cook, stirring frequently until no pink remains in the pork. Mix in the almonds, bacon, parsley, raisins, olives, eggs and soaked bread crumbs. Taste for seasoning and cool.

Drain the turkey and stuff the cavity, closing the openings with skewers or by sewing. Place the turkey in a roasting pan and roast in a 325° oven 3½ hours or until tender and browned.

Serves 10 to 12.

PUDÍN DE MAÍZ
Corn Pudding

2 12-ounce cans whole kernel
   corn, drained
3 tablespoons butter
¾ cup chopped white onions

1½ cups grated American cheese
5 eggs, beaten
¾ teaspoon salt
¾ cup milk

Grind the corn in a food chopper. Melt the butter in a skillet; sauté the onions 5 minutes. Mix into the corn with the cheese, eggs, salt and milk. Pour into a buttered 1½-quart baking dish. Bake in a pre-heated 350° oven 40 minutes, or until browned.

Serves 8.

DULCE DE PIÑA
Chilled Pineapple Dessert

¼ pound butter
1 cup packed brown sugar
3 egg yolks
1 8-ounce can crushed pineapple

¾ cup coarsely chopped nuts
3 egg whites, beaten stiff
4 cups vanilla wafer crumbs
Whipped cream

Cream the butter, then gradually add the brown sugar, beating until light and fluffy. Beat in the egg yolks until well blended, then mix in the pineapple and nuts. Fold in the egg whites.

Press ¼ of the crumbs on the bottom of a greased 9-inch square pan; over this spread ⅓ of the pineapple mixture. Continue alternating the layers until all the ingredients are used up. Place a smaller pan on top and weight it down. Chill overnight. Serve cut into squares, with a bowl of whipped cream.

Serves 8.

Finland

ALTHOUGH Finland has only had an embassy in Washington since 1955 (at which time it was raised from legation status), it has become a popular place with Washington diplomats who enjoy its pleasant atmosphere and excellent food.

The embassy building itself is comparatively small by local standards, for it is somewhat modest in scope and proportions. However, every effort has been made to create a Finnish atmosphere throughout the embassy, and the interior decor emphasizes that country's arts and crafts. Many walls are covered with fine examples of the best in Finnish modern art. In one room may be seen the traditional ryijy rug, always given to Finnish brides.

The Finns are justly proud of the national skill in creating exceptional crystal and ceramic pieces. The crystal tends to be of unusually high quality and remarkable design, modern as tomorrow. Ceramics are perhaps even more creative, executed in distinctive shapes and colors. The Finnish Embassy has numerous prize-winning examples scattered throughout its many rooms.

The dining room serves exceptionally good native dishes. Receptions are held throughout the year, particularly on each December 6 (Independence Day), and on June 24 (Midsummer Garden Party).

Embassy of Finland

FORMAL MENU

Vähänsuolattua Lohta	Maksalaatikko
Kurkkusalaati	Etikkasilliä

Lihakeitto

Murekkeela Täytetta Kana

Kermaanmuhennetut Porkkanat

Imellytetty Perunavuoka

Vispilöity Karpalohyytelö

VÄHÄNSUOLATTUA LOHTA
Fresh Salted Salmon in Dill

6 pounds salmon, in one piece
2 tablespoons salt
1 tablespoon sugar

1 tablespoon white peppercorns
12 sprigs fresh dill

Cut the salmon in half lengthwise and remove the bones. Rub insides of both halves with a mixture of the salt, sugar and peppercorns. Spread the dill on the insides and press the two pieces together. Put the fish on a plate or board and weight it down. Chill for 8 hours or overnight. To serve, cut in thin diagonal slices. Sprinkle with chopped dill.

Serves 8.

MAKSALAATIKKO
Liver Pudding

2 pounds calf's liver
3 tablespoons butter
1 cup chopped onions
1 cup fresh bread crumbs

1 cup light cream
2 teaspoons salt
½ teaspoon black pepper
2 eggs, beaten

Wash and dry the liver; put through the fine blade of a food chopper. Melt the butter in a skillet; sauté the onions until golden, then chop them very fine.

Soak the bread crumbs in the cream for 10 minutes, then mash smooth. Combine the liver, onions, mashed bread crumbs, salt, pepper and eggs. Mix thoroughly and turn into a greased 9-inch loaf pan. Cover the top with greased foil. Bake in a 350° oven 1¼ hours, or until firm. Cool, then chill in the pan, carefully turn the pudding out onto a serving dish. Cut into slices.

Serves 8.

KURKKUSALAATI
Cucumber Hors d'Oeuvre Salad

3 cucumbers	½ cup vinegar
2 teaspoons sugar	3 tablespoons ice water
2 teaspoons salt	¼ cup minced fresh dill

Peel the cucumber and cut into thin slices. Put the cucumbers, sugar and salt into a bowl. Cover with another bowl or plate and shake. Let stand 15 minutes, then drain off the liquid. Arrange the cucumbers in a serving dish, and pour the mixture of vinegar and water over them. Sprinkle with the dill.

Serves 8.

ETIKKASILLIÄ
Pickled Herring

4 salt herring fillets	¾ cup sugar
1 cup sliced red onions	1 teaspoon crushed black
½ cup vinegar	peppercorns
1 cup water	4 bay leaves

Rinse the herring fillets in cold water, cover with water and let soak overnight, changing the water once or twice. Rinse again and dry. Cut the herring crosswise into 1-inch pieces.

In a bowl or jar, make layers of the herring and onions. Mix together the vinegar, water, sugar and peppercorns. Pour over the herring and add the bay leaves. Cover and let marinate in the refrigerator 24 hours before serving.

Serves 8.

LIHAKEITTO
Beef Soup

2 oxtails
2 tablespoons butter
½ cup sliced onions
1 carrot, sliced
2 stalks celery, sliced
1 tablespoon flour
4 quarts water

2 pounds beef
1 tablespoon salt
6 peppercorns
1 clove
3 sprigs parsley
3 tablespoons dry sherry

Have the oxtails sawed into small pieces. Melt the butter in a kettle. Add the oxtail pieces, the onions, carrot and celery. Cook 15 minutes. Sprinkle with the flour, stirring until browned. Add the water and meat. Bring to a boil. Add the salt, peppercorns, clove and parsley; cover and cook over low heat 3 hours. Strain and skim the fat.

Stir the sherry into the soup, and serve with tiny cubes of the meat. *Serves 8.*

MUREKKEELA TÄYTETTA KANA
Stuffed Boned Chicken

Chicken:

2 roasting chickens or capons
1 tablespoon salt

¾ teaspoon black pepper

Have the chickens or capons boned. Rub the fowl inside and out with the salt and pepper.

Stuffing:

1 whole chicken breast
¾ pound ground veal
⅓ cup fresh bread crumbs
⅓ cup light cream
1 egg, beaten
1½ teaspoons salt

½ teaspoon white pepper
Dash nutmeg
2 tablespoons minced parsley
6 tablespoons melted butter
1 cup heavy cream

Discard the skin and bones of the chicken and grind meat in a food chopper. Add the veal and grind again.

Soak the bread crumbs in the cream, then mash smooth. Add to the ground meats with the egg, salt, pepper, nutmeg, parsley and 2 tablespoons of the melted butter. Stuff the chickens with the mixture and sew the openings. Tie the chickens to hold their shapes.

Put the chickens in a roasting pan and pour the remaining butter over them. Roast in a 375° oven 2 hours, basting and turning to brown all sides. Transfer the chickens to a platter and remove the strings. Stir the cream into the pan juices; place over high heat and bring to a boil, scraping the bottom of browned particles. Taste for seasoning and serve in a sauceboat. *Serves 8 to 10.*

KERMAANMUHENNETUT PORKKANAT
Creamed Carrots

2 bunches carrots	2 teaspoons sugar
1½ cups water	1½ cups light cream
1 teaspoon salt	2 tablespoons minced dill
2 tablespoons flour	

Peel and cube the carrots. Combine the carrots and water in a saucepan. Bring to a boil and cook over high heat until the water evaporates. Season with the salt.

Mix together the flour, sugar and cream. Add to the carrots. Cook over low heat, stirring constantly, until the mixture boils. Continue 5 minutes longer or until the carrots are tender. Sprinkle with the dill. *Serves 8.*

IMELLYTETTY PERUNAVUOKA
Potato Pudding

3 pounds potatoes	4 teaspoons salt
2 tablespoons sugar	3 cups milk
4 tablepoons flour	¼ cup melted butter

Wash the unpeeled potatoes and cook in boiling water until tender. Drain and peel the potatoes while hot, then mash smooth. Beat in the sugar and 3 tablespoons of the flour. Sprinkle the top with the remaining flour. Cover the dish with a cloth and let stand 3 hours, mixing occasionally.

To the potatoes, add the salt, milk and melted butter. Beat well and turn the mixture into a buttered baking dish. Bake in a 375° oven 25 minutes, or until browned on top.

Serves 8.

VISPILÖITY KARPALOHYYTELÖ
Cranberry Dessert

6 cups cranberry juice	¾ cup water
1 cup sugar	3 tablespoons orange liqueur
3 envelopes (3 tablespoons) gelatin	Whipped cream

Combine the cranberry juice and sugar in a saucepan; bring to a boil, stirring until the sugar dissolves, then cook 5 minutes longer.

Soak the gelatin in the water for 5 minutes, then stir into the hot cranberry juice until dissolved. Cool slightly and mix in the liqueur. Cool until mixture begins to set, then beat with a wire whisk or rotary beater until frothy. Pour into individual serving dishes and chill until set. Serve topped with whipped cream.

Serves 8.

France

THE French Embassy, needless to say, conveys an entirely Gallic atmosphere, with a lightness of style, decor and design typical of that country. At one time, the embassy building was decorated in the French fashion of centuries ago — heavy, overwhelmingly large tapestries, dark wood paneling, and somber colors — but these have been replaced by modern art, light shades of wood, and cheerful color tones.

The drawing room is extremely handsome, a room which almost everyone finds appealing. There are exceptionally fine French rugs on the floor, authentic antique furniture has been carefully placed about the room, and oil paintings by renowned masters decorate the walls.

The drawing room's colors are buoyant, with pleasing, gay shades. A large enclosed loggia has been modernized, making it a friendly, homey room.

The dining room is a small masterpiece of color and design. On the walls hang superb examples of French art; Bonnard, Vuillard and Matisse are represented. Formal dinners feature the finest of Gallic cuisine, enhanced by suitable wines; an invitation to dinner at the French Embassy is highly regarded by the diplomatic corps. The table service is superb — china by Sèvres, glassware by St. Louis and Baccarat, and flatware by Fouquet-Lapar.

Ambassade de France

FORMAL MENU

Homard à l'Armoricaine
POUILLY-FUISSÉ

Filet de Charolais
POMMARD OR CHEVAL BLANC

Salade de Saison
Fromage
LA TÂCHE

Soufflé aux Framboises

INFORMAL MENU

Oeufs Interallié

Canard aux Navets
CHÂTEAU MOUTON ROTHSCHILD

Salade de Saison
Fromage

Poires Mona Lisa

FAMILY MENU

Oeufs en Cocotte

Boeuf à la Mode
BEAUJOLAIS

Fromage

Fruits

HOMARD À L'ARMORICAINE
Lobster in Wine Sauce

8 1¼-pound live lobsters
⅓ cup olive oil
6 tablespoons butter
2 tablespoons chopped shallots
    or green onions
1 clove garlic, minced
⅓ cup warm cognac
2 cups dry white wine

2 tablespoons tomato paste
2 teaspoons salt
½ teaspoon black pepper
2 tablespoons glace de viande
    or other meat glaze
3 tablespoons minced parsley
2 teaspoons minced fresh tarra-
    gon or ¼ teaspoon dried

Have the live lobsters cut up in the shell into small pieces. Remove and reserve the soft green and yellow parts.

Heat the oil and 4 tablespoons butter in a large casserole or Dutch oven. Add the lobster pieces and cook until shells turn red, turning the pieces frequently. Add the shallots and garlic; cook 2 minutes. Pour the warm cognac over the lobster and set aflame. When flames die, mix in the wine, tomato paste, salt and pepper. Cook over low heat 20 minutes. Remove the lobster pieces and keep warm.

Cook the sauce, meat glaze, parsley and tarragon over high heat for 3 minutes. Mix the remaining butter with the reserved soft parts of the lobster and add to the sauce. Bring to a boil and cook 5 minutes. Taste for seasoning and pour over the lobsters.

Serves 10 to 16 as a first course.

FILET DE CHAROLAIS
Fillet of Beef in Pastry

Pastry:

1 pound (4 cups) flour
1 package yeast
¼ cup lukewarm water
2 teaspoons salt

3 tablespoons sugar
7 eggs
1 pound butter

Put 2 cups of the flour into a bowl. Make a well in the center and into it put the yeast and water, mixing until yeast dissolves. Gradually work the flour into the yeast mixture and shape into a ball. Cover and let rise in a warm place (about 80°) until triple its size.

Put the remaining flour in a large bowl or on a board. Make a well in the center and into it put the salt, sugar and 5 of the eggs. Beat the eggs, then work in the flour. Cream together the butter and remaining eggs, then beat in the risen yeast dough. Beat both doughs together until smooth. Put in a clean bowl; dust top lightly with flour, cover and let stand in a cool place for 4 hours. When ready to use, punch down and roll out 3 times.

Meat:

6-pound fillet of beef	1 cup Madeira
2 teaspoons salt	2 teaspoons arrowroot or
½ teaspoon black pepper	cornstarch
Chopped truffles	2 tablespoons butter
1 egg, beaten	

Trim the fat off the fillet and season with the salt and pepper. Place on a shallow roasting pan and roast in a 475° oven 15 minutes. Remove from the pan and cool. Reserve the pan juices.

Pat out the dough on a lightly floured surface 1 inch thick and large enough to completely cover the meat. Sprinkle the dough with some chopped truffles. Place the cooled fillet in the center, fold over one side of the dough and roll up. Seal edges well. Decorate the top with fancy cutouts of dough. Place on a clean baking sheet and let stand 1 hour. Just before baking, brush the dough with the egg. Bake in a preheated 400° oven for 30 minutes. Prepare the gravy while the meat is baking.

Stir the Madeira into the pan juices, scraping the bottom of any brown particles. Cook until reduced to one third. Mix the starch with a little water and add to the gravy, stirring over low heat until thickened. Mix in the butter and chopped truffles. Taste for seasoning.

Slice the meat and serve the gravy in a sauceboat. *Serves 8.*

SOUFFLÉ AUX FRAMBOISES
Raspberry Soufflé

4 packages frozen raspberries
or 1¼ pounds fresh

Sugar (¼ cup for frozen berries,
1⅛ cups for fresh)

6 egg whites

Cook the raspberries over low heat for 20 minutes without any water, then force them through a fine strainer. Return the purée to the saucepan. Add the sugar; cook over high heat until reduced to half the original quantity. Cool.

Beat the egg whites until stiff but not dry. Fold in the raspberry purée. Turn into a 1½-quart soufflé or round baking dish. Bake in a preheated 250° oven 25 minutes. Serve immediately.

Serves 8.

OEUFS INTERALLIÉ
Egg Casserole

6 tablespoons butter
4 tablespoons flour
2 cups milk
2 teaspoons salt
½ teaspoon white pepper

¾ cup freshly grated Parmesan
cheese
1 cup chopped sautéed
mushrooms
6 eggs
¼ cup light cream

Melt 4 tablespoons of the butter in a saucepan; blend in the flour, then add the milk, cooking and stirring to the boiling point. Add 1 teaspoon salt and the pepper; cook over low heat 5 minutes.

Pour half the sauce into a 1½-quart casserole or baking dish. Sprinkle with half the cheese, then spread the mushrooms over the cheese.

Beat the eggs with the cream and remaining salt, then scramble them very lightly so that they are still slightly runny. Spread over the mushrooms. Pour the remaining sauce over them, sprinkle with the remaining cheese and dot with the remaining butter. Place under a hot broiler until top is delicately browned and serve directly from the dish.

Serves 8.

CANARD AUX NAVETS
Duck with Turnips

Sauce:

3 tablespoons butter	2 tablespoons minced parsley
3 tablespoons flour	1 teaspoon salt
4 cups beef broth	½ teaspoon peppercorns
2 tablespoons tomato paste	¼ teaspoon thyme
1 glove garlic	1 bay leaf
½ cup sliced onions	

Melt the butter in a saucepan; blend in the flour until browned. Add the broth, stirring steadily until smooth and mixture boils. Add all the remaining ingredients. Cook over low heat 30 minutes, then strain.

Duck:

2 5-pound ducks	½ teaspoon thyme
2 teaspoons salt	1½ pounds turnips
½ teaspoon black pepper	2 teaspoons sugar
⅜ pound butter	36 small white onions
½ cup dry white wine	
Bouquet garni (parsley and bay leaf in a small cheese-cloth bag)	

Wash and dry the ducks; remove as much fat as possible. Season the ducks with the salt and pepper. Melt 4 tablespoons butter in a large Dutch oven or roasting pan; brown the ducks in it on all sides. Remove the ducks and drain well. Stir the wine into the pan; cook over high heat 3 minutes. Add the previously prepared sauce, the bouquet garni and thyme. Bring to a boil and return the ducks. Cook over low heat 1 hour.

Cut the turnips into large olive shapes. Melt half the remaining butter in a skillet; add the turnips and half the sugar. Sauté until browned and glazed. Remove. Melt the remaining butter in the skillet; add the onions and the remaining sugar. Sauté until browned and glazed.

Transfer the ducks to another pan; arrange the turnips and onions around them. Skim the fat off the gravy, then strain over the ducks and vegetables. Bake in a 350° oven 30 minutes, or until the ducks are tender. Carve and serve surrounded with the vegetables and covered with the gravy.

Serves 8.

POIRES MONA LISA
Pears with Chocolate Sauce in Pastry Shells

Pastry:

2¼ cups flour	½ pound plus 2 tablespoons
1 cup plus 2 tablespoons sugar	butter, melted
6 egg whites	

Sift the flour and sugar into a bowl. Mix in the egg whites until smooth, then gradually add the melted, cooled butter. Let stand 15 minutes. On a lightly floured surface, pat out the dough and cut or shape into 6-inch rounds. Transfer with a spatula to baking sheets, allowing space between each. Bake in a preheated 300° oven 10 minutes or until very delicately browned around the edges. Immediately put the cookies in cups to give them a tulip shape and allow to cool.

Pears:

8 medium-sized firm pears	1½ cups melted semi-sweet
2 tablespoons lemon juice	chocolate
2 cups sugar	Vanilla ice cream
1 quart water	Whipped cream
1 vanilla bean	

Peel the pears, cover with cold water and add the lemon juice.

Combine the sugar, the 1 quart water and vanilla bean in a sauce-pan. Bring to a boil and cook 5 minutes. Drain the pears and add to the syrup. Cook over low heat 10 minutes or until the pears are tender but still hold their shapes. Cool, drain and dry the pears. Dip into the hot melted chocolate.

Put a ball of ice cream in each pastry shell with a pear on top. Decorate with whipped cream. Arrange on an oval serving dish. At the embassy, the dish is decorated with a wreath of fresh flowers.
Makes 8.

OEUFS EN COCOTTE
Shirred Eggs

For each serving, use one or two eggs. Break the eggs carefully into individual buttered ramekins or other shallow baking dishes. Sprinkle with salt and pepper.

Place the dishes in a pan of boiling water; cover the pan and cook 2½ minutes.

BOEUF À LA MODE
Braised Beef

5 pounds rump of beef	Bouquet garni
1 calf's foot	30 small white onions
⅓ cup warm cognac	16 small scraped carrots
2 cups dry white wine	1 tablespoon arrowroot or
2½ teaspoons salt	cornstarch
¾ teaspoon black pepper	3 tablespoons cold water

Have the meat larded, wrapped in fat and tied up into a firm shape.

Have the calf's foot sawed up, but still left connected. Cover with water, bring to a boil and let stand 15 minutes. Drain, scrape and rinse under cold water.

Heat a Dutch oven and brown the meat in it on all sides. Pour off all the fat. Add the cognac and set aflame. When flames die, add the wine. Cook over high heat until reduced to half. Add the calf's foot, salt, pepper, bouquet garni and boiling water to barely cover. Cover and bake in a 350° oven 1 hour. Add the onions and carrots. Cover again and bake 2 hours longer, or until the beef is very tender. Remove the meat, foot and bouquet garni. Skim the fat from the gravy and thicken with a mixture of the starch and water. Carve the meat and serve with the vegetables and gravy.

Serves 8 to 10.

Germany

THE German Embassy is housed in a large building containing twenty rooms, handsomely located on a three-acre plot; there are spacious grounds and the building itself is well set back from the road, which lends a feeling of privacy and offers the Ambassador and his family a country-like atmosphere. Although the embassy is far from small, it is only a fraction of the size of the enormous embassy of some seventy rooms which the German government maintained before the war.

The present embassy building is air-conditioned throughout, and has an elevator. All the rooms are of good size, and well proportioned. The drawing room is generally regarded as the embassy's best room; it

is here that the many receptions and parties are held. This charming room permits a great number of people to gather without creating a sense of congestion.

The dining room, dominated by an antique Flemish tapestry, has modern furniture especially made in Germany. The china is Royal Berlin, white with a narrow gold border; the glassware is Bavarian crystal. The embassy is especially proud of its elaborate kitchen, perhaps the finest in any Washington embassy and of a size comparable to that of a medium-sized hotel. The kitchen equipment is superb, the finest obtainable, and permits the chefs and cooks to prepare food for large numbers of guests with little difficulty.

Embassy of the
Federal Republic of Germany

FORMAL MENU

Schildkrötensuppe
Hummer mit Sauce
BERNKASTELER DOKTOR

Gefüllte Filet
Herzoginnen Kartoffeln
Jerusalem Artischocken
ASAMANNSHÄUSER SPÄTBURGUNDER

Pfannkuchen
CHAMPAGNE: HENKELL TROCKEN

Demitasse

INFORMAL MENU

Consommé
Forelle Blau
Rinderroulade
Kartoffeln
Zitronen Creme
Café

SUMMER FAMILY MENU

Kalte Schale
Hühnerfrikassee
Reis
Spargel
Pfannkuchen

SCHILDKROTENSUPPE
Turtle Soup

1½ pounds turtle meat
4 quarts water
1 tablespoon salt
2 pounds stewing beef
1 veal knuckle, split
1 onion
2 stalks celery

1 carrot
½ cup Madeira
Pinch of basil, sage, marjoram,
    savory
2 teaspoons arrowroot
¼ teaspoon pepper

Wash the turtle meat and combine with the water and salt. Bring to a boil and simmer 4 hours. Remove the turtle meat. Add the beef, veal knuckle, onion, celery and carrot. Simmer 2½ hours. Strain the broth. Cut the turtle meat in small pieces and return to the broth; simmer 20 minutes. Bring the Madeira to a boil and stir in the herbs. Add the mixture to the soup. Mix the arrowroot with a little water and stir into the soup. Cook 5 minutes. Add the pepper, and salt if necessary.

Serves 10 to 12.

NOTE: Curry may be added to taste, in which case the soup is called "à la Lady Curzon."

If turtle meat is not available, use 3 quarts of canned turtle soup, and omit water. Continue preparing soup as directed.

HUMMER MIT SAUCE
Creamed Lobster

4 2-pound live lobsters
1 bottle dry white wine
1 teaspoon salt
1 large onion, sliced
1 carrot, sliced
1 stalk celery, sliced
6 parsley sprigs
1 bay leaf
6 peppercorns

½ teaspoon tarragon
⅜ pound butter
6 tablespoons flour
1 tablespoon dry mustard
Dash cayenne pepper
3 egg yolks
¾ cup heavy cream
⅓ cup brandy

Rinse the lobsters under cold running water.

Bring the wine, salt, onion, carrot, celery, parsley, bay leaf, pepper-corns and tarragon to a boil; simmer 15 minutes. Bring to a boil again and plunge the lobsters into it. Cover and cook 20 minutes. Remove the lobsters. Cook the stock until it is reduced to 3 cups. Strain. Melt half the butter; stir in the flour for 1 minute. Beat in the lobster stock and cook 3 minutes, stirring.

Split the lobsters and remove the meat from the bodies and claws discarding the black vein; cut into ½-inch pieces. Rub the coral and green matter through a fine sieve into a bowl. Mix in the mustard, pepper, egg yolks and half the cream. Gradually beat in the hot sauce. Return to the saucepan and cook, stirring with a wooden spoon, for 2 minutes. Mix in the remaining cream.

Melt the remaining butter; sauté the lobster meat 5 minutes, stirring frequently. Add the brandy; boil 3 minutes, shaking the pan frequently. Fold in the sauce. Heat and taste for seasoning. Serve on heated dishes, or stuff the shells and place in a 450° oven for 5 minutes.

Serves 8.

GEFÜLLTE FILET
Stuffed Fillet of Beef

6-pound fillet of beef	6 tablespoons butter
Salt	2 tablespoons cornstarch
Pepper	½ cup Madeira
1 8-ounce can pâté de foie gras	1½ cups beef broth

Make a deep cut in the meat lengthwise. Season the meat with salt and pepper. Mash the foie gras and stuff the fillet. Close the opening and tie the meat at 2-inch intervals.

Melt the butter in a shallow roasting pan; put the fillet in it cut side up. Roast in a 425° oven 45 minutes, basting frequently. Remove the fillet, cut away strings and keep warm.

Place pan over direct heat. Mix the cornstarch with the wine and broth. Add to the pan. Cook, stirring until thickened. Taste for seasoning. Carve the fillet and serve with the sauce.

Serves 8 to 10.

HERZOGINNEN KARTOFFELN
Duchess Potatoes

3 pounds potatoes	¼ teaspoon pepper
Boiling salted water	¼ teaspoon nutmeg
5 tablespoons butter	3 egg yolks, beaten
1½ teaspoons salt	2 whole eggs, beaten

Peel and cut the potatoes in half. Cook in boiling salted water to cover until tender. Drain well and put through a potato ricer or mash in an electric mixer. Beat in the butter, salt, pepper, nutmeg, egg yolks and eggs until fluffy. Put through a pastry tube onto a heat proof serving dish or heap in a mound. Place under the broiler until lightly browned.

Serves 8 to 10.

JERUSALEM ARTISCHOCKEN
Buttered Jerusalem Artichokes

2 pounds Jerusalem artichokes	¼ pound butter, melted
Water	2 tablespoons minced parsley
2 teaspoons salt	1 tablespoon lemon juice

Scrub the artichokes, then peel them. Drop into water to cover and add the salt. Bring to a boil and simmer 25 minutes or until tender. Drain well and toss with the melted butter, parsley and lemon juice.

Serves 8 to 10.

PFANNKUCHEN
Pancakes with Orange Liqueur Sauce

Pancakes:

1½ cups milk	⅓ cup brandy
1½ cups cold water	2½ cups sifted flour
6 egg yolks	½ cup melted butter
1 tablespoon sugar	

Beat all the ingredients together until smooth. Cover and chill at least 2 hours. Make very thin pancakes in a 5- or 6-inch skillet, piling them onto a napkin as they are finished.

Sauce:

8 lumps of sugar	¾ pound softened sweet butter
4 oranges	⅔ cup orange liqueur
½ cup fine sugar	⅔ cup brandy

Rub all sides of the sugar lumps over the orange skins to absorb the oil. Peel the oranges thinly. Squeeze the oranges and measure 1⅓ cups juice.

Mash the sugar lumps; add the peel and sugar and chop fine. Cream the butter, then beat in the sugar mixture until fluffy. Beat in the orange juice and half the orange liqueur. Put in a chafing dish and heat until mixture bubbles. One by one, dip the crêpes on both sides in the butter mixture, then fold into quarters. When all are dipped and folded, pour over them the brandy and remaining orange liqueur. Set aflame, and baste with the sauce until flames die.

Serves 8 to 10.

FORELLE BLAU
Blue Trout

8 live trout	Lemon slices
3 quarts water	Parsley sprigs
1½ cups vinegar	Melted butter

The trout must be kept alive until shortly before using, so that they will turn blue when cooked. Hold the trout by the head and clean under cold running water. Place on a wet plate. Heat a little of the water and vinegar and pour over the fish, then place in the refrigerator for 10 minutes.

Bring the remaining water and vinegar to a boil. Carefully place the fish in it and simmer 15 minutes. Drain and arrange on a hot serving dish. Garnish with the lemon and parsley and serve with melted butter.

Serves 8.

NOTE: If refrigerated trout are used, they will not turn blue, but are otherwise suitable.

RINDERROULADE
Beef Rolls

8 thin slices round steak	6 tablespoons butter
2 teaspoons salt	2 cups boiling water
½ teaspoon pepper	1 bay leaf
8 slices bacon, minced	¼ teaspoon thyme
1 cup chopped onions	¼ teaspoon rosemary
¼ cup chopped parsley	¼ teaspoon marjoram
2 teaspoons prepared mustard	¼ cup heavy cream
½ cup flour	2 tablespoons dry red wine

Pound the meat very thin and sprinkle with the salt and pepper. Mix the bacon, onions, parsley and mustard. Spread over the meat slices, roll up and tie with white thread. Dip in the flour on all sides.

Heat the butter in a deep skillet; brown the rolls in it. Add water and herbs. Simmer 1¼ hours, or until tender. Remove the rolls, cut off the thread and arrange on a hot platter. Stir the cream and wine into the gravy, then pour over the meat. Serve with boiled potatoes, brussel sprouts and broiled tomatoes.

Serves 8.

ZITRONEN CREME
Lemon Cream

2 teaspoons gelatin	¾ cup plus 2 tablespoons sugar
¼ cup water	⅓ cup lemon juice
4 eggs	1 tablespoon grated lemon rind

Sprinkle the gelatin into the water. Separate the eggs. Beat the egg yolks and sugar in the top of a double boiler. Add the lemon juice. Place over hot water and heat until mixture thickens. Stir in the gelatin until dissolved. Cool, stir in the rind and the egg whites, beaten stiff. Pour into a large bowl or 8 individual dishes. Chill. *Serves 8.*

HÜHNERFRIKASSEE
Chicken Fricassee

2 4-pound pullets, cut up	4 tablespoons flour
1 lemon	¼ pound mushrooms, chopped
3 teaspoons salt	½ cup dry white wine
5 cups water	3 egg yolks
¼ pound butter	⅓ cup heavy cream

Wash and dry the chickens. Cut the lemon in half, and with one half rub the chicken pieces. Sprinkle with half the salt. Bring the water and remaining salt to a boil. Add the chicken; cook 5 minutes. Drain and dry the chicken; reserve the liquid.

Melt half the butter in a Dutch oven. Lightly brown the chicken in it. Add the liquid. Bring to a boil and simmer 45 minutes or until chicken is tender. Remove the chicken. Reserve the stock. Carefully pull off the skin of the chicken.

Melt the remaining butter; stir in the flour. Add the stock, stirring until thickened. Add the mushrooms, wine, juice of the other half lemon, and salt and pepper to taste. Simmer 10 minutes. Beat the egg

yolks and cream. Stir in a little hot sauce, then return to balance of
sauce, stirring steadily. Add the chicken. Place pan over an asbestos
pad or hot water until heated through. Serve with rice and asparagus.

Serves 6 to 8.

KALTE SCHALE
Cold Fruit Soup

4 cups fruit in season (apples, rhubarb, gooseberries, preferably)	½ cup dry white wine
	¼ cup sugar
6 cups water	1 tablespoon lemon juice
2 tablespoons cornstarch	1 teaspoon grated lemon rind

Wash the fruit; slice the apples and rhubarb. Combine all the fruit
with the water, bring to a boil and cook 20 minutes.

Put the fruit through a fine sieve. Return to saucepan, and bring
to a boil. Mix the cornstarch with the wine, and add to the soup,
stirring until thickened. Add the sugar, lemon juice and rind. Taste
and add more sugar or lemon juice if needed. Chill and serve garnished with whole fruit or small macaroons.

Serves 8.

Greece

GUESTS at Greek Embassy dinners are seated around a handsome polished oblong table, customarily set with handmade lace place mats. The monogrammed napkins have matching lace inserts. Gleaming crystal goblets for the wines of the country provide a dramatic contrast to the dark wood of the table. Tall candelabra, along with a large floral arrangement in a silver epergne set on a lace runner, usually make up the centerpiece.

Royal Greek Embassy

FORMAL MENU

Melitzanes Salata   Midea Yemista

Soupa Avgolemono

Psari me Shordalia

Arni Yemisto

Spanakopeta

Karydopitta

MELITZANES SALATA
Eggplant Spread

2 large eggplants
½ cup grated onion
1 cup peeled diced tomatoes
3 tablespoons chopped parsley

¾ cup olive or vegetable oil
3 tablespoons vinegar
1½ teaspoons salt
¼ teaspoon black pepper

Wash the eggplants and place on a baking pan. Bake in a 400° oven 50 minutes or until tender. Dip the eggplants in cold water, then, holding them by the stems, remove the skins. Discard the stems.

Chop the eggplant, then add the onions, tomatoes and parsley. Continue chopping until fine. Gradually add the olive oil, beating constantly with a wooden spoon. Beat in the vinegar, salt and pepper. Chill. Taste for seasoning. Spread on Greek bread or crackers or thin French bread.

Serves 8.

MIDEA YEMISTA
Stuffed Mussels

36 mussels
¾ cup dry white wine
½ cup water
½ teaspoon salt
¼ cup olive oil
1 cup chopped onions
½ cup raw rice

¼ teaspoon ground allspice
¼ teaspoon black pepper
¼ cup pine nuts or slivered
    almonds
¼ cup currants or seedless
    raisins
2 tablespoons chopped parsley

Scrub the mussels under cold running water. Snip off the beards of the mussels, wash again and place in a pan. Add the wine, water and salt. Cover, bring to a boil and cook 5 minutes, or until the shells open. Discard any that don't open. Remove the mussels from the shells; reserve half the shells. Strain and reserve the liquid.

Heat the oil in a skillet; sauté the onions 5 minutes. Add the rice; cook, stirring until rice turns yellow. Add the reserved liquid. Cover and cook over low heat 15 minutes. Add the allspice, pepper, nuts, currants and parsley; cook 5 minutes longer. Taste for seasoning.

Put a mussel in each shell, and cover with the rice mixture. Serve cold.

Serves 8.

SOUPA AVGOLEMONO
Lemon Soup

8 cups chicken or beef broth	2 eggs
¼ cup rice	⅓ cup lemon juice

Bring the broth to a boil; add the rice and cook over low heat 20 minutes.

Beat the eggs and lemon juice in a bowl. Gradually add about 2 cups of the broth, stirring steadily to prevent curdling. Return to the saucepan and bring just to a boil, stirring constantly.

Serves 8.

PSARI ME SHORDALIA
Fish with Walnut Sauce

2 whole 3-pound sea bass or striped bass	1 tablespoon flour
1 tablespoon salt	4 cups boiling water
¾ teaspoon black pepper	3 cups finely ground walnuts
½ cup olive oil	1 teaspoon minced garlic
	¼ cup chopped parsley

Have the heads of the fish removed or not, as you like. Wash and dry the fish, then rub with the salt and pepper.

Heat the oil in a skillet or other pan large enough to hold the fish.

Add the flour, stirring until brown. Gradually add the water, stirring steadily. Arrange the fish in the pan. Cover, and cook over low heat 40 minutes. Taste for seasoning. Let fish cool in the stock. Transfer the fish to a serving dish.

Mix the walnuts and garlic; gradually stir in the fish broth; pour sauce over the fish and sprinkle with the parsley.

Serves 8.

ARNI YEMISTO
Roast Stuffed Crown of Lamb

Crown roast of lamb	1 cup chopped onions
¼ cup lemon juice	½ pound chicken livers, diced
4 teaspoons salt	⅓ cup currants or seedless
1 teaspoon black pepper	raisins
¼ pound butter	½ cup pine nuts or slivered
¾ cup raw rice	almonds
1¾ cups hot beef broth	¼ cup chopped parsley

A crown requires about 16 chops. Have the butcher make it for you, and have the trimmings ground. Rub the crown with the lemon juice, 3 teaspoons of the salt and ¾ teaspoon pepper. Cover the bones with foil or cubes of potatoes.

Melt 3 tablespoons of the butter in a saucepan, add the rice and cook, stirring until yellow. Add the broth, cover and cook over low heat 15 minutes.

Melt 3 tablespoons of the butter in a skillet; sauté the onions 5 minutes. Add the ground lamb and livers; sauté 10 minutes, stirring frequently. Mix together the rice, the sautéed meats, the currants, nuts, parsley and remaining salt and pepper. Taste for seasoning. Melt the remaining butter.

Place the crown in a shallow roasting pan. Put the stuffing in the center and cover the stuffing with a piece of aluminum foil. Pour the melted butter over the lamb. Roast in 350° oven 1½ hours—the lamb will be pink. Remove the covering of the bones and replace with paper frills.

Transfer the lamb to a platter, refilling the center with the stuffing. *Serves 8.*

SPANAKOPETA
Spinach Pie

12 phyllo or strudel leaves	¼ cup olive oil
2 pounds spinach	3 cups chopped onions
½ cup chopped parsley	¼ teaspoon black pepper
½ cup chopped dill	½ pound Feta cheese, crumbled
2 cups chopped green onions	¾ cup melted butter
1½ teaspoons salt	

Phyllo leaves can be purchased in Middle East food shops, and strudel leaves are available frozen in many markets. Keep the pastry leaves covered until ready to use.

Wash, clean and discard the stems of the spinach. Drain and cut into fine shreds. Combine the spinach, parsley, dill, green onions and salt in a bowl. Let stand 10 minutes, then drain, pressing out all the liquid.

Heat the oil in a skillet; sauté the chopped onions 10 minutes. Add to the spinach mixture, with the pepper and cheese. Mix well.

Brush an 11- by 14-inch baking pan with butter, then in it put 6 layers of pastry leaves, brushing each layer with melted butter. Spread the filling evenly, then cover with the remaining pastry leaves, brushing each layer with melted butter. Brush the top layer heavily. With a sharp knife, trace the top layer into squares. Bake in a preheated 375° oven 30 minutes, or until golden brown. Cut through the squares and serve hot.

Serves 8.

KARYDOPITTA
Athens Walnut Pie

Pie:

6 cups (1½ pounds) ground walnuts	12 eggs
16 zwieback, finely crushed	1½ cups sugar
1 tablespoon grated orange rind	1 teaspoon cinnamon
	2 teaspoons baking powder

Mix together the nuts, zwieback crumbs and orange rind.

Beat the eggs, gradually adding the sugar. Beat until thick and lemon colored, then mix in the cinnamon and baking powder. Fold in the nut mixture. Turn into a greased 13- by 16- by 3-inch baking pan. Bake in a preheated 350° oven 1 hour. Prepare the syrup while the cake is baking, as it must be poured over the top the moment the pan is removed from the oven.

Syrup:

1½ cups sugar	2 cups water

Bring the sugar and water to a boil, stirring steadily until sugar dissolves, then cook 5 minutes longer. Pour over the pie and cool, then cut into diamond-shaped pieces.

Serves 8.

India

THE Indian Embassy has had a most interesting history. The exterior is covered with red brick, especially made from antique bricks, and quite different in size and color from those generally seen. The front door and ironwork originally graced the main entrance of an elaborate old house in London.

The embassy building was acquired by India in 1946, and furnished in the French style. In 1961, however, with the realization that the building did not display any of the great native skills and talents of the country, it was completely redecorated in the Indian style. Now, Indian rugs cover the floors, and the furniture has been beautifully upholstered in soft-hued fabrics, handwoven in the embassy's homeland.

Walls are covered with priceless antique tapestries and modern Indian oil paintings, the old and the new blending very successfully. The lamps, vases, ceramics, drapes, brass and copper handicrafts, wood carvings and decorative screens are all intended to give an indication of the enormous artistic talents of this enormous country.

Contradictions abound, however. For example, one table displays several Hungarian (Herend) porcelain vases; the mantelpiece in the front hall came originally from Dorchester House in London; the floor in the reception room is made of antique French parquet. Nonetheless, the overall effect is that of India, and the general impression that of harmony of design and color.

Embassy of India

FORMAL MENU

Masala Fried Fish
Pulao Yakhni
Raita
Rogan Josh
Murgh Masala
Keema Curry
Mattar Panir
Fried Bhindi
Dry Dal
Poori
Chutney and Pickle
Fruits

MASALA FRIED FISH

4 fillets of sole
½ teaspoon ground dried chili
      peppers
2 cloves garlic, minced
2 teaspoons minced ginger root
1 tablespoon minced coriander
      leaves (Chinese parsley)
      or 1 teaspoon ground
      coriander seeds

¼ teaspoon turmeric
1 teaspoon salt
2 tablespoons lemon juice
1 cup vegetable oil

Wash and dry the fish. Cut each fillet in half crosswise. Rub with a mixture of the chili peppers, garlic, ginger, coriander, turmeric, and salt, then sprinkle with the lemon juice.

Heat the oil in a skillet; fry the fish until golden brown on both sides. Drain and serve hot.

Serves 8.

PULAO YAKHNI
Fried Rice Curry

Meat:

2 pounds boneless lamb
2½ teaspoons salt
2 teaspoons cinnamon
¼ teaspoon ground cloves
2 teaspoons minced fresh green
      chilies or ½ teaspoon
      dried ground chili
      peppers

1 tablespoon minced ginger
      root
2 cloves garlic, minced
4 cups water

Wash the lamb, cut up into small pieces and combine with all the remaining ingredients in a saucepan. Bring to a boil and cook over low heat 1½ hours. Remove the meat and strain the broth. Reserve.

Rice:

1 pound long grain rice	½ teaspoon ground cardamon
4 tablespoons butter	1 teaspoon cinnamon
2 large onions, peeled and sliced	½ teaspoon powdered bay leaf
2 teaspoons cumin seeds	1 teaspoon turmeric
¼ teaspoon ground cloves	2 teaspoons chili powder

Wash the rice, cover with warm water and let soak 30 minutes. Drain and dry.

Melt the butter in a saucepan. Strain off the melted butter into a large skillet, leaving the white sediment on the bottom. This clarifies the butter. Sauté the onions in the clarified butter until golden brown. Remove the onions and reserve. Brown the meat and remove. Put the spices in the skillet; cook 2 minutes, stirring constantly. Add the rice; cook until browned, stirring frequently. Add the reserved broth. Bring to a boil and cook 10 minutes. Add the reserved meat. Mix, cover and cook until all the liquid is absorbed. Garnish with the fried onions.
Serves 8.

RAITA
Cucumbers in Yogurt

3 cups yogurt	3 cucumbers, peeled and thinly sliced
¾ teaspoon salt	
½ teaspoon pepper	Paprika
3 tablespoons minced coriander leaves (Chinese parsley)	

Beat the yogurt smooth, then stir in the salt, pepper and coriander leaves. Fold in the cucumbers. Serve very cold, sprinkled with paprika.
Serves 8.

ROGAN JOSH
Lamb Curry

2 pounds boneless lamb
6 tablespoons butter
2 cups onions, chopped
2 cloves garlic, minced
1 teaspoon powdered ginger
1 teaspoon ground cumin
2 teaspoons ground coriander
    seeds

2 teaspoons salt
¼ teaspoon ground dried chili
    peppers
1 teaspoon saffron
1 large tomato, chopped
¾ cup chicken broth
½ teaspoon mace
½ teaspoon nutmeg

Cut the lamb in ½-inch cubes. Melt the butter in a saucepan; add the onions, garlic, ginger, cumin, coriander, salt and chili peppers. Cook over medium heat 5 minutes, stirring frequently. Add the meat and half the saffron; cook until meat browns. Add the tomato, broth, mace and nutmeg. Cover and cook over low heat 1 hour or until meat is tender. Stir in the remaining saffron.

Serves 8.

MURGH MASALA
Chicken Curry

2 3½-pound chickens,
    disjointed
1½ teaspoons turmeric
1½ teaspoons cumin seeds
1 teaspoon cinnamon
6 cloves
¼ teaspoon dried ground chili
    peppers
1 tablespoon minced ginger
    root

2 cloves garlic, minced
1½ cups chopped onions
½ teaspoon ground cardamon
2 pounds tomatoes, peeled
    and diced
2 teaspoons salt
Water
6 tablespoons butter

Wash the chicken pieces and combine in a Dutch oven with the turmeric, cumin, cinnamon, cloves, chili peppers, ginger, garlic, onions, cardamon, tomatoes and salt. Add enough water to reach just below the top of the ingredients. Dot top with butter. Bring to a boil, cover and cook over low heat 1 hour or until the chicken is tender. Remove the cover and cook over high heat until liquid is evaporated, turning the chicken pieces to brown.

Serves 8.

KEEMA CURRY
Ground Meat Curry

3 tablespoons butter
1 cup sliced onions
2 pounds ground lean beef or
    lamb
1½ teaspoons salt

1 teaspoon turmeric
1 tablespoon crushed
    coriander
½ cup yogurt

Melt the butter in a skillet; sauté the onions in it until very brown. Add the meat, salt, turmeric and coriander. Cook, stirring frequently, for 10 minutes. Mix in the yogurt. Cover and cook over low heat 15 minutes.

Serves 8.

MATTAR PANIR
Peas and Cheese

½ pound farmer's cheese
2 tablespoons vegetable oil
¼ pound butter
1½ cups chopped onions
½ teaspoon dried ground chili
    peppers
1½ teaspoons ground coriander

¾ teaspoon turmeric
2 teaspoons minced ginger root
1½ cups peeled diced tomatoes
1½ pounds green peas, shelled
¾ cup water
1 teaspoon salt

Cut the cheese into small cubes. Heat the oil in a skillet and brown the cheese in it over high heat. Reserve.

Melt the butter in a large skillet; sauté the onions until browned.

Stir in the chili peppers, coriander, turmeric and ginger; sauté 2 minutes, stirring almost constantly. Add the tomatoes, peas, water and salt. Bring to a boil, cover and cook over low heat 15 minutes. Add the reserved cheese and cook 10 minutes longer.

Serves 8.

FRIED BHINDI
Batter-Fried Okra

1 pound okra	½ cup flour
½ teaspoon ground cardamon	⅛ teaspoon salt
⅛ teaspoon powdered cloves	1 egg, beaten
1 teaspoon crushed cumin seeds	Water
1 teaspoon cinnamon	Vegetable oil for deep frying

Wash the okra and cut away the stem ends. Dry thoroughly and make a small slit lengthwise in each.

Place the cardamon, cloves, cumin and cinnamon in a small skillet. Cook over high heat 2 minutes, stirring constantly. Put a little in each slit of the okra.

Make a medium thick batter of the flour, salt, and egg, adding water if necessary. Dip the okra in the batter. Heat the oil to 370° and fry the okra until golden brown. Drain and serve hot.

Serves 8.

DRY DAL
Fried Lentils

2 cups lentils, preferably red	1½ teaspoons salt
3 tablespoons butter	1 teaspoon cumin seed
1 cup chopped onions	½ cup chopped coriander leaves
¼ teaspoon dried ground chili peppers	(Chinese parsley) or parsley
1 teaspoon turmeric	

Wash the lentils, cover with water and let soak 1 hour. Bring to a boil and cook 45 minutes. Drain thoroughly, and dry.

Melt the butter in a skillet; add the onions, chili peppers, turmeric and lentils. Cook over low heat, stirring frequently, for 20 minutes. Watch carefully to prevent burning. Mix in the salt. Serve sprinkled with the cumin seed and coriander, also fried onions, if desired.

Serves 8.

POORI
Fried Bread, Indian Style

1½ cups whole wheat flour	1½ tablespoons shortening
1½ cups all-purpose flour	⅔ cup water
⅛ teaspoon salt	½ pound butter

Sift together the two flours and salt. With the fingers, blend in the shortening and enough of the water to make a firm dough. Knead for a few minutes, then cover with a damp cloth and let stand 30 minutes. Knead again. Roll out thin and cut into 3-inch circles.

Melt the butter in a saucepan, then strain into a skillet, discarding the white sediment in the strainer. Heat the clarified butter and drop the circles into it in a single layer. Immediately turn them over and press each one down with a spatula. Fry until golden brown and puffed. Drain on paper towels and serve hot.

Serves 8.

Iran

THE Iranians have built a most unusual embassy building in Washington, and furnished it with exceptional skill and considerable style. Although it is now known as Iran, no one can forget that this country was once called Persia, a word which conveys thoughts of exotic architecture and furnishings. When the embassy building was planned, the architects were instructed to pattern it upon Iran's ancient city and art center, Isfahan, a place renowned for its beautiful buildings.

The embassy succeeds admirably in conveying a sense of Middle Eastern form and grace. The façade is covered by a series of intricate mosaics, set off by a number of graceful, very slim columns. The mosaic

work was done by three Iranian artisans who were brought here for that purpose; over five hundred thousand miniature pieces of baked clay were used to create a series of designs traditional to Iran, in a predominantly blue shade.

Within the building itself, there are five principal reception rooms surrounding a courtyard, according to the Isfahan style. Persian artifacts — handicraft, cushions, metalwork — are used throughout to further the local color and atmosphere. On the floor, remarkably fine Persian rugs may be seen. Elsewhere, the finest examples of both modern and ancient Iranian art are on display.

[153]

Embassy of Iran

FORMAL MENU

Caviar   Borani

Eshkaneh

Dolmeh Felfel Sabz

Morg Polo

Salade Sabzi

Paludeh

Café

CAVIAR

Heap fresh Iranian caviar in a crystal dish, on shaved ice, and serve with freshly made thin white toast. Separate small bowls of sieved hard-cooked egg yolks and egg whites, minced onions and lemon wedges may be arranged around the caviar.

BORANI
Eggplant Appetizer

2 small eggplants	2 teaspoons minced garlic
3 teaspoons salt	1 cup yogurt
⅓ cup vegetable oil	

Peel the eggplants, cut in half lengthwise, then cut into ½-inch slices crosswise. Sprinkle the eggplant with 2 teaspoons salt and let stand 30 minutes. Rinse the eggplant slices under cold running water and dry thoroughly on paper towels.

Heat the oil in a skillet; add 1 teaspoon of the minced garlic and the eggplant slices. Fry until browned on both sides. Drain on paper towels. Sprinkle with the remaining salt. Cool.

In a serving dish, spread a thin layer of yogurt, then make successive layers of the eggplant, garlic and yogurt, making as many layers as possible.
Serves 8.

ESHKANEH
Onion Soup

¼ pound butter	½ cup lime or lemon juice
2 pounds onions, peeled and sliced thin	¼ cup sugar
2 teaspoons salt	1 tablespoon dried mint
½ teaspoon turmeric	¾ teaspoon black pepper
8 cups water	½ teaspoon cinnamon
3 tablespoons rice flour or cornstarch	2 eggs

Melt the butter in a saucepan; add the onions and cook over low heat 10 minutes, stirring frequently. Add the salt, turmeric and all but ½ cup of the water. Cover loosely and cook over low heat 4 minutes.

Mix the rice flour or cornstarch with the remaining water. Add to the soup with the lime or lemon juice and sugar, stirring until the soup boils again. Cook 10 minutes. Crush the mint and add to the soup with the pepper and cinnamon.

Beat the eggs in a bowl; gradually add a little of the hot soup, stirring steadily to prevent curdling. Return to the rest of the soup. Heat, but do not let boil.

Serves 8.

DOLMEH FELFEL SABZ
Stuffed Peppers

8 green peppers	3 teaspoons salt
2½ cups water	¾ teaspoon pepper
¼ cup yellow split peas	¼ cup chopped green onions
¼ cup rice	3 tablespoons minced parsley
4 tablespoons butter	2 cups peeled chopped
¾ cup minced yellow onions	tomatoes
1 pound ground beef	Yogurt
½ teaspoon cinnamon	

Wash the peppers, cut a half-inch slice from the stem ends and reserve. Scoop out the seeds and fibers. Cover the peppers with water, bring to a boil and cook over low heat 5 minutes. Drain well.

Bring the 2½ cups water to a boil. Add the split peas and rice. Cook 25 minutes. Drain.

Melt 2 tablespoons of the butter in a skillet. Add the yellow onions and beef. Cook over medium heat, stirring frequently, for 10 minutes. Mix in the cinnamon, 1½ teaspoons salt, ½ teaspoon pepper, the green onions, parsley and cooked split peas and rice. Stuff the peppers and replace the tops.

Melt the remaining butter in a deep skillet or casserole. Arrange the peppers in it in an upright position. Mix the tomatoes with the remaining salt and pepper; pour over the peppers. Bring to a boil, cover and cook over low heat 35 minutes, or until the peppers are tender. Serve hot, topped with yogurt.

Serves 8.

MORG POLO
Chicken with Rice

Rice:

4 cups raw long grain rice	3 quarts water
4 tablespoons salt	

Put the rice in a strainer and wash it under warm running water for 5 minutes. Put the rice in a saucepan, cover with cold water, and add half the salt. Let soak 2 hours. Drain.

Bring the 3 quarts water and the remaining salt to a boil. Add the rice and cook over medium heat for 12 minutes. Drain and rinse with lukewarm water. Prepare the chicken while the rice is soaking.

Chicken:

2 3-pound fryers, disjointed	1½ cups chopped onions
2 teaspoons salt	1 cup currants or seedless
½ teaspoon black pepper	raisins
½ teaspoon cinnamon	1 cup chopped dried apricots
½ pound butter	

Wash and dry the chicken pieces; rub with the salt, pepper and cinnamon. Melt 3 tablespoons of the butter in a skillet; sauté the onions until browned. Remove the onions. Melt 5 tablespoons butter in the same skillet; brown the chicken pieces in it. Remove.

Soak the currants and apricots in hot water for 5 minutes. Drain, then sauté in the fat remaining in the skillet for 5 minutes.

Melt the remaining butter. Pour 3 tablespoons of it into a large casserole. Add 3 tablespoons water, then spread half the rice in it. Arrange the chicken, onions and fruits over it, and cover with the remaining rice. Pour the remaining butter over the top. Cover, and then place a piece of aluminum foil over the top and edges to seal. Bake in a 300° oven for 45 minutes.

Serves 8.

SALADE SABZI
Mixed Salad

2 cucumbers	½ cup chopped parsley
1 head romaine lettuce	¾ cup olive oil
3 tomatoes, peeled and diced	⅓ cup lemon juice
1 cup thinly sliced radishes	1 clove garlic, minced
½ cup thinly sliced green onions	¾ teaspoon salt
¼ cup chopped dill	½ teaspoon black pepper

Peel the cucumbers and slice thin. Wash and dry the lettuce and break into bite-sized pieces. In a salad bowl, combine the cucumbers, lettuce, tomatoes, radishes, green onions, dill, and parsley.

Make a dressing of the oil, lemon juice, garlic, salt and pepper. Pour over the salad, tossing until the vegetables are coated. Goat cheese or Feta cheese, in small pieces, may be added.

Serves 8.

PALUDEH
Melon Dessert

2 Persian melons or other melons	⅔ cup sugar
4 peaches	½ teaspoon salt
¼ cup lemon juice	3 tablespoons rose water
	Crushed ice

With a melon ball cutter, scoop out all the meat of the melons, reserving all the melon juice. Peel and thinly slice the peaches. Immediately combine with the melon balls, juice and a mixture of the lemon juice, sugar, salt and rose water. Chill. When ready to serve, divide among crystal dessert dishes and put a tablespoon of crushed ice on each.

Serves 8.

Ireland

THE new Irish Embassy was, until early 1964, the guest house of the President of the United States, while Blair House was being redecorated. It is not a huge or imposing residence, but has considerable warmth and charm.

The dining room is extremely handsome when the table is set with specially woven Irish damask or lace, and with beautifully cut Waterford crystal, an Irish specialty known the world over for its quality. The candelabra may be of silver or crystal, and casts a flattering light on the diplomatic diners.

Ambasáid na h'Éirann

FORMAL MENU

Murphy's Dream Cocktail
Dublin Bay Prawns
Roast Wicklow Capon
Baked Limerick Ham
Donegal Whole Wheaten Bread
Bombe Glacée Tullamore
Irish Coffee

INFORMAL MENU

Irish Whiskies
Clonmel Cider Fruit Cup
Aran Scallop Soup
Baked Ham Clonmel
Colcannon   Leaf Spinach
Irish Stout
Tara Salad
Flaming Beehive Enniscorthy
Irish Coffee
Irish Mist Liqueur

MURPHY'S DREAM COCKTAIL

6 ounces Irish Mist liqueur
6 ounces gin
6 ounces lemon juice

6 dashes orange bitters
2 egg whites

Combine all ingredients with a little cracked ice in a cocktail shaker and shake well. Strain into cocktail glasses and serve.
Makes 6 cocktails.

DUBLIN BAY PRAWNS

3 pounds large raw shrimp
2 cups water
1½ teaspoons salt
1 small onion
1 bay leaf
1 teaspoon dry mustard
1 cup mayonnaise

1 teaspoon sugar
½ cup tomato sauce
1 tablespoon malt vinegar
3 drops red food coloring
Lettuce
Lemon wedges

Wash the shrimp, shell and devein. Bring the water, salt, onion and bay leaf to a boil. Add the shrimp and cook over low heat 5 minutes. Drain, cool, then chill.

Blend the mustard with a little mayonnaise, then combine with all the mayonnaise, the sugar, tomato sauce, vinegar and food coloring. Taste for seasoning, adding salt and pepper, if necessary.

Arrange the shrimp on a bed of lettuce, with the lemon wedges as a garnish. Serve the sauce in a sauceboat.
Serves 8.

ROAST WICKLOW CAPON

2 5-pound capons
1 tablespoon salt
¾ teaspoon pepper
8 cups toasted fresh bread
    crumbs
1½ cups minced onions

1 cup chopped parsley
1½ teaspoons thyme
1½ teaspoons sage
1 cup milk
1 pound butter, melted

Wash and dry the capons; rub with the salt and pepper.

Mix together the bread crumbs, onions, parsley, thyme, sage, milk and all but ¼ cup of the butter. Stuff the capons with the mixture and close the openings with skewers or foil. Place in roasting pan and brush with the reserved butter. Place a piece of foil over the breasts of the capons. Roast in a 400° oven 1¾ hours, or until tender. Remove the foil after 1 hour roasting time. Serve with the ham.

Serves 8 to 12.

BAKED LIMERICK HAM

10-pound Irish ham

3 cups fine fresh bread crumbs

Wash the ham, cover with water, bring to a boil and cook over low heat 1¾ hours. Drain well and place in a covered roasting pan. Cover and roast in a 400° oven 1¾ hours. Trim off the skin of the ham, leaving the fat. Pat the bread crumbs into the fatty side of the ham and bake, uncovered, 25 minutes, or until the bread crumbs brown. Carve and serve with the capon.

Serves 12 to 15.

DONEGAL WHOLE WHEATEN BREAD

4 cups whole wheat flour
    (Donegal, if available)
1 teaspoon salt
1 teaspoon baking soda

½ teaspoon baking powder
1 teaspoon sugar
2 cups buttermilk

Mix together all the dry ingredients in a bowl. Make a well in the center and into it put the buttermilk. Work in the flour mixture until well blended. Turn out onto a lightly floured board and knead for 2 minutes, or until smooth. Shape into two loaves and place on a greased baking sheet. With the back of a knife, cut a deep cross in the center of each loaf. Bake in a preheated 400° oven 40 minutes, or until golden brown. Cool on a cake rack.

BOMBE GLACÉE TULLAMORE
Ice Cream Mold

1½ pints coffee ice cream   ½ cup Irish Mist liqueur
1 quart vanilla ice cream   1 teaspoon almond extract

Soften the coffee ice cream and spread on the bottom and sides of a 1½-quart melon or bombe mold. Freeze until firm.

Mix the vanilla ice cream with the liqueur and almond extract. Pack into the lined mold. Cover and freeze until firm. Unmold onto a serving dish covered with a linen napkin.

Serves 8 to 10.

IRISH COFFEE

For each serving, carefully warm a stemmed whiskey goblet. Into it put a jigger of Irish whiskey and a small sugar cube. Fill with strong hot black coffee to within one inch of the rim. Stir to dissolve sugar. Top with lightly whipped cream to reach the rim. Don't stir after floating the cream.

CLONMEL CIDER FRUIT CUP

½ cup powdered sugar
4 drops green food coloring
2 egg whites

5 cups diced apples, pears and
    pineapple
3 cups cider

Mix the sugar with the food coloring. Dip the rims of 8 to 10 sherbet glasses in the egg whites, then into the colored sugar. Set aside until sugar dries. Divide the fruit mixture among the glasses. Pour in enough cider to cover the fruit. Chill and serve.

Serves 8 to 10.

ARAN SCALLOP SOUP

1½ pounds scallops
1 pound fillet of sole
1 onion
1 stalk celery
6 cups water
1½ teaspoons salt
½ teaspoon white pepper
¼ pound fresh pork fat
3 cups peeled diced potatoes
3 sprigs parsley

½ teaspoon thyme
3 cups peeled diced tomatoes
1 cup crushed water biscuits,
    pilot crackers, or cream
    crackers
¼ pound butter
2 cups hot light cream
Mace
Chopped parsley

The Aran scallop is a large well-flavored scallop found around the Aran Islands. Sea or bay scallops may be used as a substitute.

Wash the scallops, cover with boiling water, drain and dice. Refrigerate until needed.

Cut the sole in pieces and combine with the onion, celery, water, salt and pepper. Bring to a boil and cook over low heat 45 minutes. Strain the stock and reserve.

Melt the pork fat in a saucepan; add the potatoes and cook over low heat 5 minutes, shaking the pan frequently. Add the fish stock, parsley and thyme. Bring to a boil and cook over low heat 20 minutes. Mix in the tomatoes and scallops; cook 20 minutes. Remove the parsley. Gradually stir in the crackers to thicken soup. Break the butter into small pieces and add to the soup; when melted, stir in the hot cream. Taste for seasoning, adding salt and pepper if necessary. Serve sprinkled with mace and chopped parsley.

Serves 8 to 10.

BAKED HAM CLONMEL

8-10 pound ham	2 cups brown sugar
2 quarts cider	3 tablespoons Irish whiskey
¾ cup flour	

Wash the ham, cover with water, bring to a boil and cook over medium heat 2 hours. Drain and trim off the rind.

Put the ham in a shallow roasting pan. Pour over it all but ⅓ cup cider. Bake in a 400° oven 1¾ hours, or until tender and browned. Baste frequently.

Put the flour in a small skillet and stir over low heat until browned. Combine with the brown sugar and remaining cider to make a paste. Spread over the ham and sprinkle with the whiskey. Bake 20 minutes longer, or until the paste is browned. Carve and serve.

Serves 10 to 12.

COLCANNON

6 tablespoons butter	Salt
5 cups mashed potatoes	Pepper
5 cups cooked finely chopped cabbage	

Melt the butter in a saucepan. Add the potatoes and cabbage, mixing well. Season to taste. Serve very hot.

Serves 8 to 10.

LEAF SPINACH

4 pounds fresh spinach   Salt
¼ pound butter

Wash the spinach thoroughly. Do not trim the stems. Drain well. Melt the butter in a large skillet. Add the spinach; cook, mixing frequently but gently, until leaves wilt. Season to taste.
Serves 8 to 10.

TARA SALAD

½ cup raw spinach or parsley   Lettuce
1½ cups mayonnaise   Celery stalks
2 hard-cooked egg yolks   Watercress

Purée the spinach or parsley in a blender, or chop very fine. Mix it into the mayonnaise. If not green enough, mix in a little green food coloring. Put the egg yolks through a fine sieve and blend into the mayonnaise.

On individual salad plates, make a bed of flat, crisp lettuce. Over it arrange watercress in the general shape of a harp. Lay across it three stalks of trimmed celery, hollow side up. With a pastry tube, fill the stalks with the mayonnaise mixture, piped to stand in curves, if possible.
Serves 6 to 8.

FLAMING BEEHIVE ENNISCORTHY

8-inch round sponge cake   2 egg yolks, beaten
¼ cup Irish Mist liqueur   Marrons (chestnuts) in syrup
¼ cup sweet sherry   Glazed fruits
1 quart Nesselrode ice cream   ⅓ cup warm Irish whiskey
5 egg whites   1½ cups whipped cream
1 cup sugar   1 teaspoon vanilla extract

The sponge cake should be about ½ inch thick. Prick it in several places and pour over it a mixture of the liqueur and sherry. Chill for 1 hour. Spread the ice cream over the cake and freeze until firm.

Beat the egg whites until peaks begin to form, then, spoon by spoon, beat in all but 1 tablespoon sugar. Beat until very stiff. Fold in the egg yolks.

Put the cake on a paper-covered board. With a pastry tube, pipe the meringue starting at the top, round and round, down to the base, to resemble a beehive. Be sure all the ice cream and cake are covered with the meringue. Make a depression in the top large enough to hold half an eggshell, which will be used later on. Place in a preheated 425° oven on the upper level for 5 minutes, or until the meringue is a pale gold color. Quickly transfer the cake to a chilled serving dish. Decorate the base with marrons and glazed fruits. Insert the eggshell in the depression and pour the warm whiskey into it. Set aflame and serve with the whipped cream, flavored with the vanilla and remaining sugar.

Serves 8 to 10.

Israel

INASMUCH as Israel is itself a young country (having come into existence in 1948), it is only natural that the nation's embassy should be quite modern in concept and design. Located on a hillside, the pleasant, well-situated building has attractive grounds. The modern design of the embassy refers chiefly to the interior, for the building's exterior is quite conservative in appearance.

The feeling of modernism may be noted immediately, for the entrance hall's chief point of interest is a tapestry with an eye-catching geometric design, much like the "op" art which has recently become so popular. Many important rooms are on the second floor, reached by a winding staircase. The living room is to the right and beyond it is the

sun room, in an unusual octagonal shape. On the left-hand side, one finds the dining room, in an interesting L-shape, created by combining two smaller rooms. The dining table is long, and has a fine wood finish; over the table there hangs a modern wheel-shaped chandelier executed in gold and white. The table china was made by Lenox, the flatware is Jensen's Cactus pattern, and the glassware is Baccarat.

The furniture throughout the embassy is quite modern, although not extreme in design or coloring; perhaps contemporary would be a more descriptive term. The library, often used as the Ambassador's private study, is a large rectangular room with a modern fireplace at one end, the remainder of the wall being paneled.

[171]

Embassy of Israel

FORMAL MENU

Chopped Liver   Gefüllte Fish

Beet and Horseradish Relish   Challah

Chicken Soup with Egg Drops

Roast Stuffed Turkey

Tzimmes   Festive Rice

Fruit Compote   Honey Cake

Tea

CHOPPED LIVER

1½ pounds chicken livers
½ cup rendered chicken fat
1½ cups diced onions
4 hard-cooked eggs

1½ teaspoons salt
½ teaspoon black pepper
Lettuce leaves

Wash and drain the livers, removing any discolored spots. Heat half the fat in a skillet; add the onions and cook over low heat 10 minutes, stirring frequently. Remove the onions.

Heat the remaining fat in the skillet and cook the livers 5 minutes, or until barely pink inside when cut. Put the livers, onions and eggs through the fine blade of a food chopper, or chop very fine. Season with the salt and pepper. Chill, form into balls and serve on lettuce leaves.

Serves 8.

GEFÜLLTE FISH
Stuffed Fish

5 pounds fillets of fresh-water
    fish
2 pounds onions
4 teaspoons salt
2 teaspoons white pepper
¼ cup cracker or matzo meal

2 eggs, beaten
½ cup cold water
2 carrots, sliced
6 cups boiling water
Head, skin and bones of fish

Use a combination of fish, like carp, whitefish and pike, or just pike and whitefish. Grind the fish fillets and 2 onions in a meat chopper. Mix the ground fish and onions, 2 teaspoons salt, 1 teaspoon pepper, the cracker meal, eggs and cold water in a wooden bowl and chop until fine and well blended. Chill while preparing the stock.

Slice the remaining onions and put in a pan with the carrots, boiling water, fish head, skin and bones and remaining salt and pepper. Bring to a boil and cook 30 minutes.

Shape ground fish mixture into 2-inch balls between wet palms and drop into pan. Cover loosely and cook over low heat 1½ hours, occasionally stirring gently. Taste for seasoning. Remove fish balls with a slotted spoon and strain stock into a bowl. Chill. Serve very cold with beet and horseradish relish.

Serves 8 to 12.

BEET AND HORSERADISH RELISH

1 cup grated horseradish	½ teaspoon sugar
¾ cup finely grated raw beets	Vinegar
½ teaspoon salt	

Use freshly grated horseradish if possible. If not available, use the bottled white horseradish. To either, add the beets, salt, sugar and vinegar to taste. The amount will depend on whether fresh or prepared horseradish is used.

Makes about 1½ cups.

CHALLAH
Egg Bread

1 cake or package yeast	1½ teaspoons salt
1 tablespoon sugar	2 eggs
½ cup lukewarm water	2 tablespoons vegetable oil
½ cup boiling water	1 egg yolk
Pinch of saffron	2 tablespoons poppy seeds
4½ cups sifted flour	

Mix together the yeast, sugar and the lukewarm water. Let stand 5 minutes.

Combine the boiling water and saffron, let stand until cool, then strain.

Sift 3 cups flour and the salt into a bowl. Make a well in the center and into it put the eggs, oil, saffron water and the yeast mixture. Work in the flour mixture gradually, then add just enough of the remaining flour to make a soft dough. Knead on a floured surface until smooth and elastic. Place in an oiled bowl and brush the top with a little oil. Cover with a towel, set in a warm place and let rise 1 hour.

Punch down, cover again and let rise until double in bulk. Divide the dough into three equal parts. Between lightly floured hands, roll the dough into three strips of even length. Braid them together and place in an oiled baking pan. Cover with a towel and let rise until double in bulk. Brush with the egg yolk and sprinkle with the poppy seeds. Bake in a 350° oven 50 minutes or until browned. Cool on a cake rack.

CHICKEN SOUP WITH EGG DROPS

Soup:

5-pound fowl	2 stalks celery and leaves
3 quarts boiling water	1 parsnip
1 tablespoon salt	3 sprigs parsley
2 carrots, sliced	2 sprigs dill
1 onion	

Wash the chicken and the giblets, and put into the boiling water. Add the salt, cover and cook over low heat 1 hour. Add the vegetables and herbs. Re-cover and cook 1½ hours longer. Strain the soup into a clean pan. Taste for seasoning.

Egg Drops:

1 egg	3 tablespoons cold water
⅛ teaspoon salt	1 tablespoon minced parsley
3 tablespoons flour	

Beat the egg with a fork, then blend in the salt, flour, water and parsley until smooth.

Bring the soup to a boil again and, with the tip of a teaspoon, pick up a little of the batter and drop it into the soup. When all the batter is added, cover the pan tightly and cook over low heat 10 minutes. *Serves 8.*

ROAST STUFFED TURKEY

10-pound turkey
1 tablespoon salt
½ teaspoon black pepper
4 tablespoons fat
1 cup sliced celery
1½ cups diced onions

½ pound mushrooms, sliced
5 cups fresh bread crumbs
1 cup hot water
½ teaspoon poultry seasoning
3 tablespoons minced parsley

Season the turkey with the salt and pepper. Chop the giblets. Heat the fat in a skillet; sauté the giblets 10 minutes. Add the celery, onions and mushrooms; cook 10 minutes. Soak the bread crumbs in the water for 5 minutes, then mix into the vegetables with the poultry seasoning and parsley. Stuff the turkey. Sew the opening or fasten with skewers. Truss the bird. Place in a roasting pan.

Roast in a 350° oven 3 hours or until the turkey is tender. Turn turkey to brown on all sides. *Serves 8.*

TZIMMES
Stewed Carrots

1 cup orange juice
2 cups water
¼ cup honey
6 tablespoons fat
¾ teaspoon salt

1 cinnamon stick
1 clove
2 bunches carrots, peeled and cubed
½ cup seedless raisins

Combine the orange juice, water, honey, fat, salt, cinnamon stick and clove in a saucepan. Bring to a boil and cook over low heat 10 minutes. Discard the cinnamon and clove. Add the carrots and raisins. Cover loosely and cook over low heat 45 minutes, or until carrots are soft and mixture thickened.

Serves 8.

FESTIVE RICE

4 tablespoons vegetable oil	4 cups chicken broth
¾ cup minced onions	½ cup toasted pine nuts or
2 cups raw rice	slivered almonds
1½ teaspoons salt	

Heat the oil in a saucepan; sauté the onions until yellow. Stir in the rice until coated with the oil. Add the salt and half the broth. Cover and cook over low heat 20 minutes, adding the remaining broth as the liquid is absorbed. With two forks, stir in the nuts.

Serves 8.

FRUIT COMPOTE

½ pound dried apricots	1 cup orange juice
½ pound dried pears	1½ cups water
1 pound prunes	½ cup sugar
½ cup seedless raisins	1 lemon, thinly sliced

Wash the apricots and pears and soak in lukewarm water for 2 hours. Drain. Wash the prunes and combine with the apricots, pears, raisins, orange juice and water. Bring to a boil, cover loosely and cook 15 minutes. Add the sugar and lemon and a little water if fruit looks too dry. Cook 15 minutes longer. Chill.

Serves 8.

0⊂⊃0

HONEY CAKE

3½ cups flour	1½ cups filberts or almonds
¼ teaspoon salt	4 eggs
1½ teaspoons baking powder	¾ cup brown sugar, packed
1 teaspoon baking soda	3 tablespoons vegetable oil
½ teaspoon ground cloves	1½ cups dark honey
½ teaspoon powdered ginger	½ cup brewed coffee

Oil an 11- by 16- by 4-inch baking pan and line it with liner paper or aluminum foil.

Sift together 3¼ cups of the flour, the salt, baking powder, baking soda, cloves and ginger. Mix the nuts with the remaining flour.

Beat the eggs and brown sugar until thick and light. Beat in the oil, honey and coffee; then stir in the flour mixture until smooth. Mix in the nuts. Turn into the pan.

Bake in a preheated 325° oven 1¼ hours, or until browned and a cake tester comes out clean. Cool on a cake rack before removing from pan.

Serves 12 to 14.

Italy

THE Italian Embassy, one of the largest in Washington, is built around a courtyard. On pleasant evenings, the doors of the embassy facing this pleasant area are opened, and guests may stroll along the gravel walks, or perhaps dine under the stars.

The main entrance of the embassy is constructed of white stone. There is a grand stairway located to the right of reception hall; marble pillars heighten the dramatic entrance area. The Ambassador's study features heavy wood paneling, in the Italian manner. The walls are upholstered with damask, creating a rich and elaborate overall effect. On one wall, there is a large stone and brick fireplace, which adds a note of simplicity.

The main drawing room is generously proportioned, with a very high ceiling, which adds to the feeling of spaciousness. From the center of the ceiling hangs a decorative chandelier that holds more than a score of lights. The floor is of inlaid parquet, set in large diamond patterns. The room is furnished in the Italianate style, with many dark wood, elaborately carved examples of various periods. The dining room is quite large, which permits large numbers of guests to be served at formal dinner parties.

Ambasciata d'Italia

FORMAL MENU

Gnocchi di Patate

Scaloppine al Marsala
Piselli alla Romana
VALPOLICELLA

Formaggio

Fruita
Café

INFORMAL MENU

Minestrone Milanese

Costolette di Vitello Milanese
Carciofi Dorati
VERDICCHIO

Fragole al Marsala
Café

GNOCCHI DI PATATE
Potato Dumplings

Sauce:

3 tablespoons olive oil	1 14-ounce can tomato sauce
¾ cup chopped onions	1 teaspoon salt
½ cup chopped celery	½ teaspoon black pepper
1 tablespoon minced parsley	½ teaspoon basil
1 clove garlic, minced	½ teaspoon oregano
1 29-ounce can Italian-style tomatoes	1 bay leaf

Heat the oil in a saucepan; add the onions, celery, parsley and garlic. Sauté until lightly browned. Add the tomatoes, tomato sauce, salt and pepper. Bring to a boil and cook over low heat 45 minutes. Add the basil, oregano and bay leaf; cook 15 minutes longer. Taste for seasoning and discard the bay leaf.

Dumplings:

3 pounds potatoes	1 tablespoon salt
4 cups flour	Grated Parmesan cheese
6 quarts water	

Scrub the unpeeled potatoes and cook in boiling water until tender. Drain, cool slightly, peel and mash very smooth. Turn out onto a floured surface and mix in just enough of the flour to make a dough. (The amount of flour required depends on the texture and moistness of the potatoes.) Knead the dough thoroughly and roll into finger-thin strips. Cut into 2-inch lengths and press each piece with a fork.

Bring the water and salt to a rapid boil. Test one, and add more flour if necessary. Cook about 20 gnocchi at a time until they come to the surface. Remove from the water with a strainer, drain well and place in a serving dish. Keep warm while cooking the balance. Always keep the water boiling briskly. When all the gnocchi are cooked, pour half the sauce over them and toss lightly. Pour the remaining sauce over the top and serve with grated cheese.

Serves 6 to 8.

SCALOPPINE AL MARSALA
Veal Sauté with Marsala

2 pounds veal cutlet, cut very thin
1½ teaspoons salt
¼ teaspoon white pepper

¼ cup flour
6 tablespoons butter
⅔ cup Marsala
3 tablespoons stock or water

Have the butcher pound the veal very thin, and then cut into even-sized pieces about 6 inches square. Sprinkle the veal with the salt and pepper, then dip lightly into the flour.

Use two large skillets and melt half the butter in each until the foam dies down. Put the veal in the skillets in a single layer. Cook over high heat until browned on both sides. Add half the Marsala to each skillet. Cook, still over high heat, for 1 minute. Transfer the meat to a serving dish. Stir the stock into the skillets, scraping the bottom and sides of browned particles. Bring to a boil and pour over the meat.

Serves 6 to 8.

PISELLI ALLA ROMANA
Peas with Prosciutto

¼ pound butter
¾ cup sliced onions
3 pounds fresh peas, shelled, or
    3 packages, frozen,
    thawed
1¼ teaspoons salt

½ teaspoon white pepper
¼ cup stock or water
¼ pound sliced prosciutto ham,
    cut julienne
½ teaspoon sugar

Melt the butter in a saucepan. Add the onions and brown lightly. Add the peas, salt, pepper and stock. Cover and cook over medium heat 10 minutes. Add the ham and a little more liquid, if necessary. Cook over low heat 10 minutes. Sprinkle with the sugar and toss.

Serves 6 to 8.

MINESTRONE MILANESE
Thick Vegetable Soup

1 teaspoon olive oil
½ pound salt pork, chopped
½ cup chopped onions
½ teaspoon minced garlic
1 teaspoon chopped parsley
¼ teaspoon sage
1 teaspoon salt
½ teaspoon black pepper
1 tablespoon tomato paste
1 cup water
1 cup chopped celery

3 carrots, sliced
2 potatoes, peeled and diced
2 cups cooked or canned pea
  beans
1½ cups shredded cabbage
½ pound zucchini, diced
1 cup shelled peas
1½ quarts beef broth or water
1 cup elbow macaroni
Grated Parmesan cheese

Combine the oil and salt pork in a large saucepan. Cook over low heat 5 minutes. Add the onions, garlic, parsley, sage, salt and pepper. Cook 10 minutes. Blend the tomato paste with the 1 cup water and add. Bring to a boil and cook 5 minutes. Add all the vegetables and the broth. Bring to a boil and cook over low heat 45 minutes. Mix in the macaroni; cook 10 minutes longer or until the macaroni is tender. Taste for seasoning. Serve with the cheese.

Serves 6 to 8.

COSTOLETTE DI VITELLO MILANESE
Breaded Veal Chops

8 veal chops, cut 1 inch thick
2 eggs
2 teaspoons salt
½ teaspoon black pepper

½ cup dry bread crumbs
½ cup grated Parmesan cheese
2 tablespoons olive oil
6 tablespoons butter

Have the chops pounded to make them thinner.

Dip the chops in the eggs beaten with the salt and pepper, then in a mixture of the bread crumbs and cheese.

Heat the oil in a skillet, then melt the butter in it. Put the chops in the skillet in a single layer and cook 10 minutes on each side, or until browned and tender.

Serves 8.

CARCIOFI DORATI
Fried Artichokes

4 artichokes	3 eggs
2 cups water	1 teaspoon salt
3 tablespoons lemon juice	½ teaspoon pepper
1 cup flour	2 cups olive oil

Cut off the tips and stems of the artichokes and discard the tough outer leaves. Wash thoroughly, then cut each artichoke in half. Remove the chokes (fuzzy centers) and cut the artichokes into very thin slices. As each piece is sliced, place it in the water mixed with the lemon juice. Drain and dry thoroughly. Roll each piece in the flour, then dip in the eggs beaten with the salt and pepper.

Heat the oil in a large skillet until it bubbles. Fry the artichokes in a single layer until golden brown. Drain and serve hot.

Serves 6 to 8.

FRAGOLE AL MARSALA
Strawberries with Marsala Wine

1½ quarts strawberries	2 cups Marsala
3 tablespoons sugar	

Hull, wash, drain and dry the berries. Toss lightly with the sugar, then pour the wine over them. Mix gently and chill 2 hours before serving.

Serves 6 to 8.

Japan

THE Embassy of Japan recreates a part of Japan in this country. The residence itself is surrounded by beautiful gardens. As is the custom in Japan, an exquisite teahouse is in the center of the garden.

In the garden, there is a stone fountain where guests on the way to the teahouse ritually rinse their hands and lips. Large stepping stones are artistically arranged as a pathway leading from the fountain to the door of the teahouse, where all shoes are removed, because that is a Japanese custom. Visitors bow and enter through a door only two

feet in height. The teahouse has no furniture, but the floor is covered with tatami, *woven mats, on which people sit. The walls have niches, in which are hung* kakemono *scrolls.*

The tea ceremony itself is very stylized, and is not meant as a social occasion, but an opportunity for contemplation of the inner self. It has been a tradition in Japan for many centuries, and the tea ceremony in the embassy follows the ritual proceedings closely.

Embassy of Japan

HORS D'OEUVRES

Seasoned Fish Roe
Raw Fish
Shredded Cucumber
SAKÉ

CLEAR SOUP

Chicken Soup, Suppon Style

BROILED DISHES

Broiled Shrimp
Broiled Butterfish

BOILED DISHES

Boiled Beans
Boiled Beef
Boiled Eggplant

SALAD

Cucumber, Abalone and Seaweed Salad

FRIED DISHES

Fried Soft-Shell Crabs
Fried Green Peppers

PICKLE

Daikon and Rice

FRUIT

Melon

Green Tea

HORS D'OEUVRES

Seasoned Fish Roe:

Seasoned herring or salmon roe is available in cans in Oriental food shops. If you can't get it, red caviar mixed with grated onion is a good substitute. Put it in a sectioned dish, with the other foods in other sections. Or put each food in an individual serving dish.

Raw Fish:

1½ pounds fresh flounder fillets

Pull out the bones with a pair of tweezers. Wrap the fish in a cloth and, holding over the sink, quickly pour boiling water over both sides. Remove the cloth and plunge the fish into cold water. Drain and dry, then slice at an angle into pieces ⅓ inch thick.

Shredded Cucumber:

3 cucumbers
1½ teaspoons salt
2 tablespoons vinegar

Peel the cucumbers and cut them into julienne strips; mix in the salt and let stand 20 minutes, or until cucumbers wilt. Mix again, then drain well, squeezing out all the liquid. Sprinkle with the vinegar and mix. Let stand 5 minutes, then drain very well.

CHICKEN SOUP, SUPPON STYLE

2 pounds chicken necks and backs
3 quarts water
1½ tablespoons minced ginger root
4 green onions, sliced
2 dried mushrooms
1 whole raw chicken breast
2 tablespoons minced green onions
1 egg
½ teaspoon salt
2 teaspoons soy sauce
½ teaspoon sugar
1 teaspoon monosodium glutamate
Narrow strips of lemon rind

Wash the chicken necks and backs and put in a saucepan with the water, ginger root and sliced green onions. Bring to a boil and cook over medium heat 1½ hours. Strain.

Wash the mushrooms and soak in hot water 30 minutes. Drain and chop very fine. Discard the skin and bones of the chicken breast and chop the meat very fine. Mix the chicken meat with the mushrooms, minced green onions, egg, salt, soy sauce, sugar and monosodium glutamate. Form the mixture into 8 flat patties. Put in a skillet with ½ cup of the soup stock. Cover and cook over low heat 15 minutes. Put a chicken patty in an individual soup bowl and pour some of the remaining hot soup over it. Garnish with a lemon strip.

Serves 8.

BROILED SHRIMP

16 large raw shrimp	½ cup lemon juice
2 tablespoons sesame seeds	½ cup soy sauce
1 teaspoon salt	

Wash the shrimp and cut a slit through the shell down the vein side, leaving the tail end connected. Pull out the vein, press the shrimp open and flatten, shell side down.

Brown the sesame seeds in a skillet. Sprinkle the sesame seeds and salt over the meat side of the shrimp and arrange on a lightly oiled broiling pan, shell side down. Broil 5 minutes, turn over and broil 3 minutes longer. Dip the shrimp in bowls of soy sauce and lemon juice.

Serves 8.

BROILED BUTTERFISH

8 small butterfish	½ cup lemon juice
Salt	½ cup soy sauce
8 strips ginger root	

Have the fish scaled and cleaned. Wash and dry the fish, then sprinkle with salt on both sides. Let stand 2 hours. Rinse and dry. The Japanese put skewers into the fish to curve it during broiling. Insert a skewer into the side of the fish through the bones and out again at the tail end. Use another skewer and insert it crosswise, so that the two skewers overlap at the tail end. Sprinkle the fish with salt again and arrange on a lightly oiled broiling pan. Broil 10 minutes on each side or until the fish flakes easily when tested with a fork. Remove the skewers carefully, garnish with the ginger (cut the ends into strips to resemble a brush) and serve small bowls of the lemon juice and soy sauce mixed together for dipping.

Serves 8.

BOILED BEANS

1½ cups dried kidney beans	1 teaspoon salt
⅓ cup sugar	

Wash and pick over the beans. Cover the beans with water, bring to a boil, cook 1 minute, remove from the heat and let soak 1 hour. Bring to a boil again, cover loosely, and cook over low heat 2 hours, or until the beans are soft. Add more boiling water if necessary. When the beans are soft, drain the water, mix in the sugar and salt and cook 5 minutes longer, stirring frequently.

Serves 8.

BOILED BEEF

1 pound onions	¼ teaspoon black pepper
1½ pounds sirloin tip or eye round	1 tablespoon rice wine or dry sherry
4 tablespoons vegetable oil	1¾ cups beef broth
4 tablespoons soy sauce	1 tablespoon cornstarch
4 teaspoons sugar	3 tablespoons water
1¼ teaspoons salt	½ cup shelled green peas

Peel the onions and cut each lengthwise into 8 wedges. Slice the beef very thin.

Heat the oil in a deep skillet; add the onions and beef. Cook over low heat 10 minutes, stirring frequently. Add a mixture of the soy sauce, sugar, salt, pepper, wine and broth. Bring to a boil and cook over low heat 20 minutes or until the meat is tender. Mix the cornstarch with the water and stir it into the mixture until thickened. Add the peas and cook 3 minutes longer.

Serves 8.

BOILED EGGPLANT

1 large eggplant	¼ cup beef or chicken broth
¼ cup sesame or vegetable oil	½ teaspoon monosodium
3 tablespoons soy sauce	glutamate
2 teaspoons sugar	

Peel the eggplant and cut as for French fried potatoes.

Heat the oil in a skillet; add the eggplant and cook until lightly browned on all sides. Add a mixture of the soy sauce, sugar, broth and monosodium glutamate. Cook over low heat 10 minutes. Serve hot.

Serves 8.

CUCUMBER, ABALONE AND SEAWEED SALAD

½ package konbu (seaweed)	2 tablespoons sugar
3 tablespoons sesame seeds	1 cup vinegar
2 cucumbers	½ teaspoon monosodium
3½ teaspoons salt	glutamate
1 can abalone	2 tablespoons cornstarch
¼ cup beef broth	¼ cup water

Seaweed is available in Oriental food shops. Wash the seaweed, cover with water, bring to a boil and cook over low heat 2 hours or until seaweed is soft. Drain and cool.

Put the sesame seeds in a small skillet and place over low heat until browned. Wash the unpeeled cucumbers and slice thin. Sprinkle with 3 teaspoons salt and let stand 30 minutes. Rinse, drain and squeeze dry. Slice the abalone thin.

Combine the broth, sugar, vinegar, monosodium glutamate and remaining salt in a saucepan. Bring to a boil, then stir in a paste of the cornstarch and water until thickened and clear. Cool and stir in the sesame seeds.

Combine the abalone, cucumbers, seaweed, and sauce. Chill.
Serves 8.

FRIED SOFT-SHELL CRABS

8 soft-shell crabs	2 eggs, beaten
Salt	Fine dry bread crumbs
Flour	Oil for deep frying

Have the crabs cleaned; wash and dry them. Sprinkle the crabs with salt and let stand 10 minutes, then dip in the flour, in the eggs and finally in the bread crumbs.

Use ⅔ sesame oil and ⅓ vegetable oil, if possible. If sesame oil is not available, use all peanut oil. Heat the oil to 360° and fry the crabs until browned. Drain and serve with tempura sauce, as a dip.

Tempura Sauce:

¾ cup dashi (fish-seaweed stock)	¼ cup rice wine or dry sherry
¼ cup soy sauce	3 tablespoons grated horseradish or white radish

Dashi is available in Oriental food shops. If you can't get it, bottled clam juice is an adequate substitute. Combine the dashi, soy sauce and wine. Bring to a boil and cool. Serve in small bowls with a little horseradish in the center of each.
Serves 8.

FRIED GREEN PEPPERS

3 green peppers   Cornstarch
Flour   Oil for deep frying
1 egg, beaten

Wash and dry the peppers. Cut each pepper lengthwise into 8 pieces, discarding the seeds. Dip the pepper strips in flour, then in the egg and finally in the cornstarch.

Heat the oil to 365° and fry the peppers until delicately browned. Drain and serve hot.

Serves 8.

DAIKON
Turnip Pickles

2 pounds white turnips   ¼ cup salt
1 cup water   ¼ cup rice wine vinegar or
1 cup sugar   white vinegar

Wash the turnips, peel and cut in thin slices. Combine and bring to a boil the water, sugar, salt and vinegar. Cool, then pour over the turnips. Cover and let pickle in the refrigerator 3 days before serving. Serve with rice.

Korea

THE Korean Embassy, handsome and attractive in appearance, is generally furnished and decorated in Western style. The building itself is not large by embassy standards. As in Korea, the embassy's parquet floors are polished to a high degree.

The rooms are decorated with remarkable examples of Korean art and handicrafts, including many fine paintings, cloissoné vases and bowls, and large dolls dressed in Korean national costumes. Especially fine examples of celadon ware, ceramics executed in a pale green color, may be found in the main rooms. The Koreans are experts in lacquerwork, and there are low tables, cabinets and chests inlaid with mother-

of-pearl in classic flower and bird designs. The country's national emblem is the tiger, and its representation may be found frequently in the furniture and art of the embassy.

On important ceremonial occasions, the embassy brings forth its great treasure, a world-famous rug made from sixty-four specially selected leopard skins. It originally belonged to a palace in Seoul from which it was stolen; later it was returned to the embassy.

Western food is often served at cocktail parties and receptions. When Korean meals are offered, most of the dishes are brought to the table at the same time.

Embassy of Korea

Ku-Jul-Pan

Sang-Suhn Jim

Ko-Kee Kui

Dahk Kook

Yak-Kwa

KU-JUL-PAN
Appetizers, Korean Style

These appetizers are customarily served in a nine-sectioned dish. They can also be arranged on any large round serving dish, the pancakes in the center and the other foods in a spokelike effect.

Pancakes:

1 egg
1½ cups water

1½ cups flour
Oil

Beat the egg, stir in the water and then the flour. Strain. Using a 5-inch hot oiled skillet, make paper-thin very lightly browned pancakes.

Shrimp in Soy Sauce:

1 pound raw shrimp, shelled and deveined
3 tablespoons sesame or vegetable oil

½ cup chopped green onions
1 clove garlic, minced
¼ cup soy sauce
Dash cayenne pepper

Wash and dry the shrimp. Heat the oil in a skillet; add the shrimp and cook over high heat 2 minutes. Mix in the green onions, garlic, soy sauce and cayenne pepper. Cook 3 minutes longer.

Sautéed Bamboo Shoots:

1 can bamboo shoots
2 tablespoons sesame or vegetable oil
1 teaspoon sugar
1 tablespoon soy sauce

1 tablespoon minced green onions
1 tablespoon ground sesame seeds
1 teaspoon monosodium glutamate

Drain the bamboo shoots and dry. Cut into narrow strips. Heat the oil in a skillet; add the bamboo shoots; cook over high heat 1 minute. Add the remaining ingredients. Cook over low heat 5 minutes.

Fried Mushrooms:

1 pound mushrooms
2 tablespoons sesame or vegetable oil

2 tablespoons soy sauce
2 tablespoons chopped green onions

Wash the mushrooms and slice thinly. Heat the oil in a skillet; add all the ingredients and cook over high heat 3 minutes, stirring almost constantly.

Raw Meat:

¾ pound fillet of beef
1 tablespoon sugar
3 tablespoons soy sauce
2 tablespoons minced green
onions
1 teaspoon minced garlic
1 teaspoon minced ginger root

4 tablespoons chopped pine
nuts or almonds
3 tablespoons ground sesame
seeds
¼ teaspoon black pepper
1 tablespoon sesame or vegetable oil

Slice the beef very thin and then into narrow strips. Combine all the remaining ingredients and marinate the meat in the mixture for 30 minutes.

Cucumber Sauté:

2 cucumbers
1 teaspoon salt
1 tablespoon sesame or vegetable oil

1 tablespoon soy sauce
1 tablespoon minced green
onions
1 teaspoon ground sesame seeds

Peel the cucumbers, cut in half crosswise and cut into julienne strips. Sprinkle with the salt and let stand 15 minutes. Drain well, squeezing out all the liquid. Heat the oil in a skillet, add the cucumbers and cook over high heat 1 minute. Add the remaining ingredients and cook 1 minute longer.

Eggplant Sauté:

1 eggplant
¼ cup sesame or vegetable oil
1 tablespoon soy sauce
1 teaspoon salt
1 tablespoon minced green
onions

½ teaspoon minced garlic
2 teaspoons ground sesame
seeds
Dash cayenne pepper

Peel and slice the eggplant. Cut as for French fried potatoes. Heat the oil in a skillet; fry the eggplant until browned. Add all the remaining ingredients and cook over high heat 1 minute.

Carrot Sauté:

- 5 young carrots
- 2 tablespoons sesame or vegetable oil
- 1 teaspoon sugar
- 1 tablespoon minced green
  onions
- 1 tablespoon ground sesame
  seeds
- 1 tablespoon soy sauce

Scrape the carrots and cut in matchlike strips. Heat the oil in a skillet; add all the remaining ingredients and cook over high heat 5 minutes, stirring frequently.

Egg Shreds:

- 2 eggs
- ¼ teaspoon salt
- 1 tablespoon oil

Beat the eggs and salt. Heat a little oil in a 6-inch skillet and pour in ¼ of the eggs. Cook until set, turn over for a few seconds, turn out and roll up. Cut into narrow strips. Repeat with balance of eggs.

SANG-SUHN JIM
Fish in Soy Sauce

- 3-pound white fish, cod or bass
- ¾ cup soy sauce
- 3 tablespoons vinegar
- Vegetable oil for deep frying
- 2 tablespoons cornstarch
- 1½ cups water
- ⅓ cup sugar
- ¼ cup grated carrots
- ¼ cup julienne-cut bamboo
  shoots
- ¼ cup sliced canned mushrooms

Wash and dry the fish. Make several cuts on both sides of the fish. Mix together ½ cup soy sauce and 2 tablespoons vinegar. Pour over the fish, and let marinate 45 minutes, basting and turning the fish several times. Drain well. Heat the oil to 365° and fry the fish in it until browned on all sides. Drain, place on a serving dish and keep hot.

In a saucepan mix the remaining soy sauce and vinegar with the cornstarch. Add the water gradually, stirring until smooth. Mix in the sugar. Bring to a boil, stirring steadily. Add the carrots, bamboo shoots and mushrooms. Cook over low heat 10 minutes. Pour over the fish. *Serves 8.*

KO-KEE KUI
Broiled Marinated Beef

3 pounds fillet of beef
⅓ cup sesame or vegetable oil
4 tablespoons sugar
½ cup sesame seeds
¾ cup soy sauce

½ teaspoon black pepper
½ cup chopped green onions
2 cloves garlic, minced
3 tablespoons flour

Cut the meat in very thin slices. Mix with the oil and sugar. Let stand 10 minutes.

Put the sesame seeds in a skillet and cook, stirring frequently, until lightly browned. Add to the meat with the soy sauce, pepper, onions, garlic and flour. Mix well and let marinate 30 minutes; mix a few times.

The meat can be broiled over a charcoal fire, in a very hot broiler, or sautéed in a little oil. Broil or sauté until browned on both sides and serve hot. Serve with spiced dill pickles. *Serves 8.*

DAHK KOOK
Chicken Soup

5-pound roasting chicken
9 cups water
1 onion
1 stalk celery
2 teaspoons salt
⅓ cup soy sauce

¼ teaspoon black pepper
2 green onions, chopped
1 clove garlic, minced
3 tablespoons vegetable oil
1 egg

Wash and clean the chicken. Cut all the meat off the bones into 1-inch pieces. Combine the bones, skin, giblets, water, onion, celery and salt in a saucepan. Bring to a boil, cover and cook over medium heat 1½ hours. Strain.

While the broth is cooking, combine the chicken pieces, soy sauce, pepper, green onions and garlic in a bowl. Let stand 30 minutes. Heat 2 tablespoons of the oil in a saucepan; add the chicken mixture and cook, stirring frequently, until chicken is seared on all sides. Add the strained broth, cook over low heat 20 minutes.

Separate the egg; beat the white and yolk separately. Heat a little of the remaining oil in a 6-inch skillet, and pour in the egg white, turning the pan quickly to coat the bottom. Cook until lightly browned on both sides. Turn out, roll up and cut in narrow pieces. Prepare the yolk in the same manner. Sprinkle over the soup.

Serves 8.

YAK-KWA
Fried Honey Cookies in Syrup

2¾ cups water	½ cup oil
2½ cups sugar	Fat for deep frying
½ teaspoon ground ginger	¾ cup chopped pine nuts or
¼ cup honey	almonds
5 cups sifted flour	

Combine 2 cups of the water and 2 cups of the sugar in a saucepan. Bring to a boil, stirring steadily until the sugar melts, then cook over high heat for 5 minutes. Mix in the ginger and cool.

Combine the remaining sugar and water with the honey. Bring to a boil and cook 1 minute. Cool.

Sift the flour into a bowl; make a well in the center and into it put the honey syrup and the oil. Gradually mix the flour into the well with the hands until a dough is formed. Form tablespoons of the dough into balls, then press each into a ¼-inch-thick circle.

Heat the fat to 375°. Fry a few circles at a time until light brown, turning them frequently. Drain and place in the sugar-ginger syrup; let soak 2 minutes, then remove and sprinkle one side with the nuts.

Makes about 50.

Lebanon

THE Lebanese Embassy, a large and comfortable house, was formerly one of Washington's most imposing private residences.

A wide center hall is flanked on one side by a large graceful drawing room and on the other by a well-proportioned dining room where formal diplomatic dinners are served. A charming garden suitable for entertaining small groups of guests is at the back of the house.

Embassy of Lebanon

INFORMAL MENU

Homos   Kabees El Lift

Shourabit Djaaj

Kibbe

Yogurt

Ghurayba

Fruits, Dates and Nuts

Arabian Coffee

HOMOS
Chick Pea Appetizer

1 pound chick peas
½ teaspoon baking soda
3 teaspoons salt
1 cup taheeni (sesame-seed
     paste)

1 cup lemon juice
3 cloves garlic
3 tablespoons minced parsley

Wash the chick peas and discard any imperfect ones. Cover with water, mix in the baking soda and let soak overnight. Drain, wash under cold running water, place in a saucepan and cover with water. Bring to a boil, and cook over low heat 3 hours, adding 1½ teaspoons salt after 1 hour cooking time. Drain. Purée the chick peas in an electric blender or put through a food mill.

Taheeni can be bought in Middle East food shops. (If it is not available, use ¾ cup sesame or vegetable oil, and make a dressing with the lemon juice, beating until thickened, then add gradually to the chick peas.) Gradually alternately add the taheeni and lemon juice to the chick peas. Crush the garlic with the remaining salt, and beat into the bean mixture. Spread on a serving dish and sprinkle with the parsley. Serve with Arabic or French bread.

Serves 10 to 12.

KABEES EL LIFT
Pickled Turnips

2 pounds turnips
2 beets
½ cup salt

4 cups water
3 cloves garlic
2 cups white vinegar

Wash and pare the turnips. Cut in half lengthwise and dry on paper towels. Scrub the beets with a brush, but do not pare. Cut into quarters.

Dissolve the salt in the water. In a large glass jar, put the turnips, beets and peeled garlic. Mix the vinegar with the salt solution and fill the jar. Cover the jar with the lid lightly and let stand 3 to 4 days. Chill before serving.

SHOURABIT DJAAJ
Chicken Soup with Parsley

4-pound fowl	1 tablespoon salt
3 quarts water	¼ teaspoon white pepper
1 onion	¾ cup rice
2 stalks celery	¼ cup chopped parsley

Wash and clean the chicken. Combine in a saucepan with the water and onion. Bring to a boil, cover loosely and cook over low heat 1 hour. Add the celery, salt and pepper; cook 1½ hours longer. Remove the chicken and discard the onion and celery. (Use chicken for salad or other purpose.) Add the rice to the broth; cook 20 minutes. Serve sprinkled with the parsley.

Serves 8 to 10.

KIBBE
Baked Meat and Wheat

Wheat Mixture:

1 pound borghul (fine crushed wheat)	½ cup grated onions
2 pounds lean twice-ground lamb	2 teaspoons salt
	½ teaspoon black pepper
	¼ teaspoon cinnamon

Borghul is available in Middle East or other specialty food shops. Soak the wheat in cold water to cover for 30 minutes, kneading it several times. Drain thoroughly, then mix in the lamb, onions, salt, pepper and cinnamon. Knead for a few minutes, then put through the fine blade of a food chopper, adding ¼ cup ice water as you grind.

Filling:

1 tablespoon butter	¼ teaspoon black pepper
¾ cup chopped onions	¼ cup pine nuts
½ pound ground lamb	½ cup melted butter
½ teaspoon salt	

Melt the butter in a skillet; brown the onions in it. Add the meat, salt and pepper. Cook, stirring frequently, for 5 minutes. Add the nuts. Cook, stirring frequently, until browned.

Pat half the wheat mixture into a greased 9- by 12-inch baking pan. Spread the filling over it. Cover with the remaining wheat mixture, pressing down until firm. With a sharp knife, cut diagonal lines across the top to form a diamond pattern. Pour the melted butter over the top. Bake in a preheated 400° oven 30 minutes. Reduce heat to 350° and bake 30 minutes longer. Cut into squares and serve. This dish may be eaten hot or cold.

Serves 8 to 10.

GHURAYBA
Short Cookies

½ pound butter	¼ pound shelled almonds,
1 cup sugar	blanched and split
2 cups sifted flour	

Cream the butter until very light and fluffy. Gradually beat in the sugar. Work in the flour until a dough is formed.

On a lightly floured surface, roll out the dough ⅓-inch thick. Cut with a doughnut cutter. Transfer the cookies to a baking sheet. Arrange 3 half almonds on top of each. Bake in a preheated 300° oven 25 minutes, or until delicately browned.

Makes about 3 dozen.

Mexico

THE Mexican Embassy has large, sometimes enormous, rooms and superb facilities for entertaining the diplomatic corps of Washington.

The entrance hall is attractive, brightened by tall windows hung with silk drapes; at the left there is a small poudreuse. Most of the important reception rooms are upstairs, reached by a wide staircase flanked on all sides by an elaborate series of murals. The drawing room is rather handsome, and the furniture is appropriate in a formal style; upholstered pieces are covered in antique satin. It is a custom of the embassy to fill this room with banks of tropical flowers on evenings

when guests are expected. The large ballroom has lovely frescoes on the walls and ceilings, and it features a gilded pipe organ.

The embassy's dining room has massive furniture of the Spanish Colonial period; the table is laden with Mexican flatware and silver table service. On the walls are hung ancient Spanish embroideries, and there is a fine, thick rug on the floor. One of the loveliest areas of this embassy is the conservatory, a room usually filled with thousands of Mexican blossoms and plants for special holidays or receptions.

Embajada de Mexico

MANZANILLA SHERRY

Camarónes en Salsa Jitomate
Pastel de Mole
Sopa de Espuma
AMONTILLADO SHERRY

Huachinango Relleno
CHABLIS

Tournedos al Embajador
BURGUNDY

Bombe aux Fruits
CHÂTEAU YQUEM OR CHAMPAGNE

CAMARÓNES EN SALSA JITOMATE
Shrimp in Tomato Sauce

3 pounds raw shrimp
3 cups chicken broth
3 cups water
1 carrot, sliced
2 stalks celery, sliced
6 peppercorns
1 bay leaf
½ teaspoon thyme
2 teaspoons salt
1 cup olive oil

1 cup vegetable oil
1 cup wine vinegar
1½ cups peeled chopped
  tomatoes
½ cup thinly sliced green onions
2 cloves garlic, minced
⅛ teaspoon dried ground chili
  peppers
2 tablespoons minced parsley

Wash and drain the shrimp. Combine and bring to a boil the broth, water, carrot, celery, peppercorns, bay leaf, thyme and 1 teaspoon of the salt. Cook over medium heat 15 minutes. Add the shrimp, cover loosely, bring to a boil and cook over low heat 5 minutes. Let cool in the liquid, then drain, shell and devein.

Mix together the oils, vinegar, tomatoes, green onions, garlic, chili peppers, parsley and remaining salt. Pour over the shrimp and let marinate in refrigerator 4 hours. Drain off most of the liquid and serve on shredded lettuce.

Serves 12.

PASTEL DE MOLE
Pastry Shells with Poultry Stuffing

1 can Mole Poblano
3 tablespoons olive oil
¾ cup peeled seeded chopped
  tomatoes
1 teaspoon sugar

2 cups chicken broth
3 cups diced cooked turkey or
  chicken
12 heated patty shells

[215]

Mole Poblano is available in Mexican, Spanish or specialty food shops. Heat the oil in a saucepan; stir in the Mole and cook, stirring almost constantly, for 2 minutes. Add the tomatoes and sugar; cook over low heat 3 minutes. Gradually add the broth, stirring constantly. Cook over low heat 20 minutes. Mix in the chicken and cook 5 minutes longer. Fill the shells and serve hot.

Serves 12.

SOPA DE ESPUMA
Soup with Fluffy Dumplings

¾ cup sifted flour	2 tablespoons grated Parmesan
1 teaspoon baking powder	cheese
¼ cup melted butter	4 quarts chicken broth
3 eggs	

Sift together the flour and baking powder, then stir into the melted butter. Add the eggs one at a time, beating until well blended after each addition. Stir in the cheese.

Bring the broth to a rolling boil and drop the batter into it by the teaspoon. Cover and cook over medium heat for 10 minutes without raising the cover. Serve hot in consommé cups.

Serves 12.

HUACHINANGO RELLENO
Stuffed Fish Fillets

6 tablespoons butter	1 teaspoon white pepper
6 tablespoons flour	12 fillets of red snapper or sole
1½ cups chicken broth	24 shucked oysters
1½ cups light cream	¾ pound sliced sautéed mush-
⅛ teaspoon mace	rooms
3 teaspoons salt	

Melt the butter in a saucepan; blend in the flour. Add the broth and cream, stirring steadily over low heat until smooth and thickened. Add the mace, 1 teaspoon of the salt and ½ teaspoon pepper and cook 5 minutes longer.

Rinse and dry the fillets. Sprinkle with the remaining salt and pepper. Dip the oysters in the sauce and place two on each fillet. Divide the mushrooms among the fillets, then roll up like a jelly roll. Arrange in a single layer in a shallow buttered baking dish and pour the remaining sauce over them. Bake in a 375° oven 25 minutes, or until the fish flakes easily when tested with a fork.

Place under the broiler until top is delicately browned. Serve garnished with cooked green peas and parsley.

Serves 12.

TOURNEDOS AL EMBAJADOR
Fillet of Beef with Stuffed Artichokes

12 canned artichoke bottoms	Salt
1 8-ounce can pâté de foie gras	Black pepper
¼ cup heavy cream	¼ cup cognac
12 slices of truffles	¼ cup beef broth
12 fillets of beef, cut 2 inches thick	3 tablespoons minced parsley
⅜ pound butter	Watercress sprigs

Heat the artichoke bottoms in a double boiler. Mash the pâté in a saucepan and blend in the cream. Heat. Fill the artichokes with the mixture and garnish each with a slice of truffle. Keep hot while preparing the meat.

Melt half the butter in a skillet. Add the fillets and cook over high heat 3 minutes on each side, or to desired degree of rareness. Transfer to a serving dish, sprinkle with salt and pepper and keep hot.

Pour the cognac into the skillet and set aflame. When flames die, add the broth and bring to a boil, scraping the bottom of browned particles. Break the remaining butter into small pieces and swirl it into the sauce. Stir in the parsley. Pour over the fillets and arrange the stuffed artichokes around them. Garnish with watercress sprigs.

Serves 12.

BOMBE AUX FRUITS
Frozen Fruit Mousse

1½ cups chopped candied fruits
½ cup cognac
1½ cups sugar
1 cup water

8 egg yolks
1 cup chopped almonds
4 cups heavy cream

Marinate the fruits in the cognac for 30 minutes.

Bring the sugar and water to a boil; cook 5 minutes, or until thick and syrupy. Cool. Beat the egg yolks in the top of a double boiler; gradually stir in the syrup. Place over hot water and cook, stirring steadily, until thick and mixture coats spoon. Strain through a fine sieve. Cool. Mix in the undrained fruits and the nuts.

Whip the cream and fold it into the mixture. Turn into a 3-quart or two 1½-quart bombe or other molds. Cover with a piece of buttered waxed paper, then with the mold cover. Freeze for 12 hours. Unmold onto a chilled serving dish. Decorate with whipped cream and candied fruits and leaves.

Serves 12.

Morocco

THE embassy of this North African country is situated on commodious grounds, well set back from the road. The building is white, and the green shutters next to the upper floor windows offer a cheerful note of contrast. Behind the house, one finds a fine garden and a swimming pool, the whole enclosed by hedges of tall rhododendrons which create a feeling of privacy. In the building itself, the drawing room, the embassy's main reception area, is reached by a step down to a lower level. It is executed in the classic French style, with gray satin drapes hung alongside tall, arched windows. A fine example of the Moroccan skill in rugmaking, with an unbelievably heavy pile, covers much of the floor. The furniture is chiefly French, with many fine pieces, mostly

Regency or Louis XVI; the upholstered furniture is covered in satin and silk. The embassy also has a typically Moroccan room, decorated in very bright, gay colors; guests sit on brilliant yellow banquettes and dine informally off extremely low tables.

However, on formal occasions the main dining room is used; it is exceptionally large and handsome, facing onto a patio. The table is long and impressive; the chairs are covered with a dull white silk. Nearby there's a superb library, with a most unusual paneling decorated with Latin mottoes, executed in gold, which reach from floor to ceiling. The decor is charming, the colors being green, gold and white; it is often considered the most inviting and gracious room in the embassy.

Embassy of Morocco

FORMAL MENU

Bstila

Shad with Dates

Kabab

Couscous

Hearts of Lettuce Salad

El Majoun

BSTILA
Pastry Hors d'Oeuvres

The pastry for bstila is very difficult to make, but an adequate substitute is either phyllo leaves (available in Greek or Middle East food shops) or packaged strudel leaves. Buy two pounds phyllo leaves or ten packages strudel leaves. Usually bstila is prepared in a round shape, but with the prepared pastry it will be oblong.

1 cup water	½ teaspoon saffron
1 pound butter	½ teaspoon crushed coriander
¾ teaspoon salt	½ cup minced onions
½ teaspoon ground cardamon	¼ cup minced parsley
⅛ teaspoon mace	4 pigeons or squabs
¼ teaspoon ginger	6 eggs
⅛ teaspoon nutmeg	¼ cup sugar
Dash cayenne pepper	½ pound shelled almonds
Dash powdered cloves	2 teaspoons cinnamon
⅛ teaspoon powdered fennel	3 tablespoons confectioners'
¼ teaspoon black pepper	sugar

Combine the water, half the butter, the spices, onions, parsley, pigeons and their gizzards and livers in a saucepan. Bring to a boil, cover and cook over low heat 2 hours. Remove the pigeons, discard the skin and bones and cut the pigeon meat, gizzards and livers into small pieces.

Beat 4 eggs in a bowl; gradually add the hot sauce, beating until thickened. Beat the remaining eggs separately.

Use 10 sheets of pastry for the bottom layer, piling one sheet on top of the other and brushing each with beaten egg. Leaving a 2-inch

[223]

border, sprinkle the sugar over the top sheet, then the almonds and 1 teaspoon cinnamon. Cover with 10 sheets of pastry, brushing each with beaten egg. Leaving a 2-inch border, spread the pigeon meat and cover with the sauce. Cover with the remaining sheets of pastry, brushing each with beaten egg yolk. Tuck in all the edges to seal.

Melt the remaining butter in a baking pan; pour off half. Put the pastry in it and pour the melted butter over the top. Bake in a preheated 425° oven 25 minutes, or until golden brown. Sprinkle the top with the confectioners' sugar and the remaining cinnamon. While hot, cut into squares.

SHAD WITH DATES

2 whole shad or other fish	¼ pound butter
1 pound dates	1 teaspoon salt
½ cup cooked rice	1½ teaspoons black pepper
½ cup ground almonds	¾ cup chopped onions
1 teaspoon sugar	½ cup water
½ teaspoon ginger	⅓ teaspoon cinnamon

Have the shad split for stuffing. Wash the shad and let stand in salted water for 5 minutes. Drain and dry.

Remove the pits of the dates carefully. Mix together the rice, almonds, sugar, half the ginger and 2 tablespoons of the butter. Stuff the dates with the mixture, then stuff the fish with them. Sew the opening, or close with skewers. Melt half the remaining butter in a baking dish. Arrange the fish in it. Sprinkle with the salt, pepper and remaining ginger, dot with the remaining butter and add the onions and water. Bake in a 350° oven 1¼ hours, basting frequently. Sprinkle with the cinnamon, raise heat to 450° and place fish on the upper rack of the oven until browned. Remove the threads or skewers and arrange the dates around the fish.

Serves 10.

KABAB
Meat on Skewers

3 pounds fillet of beef
1 pound beef fat
2 cups minced onions

1 cup minced parsley
2 teaspoons salt
1 teaspoon black pepper

Cut the beef into pieces 1 inch square and about ½ inch thick. Cut the fat into slightly smaller, thinner pieces.

Combine the meat, fat, onions, parsley, salt and pepper in a bowl. Mix well and let stand 4 hours. Using ten skewers, alternately thread the meat and fat on them, starting and ending with the meat. Broil in a hot broiler close to the source of heat 10 minutes, turning the skewers to brown all sides.

Serves 10.

COUSCOUS
Mixed Meats and Semolina

3 cups faufal
3 cups water
1½ tablespoons salt
1 cup dried chick peas, or 2 cups canned, drained
¼ cup olive oil
½ pound butter
2 cups chopped onions
4 pounds boneless lamb, cubed
5-pound chicken, disjointed
3 cups chicken broth
2 carrots, sliced

2 green peppers, sliced
3 tomatoes, peeled and cubed
¼ teaspoon saffron
1 teaspoon freshly ground black pepper
½ teaspoon cayenne pepper
2 cups shredded cabbage
2 cups seedless raisins
1 pound fresh green peas, shelled, or 1 package frozen

Faufal is tiny pellets of wheat. It can be found in Near Eastern or Oriental food shops. If unobtainable, you may substitute cracked wheat, wheat semolina or even farina.

Put the faufal in a bowl and stir in the 3 cups water and 1 teaspoon salt. Rub mixture between the hands about 1 foot above the bowl, letting it fall into bowl. Do this several times. Do not allow lumps to form. Let faufal soak until all the water is absorbed.

If you are using dried chick peas, cover with water, bring to a boil and let soak 1 hour. Drain.

Heat the oil and half the butter in a large saucepan; brown the onions, lamb and chicken in it. Add the broth and the soaked chick peas (if canned chick peas are used, add later, with the green peas). Mix in the carrots, green peppers, tomatoes, saffron, black pepper, cayenne pepper and remaining salt. Turn the faufal into a large strainer or colander and place over the saucepan. Cover as tightly as possible. Cook over low heat 1½ hours, then to the chicken mixture add the cabbage, raisins, green peas (and canned chick peas). Re-cover and continue cooking 45 minutes longer, or until chicken is tender. Stir remaining butter into faufal with a fork. Heap the faufal in the center of a platter with the chicken, lamb, vegetables and sauce around it.

Serves 10.

HEARTS OF LETTUCE SALAD

6 hearts of lettuce	2 teaspoons sugar
¾ teaspoon salt	½ cup olive oil
1 teaspoon black pepper	3 tablespoons white wine
⅛ teaspoon cinnamon	vinegar

Wash and dry the lettuce, then chop it up. Sprinkle with the salt, pepper, cinnamon and sugar. Just before serving, sprinkle with the olive oil and toss, then add the vinegar and toss again.

Serves 10.

EL MAJOUN
Nut-Honey Dessert

1 pound toasted blanched
    almonds
½ pound shelled almonds
1 pound seedless raisins
3 tablespoons preserved ginger
1 teaspoon ground cardamon
¼ teaspoon mace
¼ teaspoon nutmeg

½ teaspoon cinnamon
½ teaspoon saffron
¼ teaspoon fennel seeds
⅛ teaspoon cayenne pepper
½ pound honey
¼ pound butter
1½ cups sesame seeds

Grind the nuts and chop the raisins and ginger fine. Pound together all the spices. Use a heavy-bottomed saucepan, and in it combine the nuts, fruits, spices, honey and butter. Cook over low heat, stirring frequently, until mixture turns very thick, about 1 hour. Watch carefully to prevent burning.

Let stand until cool enough to handle, then form into walnut-sized balls and roll heavily in the sesame seeds. Keep in a cool dry place.

Makes about 60.

Netherlands

THE Embassade Van Het Koninkrijk der Nederlanden, the correct name, is housed in a handsome building designed by a Washington architect, Ward Brown. The interior is charmingly Old World in design and decor.

The first floor has a comfortable entrance hall containing various examples of Dutch art from the sixteenth and seventeenth centuries, including sculptures, woodwork and tapestries. Even the adjacent cloakrooms have period marquetry furniture. The main rooms of the embassy are reached by a rather broad marble staircase which rises from the center of the entrance hall. On the second floor are situated most of the principle rooms, of which the drawing room is the most imposing. The walls are decorated in light colors, the curtains are made of a sheer

fabric framed by pastel silk drapes, and even the carpeting — hand loomed in the Netherlands — is an off-white shade. There are many notable paintings representative of Dutch art on the walls of the drawing room, including examples by van Honthorst, Eijck and Moreelse. The furniture is mainly French, of the Louis XV, Louis XVI and Directoire periods. At the far end of the drawing room, down a few steps, is a paneled book-lined library, decorated in Delft blue and white; the Dutch paintings here are by Maes, van de Velde and Cuyp.

The embassy's dining room is large but nevertheless has an intimate feeling. It features a large Dutch cupboard dating back to the seventeenth century. The outstanding example of art upon the walls is a painting of a husband and wife by Cornelis de Vos.

[229]

Ambassade Van Het Koninkrijk der Nederlanden

FORMAL MENU

Kaastruffels
Paling Soep
Hazepeper
Roompudding

INFORMAL MENU

Bitterballen
Kerry Soep
Gevulde Kalfsborst
Appelschoteltje

KAASTRUFFELS
Cheese Truffles

¼ pound butter
½ cup grated Gouda or cheddar
    cheese
⅛ teaspoon pepper

⅛ teaspoon celery salt
¼ teaspoon paprika
1 cup stale pumpernickel or rye
    bread crumbs

Soften the butter and beat until smooth, then mix in the cheese, pepper, celery salt and paprika. Shape into olive-sized balls. Use a warm teaspoon, and roll each ball in the bread crumbs. Chill several hours, then serve.

Makes about 60 balls.

PALING SOEP
Eel Soup

1½ pounds eel
2 quarts water
1 tablespoon salt
8 peppercorns
1 small bay leaf

6 tablespoons butter
6 tablespoons flour
1 tablespoon chopped parsley
2 egg yolks

Have the skin of the eel removed, wash and cut into 1-inch pieces.

Bring the water, salt, peppercorns and bay leaf to a boil. Add the eel and simmer for 20 minutes. Remove the eel.

Melt the butter in a large saucepan; mix in the flour. Add the eel stock; simmer for 15 minutes. Strain. Add the eel and parsley and re-heat. Beat the egg yolks in a bowl; mix in a little hot soup, then return to balance of soup and serve.

Serves 8.

HAZEPEPER
Marinated Rabbit

1 large hare or 2 rabbits	2 teaspoons sugar
1 cup vinegar	1 teaspoon salt
3 cups dry red wine	½ teaspoon pepper
½ pound butter	1 bay leaf
2 onions, sliced	4 cloves
2 tablespoons flour	2 tablespoons soy sauce

Have the hare or rabbits skinned, cleaned and cut into serving-sized pieces. Pour boiling water over them, drain and dry.

Combine the vinegar and wine in a large bowl; marinate the pieces in the mixture overnight in the refrigerator. Drain, reserving the marinade. Dry the pieces.

Melt half the butter in a skillet; add the rabbit pieces and cook over medium heat until browned on all sides. Melt the remaining butter in a Dutch oven; brown the onions in it. Mix in the flour until browned. Add the marinade and bring to a boil, stirring. Add the sugar, salt, pepper, bay leaf, cloves, soy sauce and browned rabbit. Cover and simmer 3 hours, or until the rabbit is tender. Serve with potatoes or rice and mixed vegetables.

Serves 6 to 8.

ROOMPUDDING
Fruit-Nut Pudding

1 envelope (1 tablespoon) gelatin	½ cup milk
3 tablespoons water	3 cups heavy cream
½ cup sugar	¼ cup ground almonds
1½ teaspoons vanilla	¼ cup chopped candied fruits

Sprinkle the gelatin into the water. Combine the sugar, vanilla, milk and 2 cups of the cream and bring to a boil; stir in the gelatin until dissolved. Cool until mixture begins to thicken. Stir in the nuts and fruits. Whip the remaining cream and fold it into the gelatin mixture.

Rinse a 1½-quart mold with cold water, drain, then pour the pudding mixture into it. Chill until firm enough to unmold.

Serves 8.

BITTERBALLEN
Meat Balls

3 tablespoons butter	½ teaspoon nutmeg
4 tablespoons flour	1 tablespoon chopped parsley
1 cup milk	1½ cups ground cooked meat
1 tablespoon grated onion	1 cup dry bread crumbs
1 teaspoon Worcestershire	2 eggs
sauce	Fat for deep frying
1 teaspoon salt	Dutch-style mustard

Melt the butter in a saucepan; stir in the flour, then the milk, stirring steadily until sauce thickens. Add the onion, Worcestershire sauce, salt, nutmeg, parsley and meat. Simmer 5 minutes, stirring frequently. Spread on a plate or board until cool, then shape into ½-inch balls. Roll the balls in the bread crumbs, then in the eggs beaten with a little water, and again in the bread crumbs. Let stand 1 hour.

Heat deep fat to 370°. Drop the balls into it, not too many at once, and fry until browned. Drain, put a cocktail pick into each, and arrange around a small bowl of mustard.

Makes about 60.

◦⟨⟩◦

KERRY SOEP
Curried Pea Soup

3 cups green split peas	1 celery root, peeled and cubed
3 quarts water	3 tablespoons butter
2 pig's feet	2 onions, chopped
1 pound slab bacon	1 tablespoon flour
3 leeks, sliced	1 tablespoon curry powder
2 whole onions	Salt and pepper to taste
2 tablespoons chopped parsley	Croutons
1 cup chopped celery and leaves	

Wash the split peas and cook in the water for 2 hours. Rub through a sieve. Add the pig's feet and bacon; simmer for 2 hours. Add the leeks, whole onions, parsley, celery, and celery root. Simmer 1 hour. Cool, then refrigerate overnight. Remove the pig's feet, bacon, and onions.

Melt the butter in a large saucepan; cook the chopped onions in it until golden. Blend in the flour and curry powder. Slowly add the pea soup; bring to a boil and cook 10 minutes. If too thick, add boiling water. Season to taste with salt and pepper. Serve with croutons. *Serves 6 to 8.*

◦⟨⟩◦

GEVULDE KALFSBORST
Stuffed Breast of Veal

3 slices white bread	½ teaspoon pepper
½ cup milk	½ pound butter
1 pound ground veal	2 tablespoons flour
2 eggs	1 cup hot water
¼ teaspoon nutmeg	¼ teaspoon tarragon
3 teaspoons salt	1 tablespoon dry sherry
1 breast of veal, with pocket for stuffing	

Cut the crusts from the bread, then soak bread in the milk for 10 minutes. Mash smooth. Mix with the ground veal, eggs, nutmeg and

1 teaspoon of the salt. Season breast of veal with the pepper and remaining salt and stuff the pocket with the ground veal mixture.

Melt all but 2 tablespoons of the butter in a roasting pan. Place the veal in it. Roast in a 300° oven for 3½ hours, or until the meat is tender. Baste frequently and add a little boiling water every once in a while.

Melt the remaining butter in a saucepan; mix in the flour, then the water, tarragon and pan drippings. Simmer for 10 minutes. Strain and mix in the sherry. Carve the veal and serve with the sauce, and tiny peas, applesauce, mashed potatoes or rice.

Serves 4 to 6.

APPELSCHOTELTJE
Dutch Apple Pudding

8 zwieback	½ cup flour
1 cup milk	8 sour apples, peeled and thinly
¼ teaspoon grated lemon rind	sliced
Pinch of salt	10 tablespoons sugar
¼ pound plus 2 tablespoons	3 egg yolks
butter	3 egg whites, beaten stiff

Crush the zwieback into fine crumbs. Bring the milk, lemon rind and salt to a boil. Knead 3 tablespoons of the butter with the flour and stir into the hot milk, cooking and stirring until thickened.

Melt 2 tablespoons butter in a skillet; add the apples and half the sugar. Simmer 10 minutes.

Stir the remaining sugar and all but 2 tablespoons of the remaining butter into the sauce. Beat the egg yolks; gradually stir in the hot sauce, then the apples. Cool. Fold in the egg whites.

In a buttered 1½-quart baking dish, make layers of the zwieback crumbs and apple mixture, starting and ending with the crumbs. Dot with the remaining butter. Bake in a preheated 325° oven 45 minutes. Serve warm with whipped cream, if desired.

Serves 6 to 8.

New Zealand

THE New Zealand Embassy is housed in a huge mansion, a most attractive and pleasant building. From the moment that guests step into the elaborate marble entrance hall, a feeling of graciousness pervades. On one wall hangs a portrait of a chieftain of the Maori, who were among earliest inhabitants of New Zealand.

On the right-hand side of the first floor is the sun room, with light-colored walls and bright, attractive decor; the overall effect is cheerful and warm. The reception room, formal but not austere, has good proportions and is quite elegant. The color scheme is fairly light, with some accents in darker shades. The dining room has a large fireplace at one end,

with a good-sized portrait over it; the dining room's mahogany chairs are covered in brocade, and complement the table.

Upstairs, the master bedroom is painted in pale colors, and the drapes, furniture and decorations are of similar or matching shades. A favorite retreat of the Ambassador and his family is the library, which has knotty pine paneling; the walls are lined with bookcases. There are various New Zealand landscapes and scenes in this room, as well as in other rooms of the house. New Zealanders are inordinately fond of gardens, and this embassy's garden reflects the national love of flowers and all growing things.

New Zealand Embassy

Toheroa Soup

Roast Leg of Lamb

Broiled Tomatoes   Baby Peas and Onions

Spring Potatoes

Curried Relish

Pavlova Cake   Coffee

TOHEROA SOUP

1 15-ounce can toheroa con-
    centrate
3 cups milk
1 teaspoon sugar

⅛ teaspoon nutmeg
2 tablespoons butter
3 tablespoons cornstarch
½ cup water

Toheroa is a shellfish found only in the waters of New Zealand. The canned concentrate or condensed soup is available in the United States in many specialty food shops. (If you can't get it, an alternate recipe below will give an adequate substitute.)

Pour the toheroa concentrate into a heavy saucepan. Bring to a boil and cook over low heat 30 minutes. Pour into a clean saucepan, being careful to leave any sandy residue in the first saucepan. To the concentrate, add the milk, sugar, nutmeg and butter. Bring to a boil. Mix the cornstarch with the water. Add to the soup, stirring until smooth and thickened. Serve hot in soup cups.

Serves 6.

Toheroa Substitute:

2 10-ounce cans minced clams
¾ canned condensed pea soup

1 tablespoon cornstarch
3 cups milk

Purée the undrained clams in an electric blender. Pour into a saucepan, bring to a boil and cook over low heat 15 minutes. Mix the pea soup, cornstarch and milk until smooth and stir into the clams. Cook, stirring steadily, until mixture boils and is smooth and thickened.

Serves 6.

ROAST LEG OF LAMB

5-pound leg of lamb
3 cloves garlic, slivered
2 teaspoons salt
½ teaspoon black pepper
½ teaspoon rosemary
3 tablespoons butter

2 stalks celery, sliced
1 carrot, grated
¾ cup chopped onions
¾ cup water
¾ cup dry sherry

Make several shallow cuts in the leg and into them insert the garlic slivers. Season with the salt, pepper and rosemary. Place the leg in a roasting pan and dot with the butter. Surround the leg with the celery, carrot and onions. Pour the water into the pan. Roast in a 300° oven 25 minutes a pound. Baste and turn frequently, and add the sherry 30 minutes before end of roasting time. Pour off the pan juices and skim the fat. Serve with the carved lamb.

Serves 6.

BROILED TOMATOES

6 tomatoes
1 teaspoon salt
¼ teaspoon black pepper

½ teaspoon tarragon
2 tablespoons butter

Wash and dry the tomatoes and cut in half crosswise. Sprinkle the cut halves with the salt, pepper and tarragon. Arrange on a buttered baking pan and dot with the butter. Broil 10 minutes, or until tender.

Serves 6.

BABY PEAS AND ONIONS

2½ pounds peas, shelled
2 cups water
¾ cup sliced green onions
1 teaspoon salt

⅛ teaspoon white pepper
3 tablespoons butter
2 tablespoons minced parsley

Buy very small peas. Bring the water to a boil and add the shelled peas. Cook over low heat 5 minutes. Add the green onions, salt and pepper; cook 5 minutes longer, or until the peas are tender. Drain and add the butter and parsley; toss until butter melts and peas are coated.

Serves 6.

ᴑ

SPRING POTATOES

2 pounds small new potatoes
3 cups water
2 teaspoons salt

3 tablespoons butter
2 tablespoons minced parsley

Peel the potatoes. (If small new potatoes are not available, make potato balls of larger potatoes.) Bring the water and salt to a boil; add the potatoes and cook 12 minutes, or until the potatoes are tender but slightly firm. Drain. Return to a saucepan and shake the pan over low heat until the potatoes are dry. Add the butter and parsley. Toss until butter melts and potatoes are coated.

Serves 6.

ᴑ

CURRIED RELISH

4 pounds tomatoes, cubed
2½ cups chopped onions
1½ tablespoons salt
Cider vinegar
1 tablespoon flour

1 tablespoon dry mustard
2 tablespoons curry powder
1 tablespoon brown sugar
1½ teaspoons dried ground chili
    peppers

Put the tomatoes and onions in a bowl in layers, sprinkling each layer with salt. Let stand overnight.

Drain off the accumulated liquid and turn the tomato-onion mixture into a heavy saucepan. Add enough vinegar to cover. Bring to a boil and cook over high heat 5 minutes. Mix the flour, mustard, curry powder, brown sugar and chili peppers with a little vinegar and stir into the tomato mixture. Cook over low heat 1 hour, stirring occasionally. Cool and turn into glass jars. Cover and refrigerate. The relish will keep indefinitely.

Makes about 1½ pints.

PAVLOVA CAKE

4 egg whites
⅛ teaspoon salt
1 cup superfine sugar
¾ teaspoon vanilla extract

1½ teaspoons vinegar
1½ cups heavy cream
Strawberries, sliced peaches, or
    raspberries

Cut an 8-inch circle of baking lining paper or waxed paper and place it on a greased baking sheet.

Beat the egg whites and salt until stiff peaks form, then beat in 1 tablespoon sugar at a time. Add the vanilla and vinegar and beat again. Spread on the paper circle, smoothing the top with a wet spatula. Bake in a preheated 250° oven 1¼ hours, or until the meringue is dry. Immediately peel the paper from the bottom. Cool the meringue on a cake rack.

Whip the cream and heap on the top. Arrange the selected fruit on the cream. Canned fruit may be used, in place of the fresh.

Serves 6.

Pakistan

THE Pakistani Embassy obtained its fine property from Leland Har-
rison, once United States Minister to Switzerland. The building itself
is of moderate size, well proportioned and pleasing in appearance. The
exterior is quite formal, and constructed along traditional lines. Behind
the house there is a good-sized square area of grass, bordered with box
shrubs and lovely rose bushes. From the point of view of outdoor dining, it has one of the best and most convenient gardens of all diplomatic
Washington. The embassy's parties and receptions are often held in
mild weather so that alfresco entertaining is possible. Buffet tables are
arranged outdoors, a large, many-branched oak tree covering the tables

and guests like a verdant canopy. At night, small colored lights are hung from the tree, creating additional atmosphere.

The main reception area of the embassy is its formal drawing room, decorated in various harmonizing soft and pastel shades. At one end is a good-sized fireplace, and over it hangs a portrait of Mohamed Ali Jinnah, sometimes called the George Washington of Pakistan. The furniture is mostly French, chiefly Louis XVI, intermixed with a few Chinese pieces; upholstered pieces are mostly covered with silk or silk damask.

Embassy of Pakistan

FORMAL MENU

Roughan Josh and Samosas
Veal Polao
Chicken Chargha
Paratha
Bhujia
Firni

INFORMAL MENU

Dham-Ka-Kabab and Nan Roti
Chicken Biriani
Shrimp Korma
Okra Bhujiya
Assorted Fruits

LUNCHEON MENU

Fried Fish and Chilly Sauce
Egg and Potato Curry
Masur Dal and Papadams
Shahi Tukra

ROUGHAN JOSH
Lamb Stew

4 pounds lamb shanks
3 tablespoons vegetable oil
1½ cups sliced onions
1½ cups diced tomatoes

12 peppercorns
6 cloves
2 teaspoons salt
6 cups boiling water

Have the shanks cut up into small pieces. Heat the oil in a Dutch oven. Add the lamb, cover and cook over low heat 30 minutes, turning the pieces to brown all sides. Add all the remaining ingredients. Cover and cook 5 hours. Mix occasionally and add a little boiling water if necessary. Discard the bones before serving and skim the fat.
Serves 8.

SAMOSAS
Meat Pastries

2 cups flour
1½ teaspoons salt
¼ cup melted butter
¼ cup yogurt
1 tablespoon vegetable oil
½ pound ground beef

1½ cups chopped onions
2 green chilies, minced
¼ teaspoon minced fresh or
preserved ginger root
Vegetable oil for deep frying

Sift the flour and half the salt into a bowl; stir in the melted butter and yogurt until a dough is formed. Cover and let stand while preparing the filling.

Heat the 1 tablespoon oil in a skillet. Add the meat, onions, chilies, ginger and remaining salt. Cover and cook over low heat 15 minutes stirring frequently. Cool.

On a lightly floured surface roll out the dough very thin. Cut into 3-inch squares. Put a little filling on one side, and fold over into triangles, sealing the edges with a little water or egg white.

Heat the oil to 370°. Fry a few pastries at a time until golden brown. Drain and serve hot.

Makes about 24.

VEAL POLAO
Veal Curry or Stew

6 tablespoons butter	¾ teaspoon cumin seed, crushed
2 cups chopped onions	4 bay leaves
3 pounds boneless veal, cut into	3 cardamon seeds
1-inch cubes	6 cloves
2 cloves garlic, minced	5 cups boiling water
1 teaspoon minced fresh or	3 cups rice
preserved ginger root	2½ teaspoons salt

Melt the butter in a Dutch oven; add the onions and cook until golden. Add the meat and spices. Cover and cook over low heat 15 minutes, shaking the pan frequently. Add ½ cup of the water. Cover and cook 1¼ hours. Mix in the rice, then add the salt and remaining water. Cover and cook over low heat 25 minutes, or until the rice is tender. Shake pan frequently.

Serves 8.

CHICKEN CHARGHA
Broiled Spiced Chicken

2 2½-pound broilers, quartered	1½ teaspoons cinnamon
2 cups yogurt	1 teaspoon dried mint
2 teaspoons salt	½ teaspoon ginger
2 teaspoons black pepper	3 tablespoons lemon juice
2 teaspoons ground cumin seed	

Wash and dry the chickens, then marinate in a mixture of all the remaining ingredients for three hours at room temperature. Be sure the chicken quarters are well covered with the yogurt mixture, spreading it on if necessary.

Arrange the chicken on an oiled broiling pan, and broil on the lowest rack for 30 minutes on each side.

Serves 8.

PARATHA
Bread-Pancake, Pakistan Style

2 cups flour	2 cups milk
1 egg	6 tablespoons butter

Mix the flour with the egg, then add just enough of the milk to make a dough. Cover with a damp cloth and let stand 30 minutes. Divide dough into eight pieces; pat each piece, dot with butter, fold over and roll out into a circle.

Melt some butter in a skillet; put one piece of dough into it at a time and fry until golden brown on both sides.

Makes 8.

CHICK PEA AND CAULIFLOWER BHUJIA

3 tablespoons vegetable oil	1½ teaspoons salt
1½ cups sliced onions	¼ teaspoon cumin seed
¾ cup chopped tomatoes	¾ teaspoon ginger
3 packages frozen cauliflower	¼ teaspoon dried ground red
2 cans chick peas, drained	peppers

Heat the oil in a deep skillet; sauté the onions until golden. Add the tomatoes, cauliflower, chick peas, salt, cumin, ginger and red pepper. Cover and cook over low heat 20 minutes, shaking the pan frequently. Serve hot.

Serves 8.

FIRNI
Rice Flour Pudding

4 cups milk	¼ cup seedless raisins
3 tablespoons rice flour	Rose water
½ cup sugar	Silver cake dusting (available in
¼ cup blanched sliced almonds	Oriental stores)

Bring the milk to a boil. Mix the rice flour with a little of the milk until smooth, then stir into all the milk. Cook over low heat, stirring steadily until thickened. Add the sugar, almonds and raisins. Cook, stirring very frequently, for 15 minutes. Stir in 6 drops of rose water and remove from the heat. Cool slightly, then pour into a serving dish. Serve chilled sprinkled with the silver cake dusting.

Serves 8.

DHAM-KA-KABAB
Spiced Beef Slices

3 pounds chuck steak	2 teaspoons cinnamon
½ cup shredded coconut	½ teaspoon ground cardamon
1 tablespoon sesame seeds	½ teaspoon powdered cloves
3 cups yogurt	½ cup vegetable oil
4 cloves garlic, minced	1 cup sliced onions
2 tablespoons minced fresh or	2 teaspoons salt
preserved ginger root	¼ cup sliced green chili peppers

Cut the meat into ½-inch-thick slices. Brown the coconut and sesame seeds in a small skillet, then pound very fine. Combine the coconut mixture with the yogurt, garlic and all the spices. Marinate the meat in the mixture 4 hours at room temperature, or overnight in the refrigerator.

Heat the oil in a Dutch oven or casserole; brown the onions in it. Add the meat mixture and salt. Bake in a 350° oven 1½ hours. Garnish with the chili peppers.

Serves 8 to 10.

⊶⊷

NAN ROTI
Unleavened Bread

2 cups all-purpose flour	1½ teaspoons sugar
2 cups whole wheat flour	½ cup yogurt
½ teaspoon salt	½ cup warm water

Mix all the ingredients together until smooth. Cover the dough and let stand for 2 hours. Divide the dough into 8 pieces and pat each piece thin. Arrange on a lightly oiled baking sheet, leaving space between each. Bake in a preheated 350° oven 20 minutes. Serve warm, spread with sweet butter.

Makes 8.

⊶⊷

CHICKEN BIRIANI

4 whole chicken breasts	2 cardamon pods
3 teaspoons salt	2 cloves
½ teaspoon black pepper	2 tablespoons yogurt
½ teaspoon ginger	½ teaspoon cumin
1 clove garlic, minced	½ teaspoon saffron
1 pound rice	10 almonds
1 teaspoon cinnamon	10 raisins
6 tablespoons butter	¼ cup sliced onions

Cut the chicken breasts in half through the breastbones, wash and dry. Rub the breasts with a mixture of half the salt, the pepper, ginger and garlic. Let stand at room temperature 30 minutes.

Half cook the rice with the cinnamon and remaining salt. Drain.

Heat 4 tablespoons of the butter in a skillet. Break the cardamon pods and add the seeds and the cloves to the butter. Add the chicken and let brown on both sides, adding the yogurt when turning the chicken.

Spread half the rice in a greased casserole or deep skillet. Arrange the chicken over it and cover with the remaining rice. Pour pan juices on rice and sprinkle with the cumin and saffron. Place over medium heat for 5 minutes, then over low heat for 15 minutes.

Sauté the almonds, raisins and onions in the remaining butter until golden in color. Arrange on top of the rice before serving.

Serves 8.

SHRIMP KORMA

2 pounds raw shrimp, shelled and deveined	3 teaspoons powdered cumin
1 cup minced onions	1 teaspoon ginger
1 teaspoon salt	6 tablespoons butter
¼ teaspoon crushed dried red pepper	2 cups fresh tomato sauce
	3 cardamon pods
	10 black peppercorns

Wash and dry the shrimp; toss with the onions, salt, red pepper, cumin, and ginger. Let stand 10 minutes.

Melt the butter in a casserole or deep skillet. Add the shrimp mixture and cook over low heat 15 minutes, stirring occasionally. Add the tomato sauce; cook and stir until sauce turns brown. Stir in the cardamon seeds out of pods and the peppercorns.

Serves 8.

OKRA BHUJIYA

2 tablespoons vegetable oil	3 packages frozen okra or 2 cans, drained
1 cup chopped onions	
1½ cups chopped tomatoes	1¼ teaspoons salt
½ teaspoon cumin	

Heat the oil in a skillet; sauté the onions until golden brown. Add the tomatoes and cumin; bring to a boil and add the okra and salt. Cover and cook over low heat 20 minutes, or until the okra is very tender.

Serves 8.

FRIED FISH AND CHILLY SAUCE

Sauce:

½ pound cream cheese
⅓ cup evaporated milk
1 teaspoon Worcestershire
　　sauce
½ teaspoon salt
¼ teaspoon pepper
½ teaspoon paprika
1 tablespoon lemon juice

3 drops Tabasco
1 tablespoon chopped green
　　pepper
1 tablespoon chopped fresh
　　mint or ¼ teaspoon dried
¼ cup chopped parsley
¼ cup chopped green onions

Beat the cheese and evaporated milk until smooth. Blend in the Worcestershire, salt, pepper, paprika, lemon juice and Tabasco. Fold in the green pepper, mint, parsley and green onions.

Fish:

8 slices fish (sea bass, mackerel,
　　snapper) cut ¼ inch
　　thick
½ teaspoon salt

¼ teaspoon cayenne pepper
½ teaspoon turmeric
2 tablespoons onion powder
1 cup vegetable oil

Rinse and dry the fish. Rub with a mixture of the salt, cayenne pepper, turmeric and onion powder. Let stand 30 minutes. Heat the oil in a skillet. Add the fish in a single layer and fry until cooked and browned on both sides. Drain, and serve with the sauce.

Serves 8.

EGG AND POTATO CURRY

6 tablespoons butter
6 potatoes, peeled and quar-
　　tered
2 cups diced onions
½ teaspoon turmeric
½ teaspoon ground coriander
⅛ teaspoon cayenne pepper

1 teaspoon finely crushed bay
　　leaf
Water
1¼ teaspoons salt
8 hard-cooked eggs, shelled
1 cardamon pod

Melt 4 tablespoons of the butter in a skillet. Add the potatoes and fry until golden on all sides. Remove the potatoes. Melt the remaining butter in the skillet; sauté the onions until golden. Stir in the spices, 3 tablespoons water and the salt. Cook 3 minutes. Return the potatoes and add the whole eggs. Cook over low heat 5 minutes. Add ¼ cup more water and cook 5 minutes, or until the potatoes are tender. Stir in the cardamon seeds out of pod.

Serves 8.

MASUR DAL
Curried Lentils

1 pound Dal Masur (orange-red lentils)	1 cup chopped onions
6 cups water	2 teaspoons salt
2 tablespoons minced fresh or preserved ginger root	4 tablespoons butter
¾ teaspoon turmeric	2 tablespoons chopped coriander leaves or Chinese parsley
1 bay leaf	

The red lentils are available in Oriental, Middle East or specialty shops. If you can't get them, ordinary lentils can be prepared in the same way.

Pick over and wash the lentils until the water runs clear, then soak in water to cover for 1 hour. Drain. Combine the lentils in a saucepan with the 6 cups water, the ginger, turmeric, bay leaf and half the onions. Bring to a boil, cover and cook over low heat 45 minutes or until the lentils are tender, adding the salt after 30 minutes cooking time. Drain if any water remains and discard the bay leaf.

Melt the butter in a skillet; sauté the remaining onions until golden brown. Stir in the drained lentils; cook and stir for 2 minutes. Serve sprinkled with the coriander leaves and accompanied by rice.

Serves 8.

PAPADAMS

Papadams are available in cans or packages in specialty food shops; they are thin, small circles, made of lentil flour. Fry the papadams in deep fat (375°) until they puff up and brown lightly. Drain and serve.

SHAHI TUKRA
Sweet Bread Dessert

8 slices bread
¼ pound sweet butter
1 cup sugar
2 cups water

5 cups milk
1 teaspoon saffron
¼ cup pistachio nuts

Cut off the crusts of the bread. Melt the butter in a skillet and fry the bread in it until golden on both sides.

Cook the sugar and water until thick and syrupy. Soak the fried bread in the syrup, and then in a mixture of 1 cup of the milk and the saffron.

Cook the remaining milk over medium heat 30 minutes, stirring frequently. At this point the milk should have thickened to a spreadable consistency. Cool and, just before serving, spread on the bread slices, then sprinkle with the pistachios. (Whipped cream can be substituted for the cooked milk, if desired. Also, if edible silver leaf is available, in Middle East or Oriental shops, spread it over the cream.)
Serves 8.

Peru

THIS South American nation occupies a most historic area in a part of Washington known as Battery Terrill, where numerous skirmishes of the Civil War were fought. The embassy property encompasses twenty-five acres of lovely woodland, several miles from central Washington. The three-story building combines in its design the best features of a classic Grecian mansion and a palatial Southern-style American country home. The front entrance is surrounded by twin pairs of double white columns, located on either side of the double doors; overhead, there is a Grecian pediment. The pediment design is repeated on the third floor, where the walls are covered with eighteenth- and

nineteenth-century etchings and engravings, including one by Goya. The drawing room is elaborate and impressive, featuring a large Gobelin tapestry. It is a traditional room, with a heavy Spanish rug on the floor, furniture covered with silk brocade, and the walls hung with renowned oil paintings, mainly religious in theme, including a Madonna by Murillo. The dining room, too, is quite regal. On formal occasions, when the Ambassador entertains his colleagues, all of the finest china, glassware, candelabra and, especially, the best examples of handmade Peruvian silverware are brought forth.

Embajada de Peru

Cebiche

Tamales

Ají de Gallina

Ensalada Verde

Maná

CEBICHE
Marinated Raw Fish

2 pounds fillet of flounder or
    scallops
1½ teaspoons salt
½ teaspoon white pepper
1¼ cups lemon juice
1 cup orange juice (sour
    oranges)

1½ cups minced onions
½ teaspoon dried ground chili
    peppers
3 sweet potatoes, cooked
3 ears of corn, cooked

Be sure the fish or scallops are fresh, not frozen. Wash and drain. Cut in small pieces and put in a bowl. Mix together the salt, pepper and half the lemon and orange juice. Pour over the fish and let marinate in the refrigerator for 5 hours. Drain very well, then add the remaining juices, the onions and chili peppers. Mix again and let marinate in the refrigerator for 2 or more hours.

Slice the sweet potatoes and cut the corn, on the cob, into 2-inch rounds. Garnish the fish with the sweet potatoes and corn.

Serves 8 to 10.

NOTE: The citrus juices "cook" the fish.

TAMALES

5-pound duck
2½ pounds pork
2 slices salt pork
2 quarts water
1 tablespoon salt
4 16-ounce cans white corn
½ cup lard or oil
1 teaspoon ground cumin
2 teaspoons ground sesame
    seeds
½ teaspoon powdered anise

4 cloves garlic, minced
1 6-ounce can evaporated milk
2 pounds onions, peeled and
    chopped
1 teaspoon dried ground chili
    peppers
1 teaspoon annatto or paprika
¾ cup toasted peanuts
¾ cup small pimiento-stuffed
    olives
4 hard-cooked eggs, sliced

[259]

Wash the duck and pork and combine in a large saucepan with the salt pork, water and salt. Bring to a boil, cover and cook over low heat 2 hours. Drain the meats, reserving the broth. Remove the skin and bones of the duck and cut the meat into small pieces. Cut the pork and salt pork in small pieces. Skim the fat off the broth.

Drain the corn and purée in an electric blender or put through a food chopper twice.

Heat half the lard or oil in a large skillet; stir in the cumin, sesame seeds, anise and half the garlic. Cook 2 minutes, stirring. Add the evaporated milk, corn and ¾ cup of the broth. Cook, stirring constantly, until thick enough to spread.

Heat the remaining lard or oil in a skillet; add the onions, chili peppers, annatto, and remaining garlic. Sauté until browned. Add ¼ cup broth and bring to a boil. Mix in the meats.

In Peru, banana leaves are used for making tamales. Aluminum foil may be used. Cut pieces about 4 by 6 inches. Spread a little corn mixture over the foil, leaving a 1½-inch border all around. In the center, put some meat mixture, peanuts, an olive, and a slice of egg. Cover with a thin layer of corn mixture. Roll up and twist the ends securely, so mixture won't leak out.

Cook in deep boiling salted water 2 hours, turning them after half the cooking time.

Serves 8 to 10.

AJÍ DE GALLINA
Chicken in Pepper-Bread Sauce

2 teaspoons dried ground chili
    peppers
3 5-pound chickens, disjointed
2 quarts water
2 teaspoons salt
10 slices white bread, trimmed
1 14½-ounce can evaporated
    milk

1 cup olive or vegetable oil
1 cup minced onions
1 teaspoon crushed cumin seed
1 teaspoon crushed coriander
1 cup freshly grated Parmesan
    cheese
6 hard-cooked eggs, quartered

Soak the chili peppers in water overnight, changing the water twice. Drain.

Wash the chickens and combine in a saucepan with the water and salt. Bring to a boil, cover and cook over low heat 1¼ hours, or until chickens are tender. Drain, remove the skin and bones and coarsely shred the meat.

Soak the bread in the evaporated milk for 15 minutes. Drain and mash.

Heat some of the oil in a skillet; sauté the onions 5 minutes. Mix in the cumin, coriander and chili peppers. Cook 5 minutes. Stir in the cheese, bread, chicken, and remaining oil. Taste for seasoning. Cook over low heat 30 minutes. Serve garnished with the hard-cooked eggs and with boiled potatoes.

Serves 8 to 10.

MANÁ
Almond Dessert

1 pound shelled almonds, blanched	½ cup water
2½ cups sugar	8 egg yolks
	¼ cup port wine

Grind the almonds in an electric blender, or put through a Mouli grater, or through the fine blade of a food chopper twice.

Combine the sugar and water in a saucepan; cook over low heat, stirring constantly until sugar dissolves, then cook without stirring until syrupy. Mix in the almonds; cook until slightly thickened. Remove from heat.

Beat the egg yolks well and stir in the port. Add to the almond mixture. Cook, stirring frequently, until solid. Remove from the heat, and beat for a couple of minutes. Turn into a buttered mold, cover and let stand in a cool place overnight.

Serves 8 to 10.

Philippines

THE Embassy of the Philippines was originally built about the turn of the century for General Fitzhugh; later, it became the property of Fred A. Britten, a Congressman from Illinois. The Philippine government purchased it from the Brittens in 1946.

Guests enter the embassy by means of a foyer on the first floor. Just off this entrance area is the famous Philippine Room, noteworthy as a reflection of island living. It is thought that, other than in the Philippines itself, there is no similar room in the world. Every possible item — including wood, cement, nails, shells, abaca, furniture, lamps and fabric — was produced in the Philippine Islands. The walls of this room are of dao wood, with contrasting inserts of natural color hemp fabric. The cornice is decorated with Manila rope and abaca, harmon-

izing with the wall treatment. The doors are a combination of dao wood
and rattan. Both the dao wood paneling and the parquet floors are finished in their natural colors. The overall effect generally suggests the
tropics and, in particular, the Philippines.

On the second floor, the visitor enters the anteroom, where reception
lines usually form. From this foyer, the dining room may be reached.
The Queen Anne dining table seats twenty-four guests, and has matching period chairs upholstered in blue and gold. The drapes and Chinese
gold and blue rug help to carry out the room's attractive color scheme.
Adjoining the dining room, on the right-hand side, is a bar paneled in
Philippine mahogany, with wicker chairs and a table which were made
on the islands.

Embassy of the Philippines

FORMAL MENU

Pancit Molo
Balao Balao
Pollo Relleno
Leche Flan
Café

INFORMAL MENU

Sabaw Almondigas
Escabeche
Morcón
Buco Pastelitos
Café

PANCIT MOLO
Soup with Stuffed Dumplings

Dumpling Dough:

1½ cups flour
2 egg yolks
¼ teaspoon salt
3 tablespoons water

Sift the flour and salt into a bowl. Work in the egg yolks with the fingers, then the water. Knead until very smooth and elastic. Cover with a cloth and let stand while preparing the filling.

Filling:

½ cup ground pork
¼ cup chopped water chestnuts
¼ cup chopped cooked chicken
¼ cup chopped raw shrimp
1 egg
1 teaspoon minced garlic
4 tablespoons chopped green onions
2 tablespoons soy sauce

Mix all the ingredients together. Roll out the dough paper thin and cut into 3-inch squares. Place a teaspoon of the filling on each square and fold over into triangles. Seal the edges with a little water. Reserve the balance of the filling for the soup.

Soup:

2 tablespoons lard or butter
10 cups chicken broth
¼ cup chopped onions
3 tablespoons chopped green onions
1 clove garlic, minced
Dash cayenne pepper

Melt the lard or butter in a large saucepan; sauté the onion and garlic 5 minutes. Add the reserved filling; cook 5 minutes, stirring frequently. Add the cayenne pepper and broth. Bring to a boil, and one by one, drop in the dumplings. Cover and cook over medium heat 15 minutes. Add green onions. Taste soup for seasoning.

Serves 8 to 10.

BALAO BALAO
Shrimp in Coconut Milk

1 cup packaged flaked coconut
3 cups milk
2 pounds raw shrimp, shelled
    and deveined
3 tablespoons butter

1 pound tomatoes, peeled and
    sliced
1½ teaspoons salt
⅛ teaspoon cayenne pepper

Rinse the coconut under cold running water. Combine with the milk in a saucepan; bring to a boil and let soak for 30 minutes. Run in a blender for a few seconds or strain, pressing out all the liquid.

Wash and dry the shrimp. Chop very fine. Melt the butter in a skillet; add the shrimp and stir over low heat for 2 minutes. Add the tomatoes, salt and cayenne. Cook 10 minutes. Stir in the coconut milk and cook until almost all the liquid is evaporated. Serve in ramekins or shells.

Serves 8.

POLLO RELLENO
Stuffed Chicken

Chicken:

2 6-pound roasting chickens
½ cup lime or lemon juice
½ cup soy sauce
3 pounds ground pork
4 Spanish or Italian sausages,
    finely chopped
1 cup grated Edam or cheddar
    cheese
5 raw eggs

1½ teaspoons salt
½ teaspoon black pepper
4 hard-cooked eggs, quartered
1 pound ham, cut into strips
4 sweet pickles, cut into eighths
    lengthwise
6 cups chicken broth
Vegetable oil for deep frying

Have the chickens boned, leaving wings and legs intact. Brush with a mixture of the lime juice and soy sauce. Let stand 1 hour, then drain.

Mix together the pork, sausages, cheese, raw eggs, salt and pepper. Stuff each chicken, then press 2 hard eggs, half the ham and 2 pickles into the center of the stuffing of each. Sew up or skewer the openings of the chickens. Place in a large Dutch oven. Add the broth, bring to a boil, cover and cook over low heat 2 hours, turning the chickens carefully once or twice. Drain well and dry. Reserve the broth.

Heat the oil to 375° and fry one chicken at a time until browned. Drain and keep hot.

Sauce:

    3 tablespoons lard or butter   3 cups reserved broth
    2 cloves garlic, minced   2 tablespoons soy sauce
    3 tablespoons flour

Melt the lard or butter in a saucepan; sauté the garlic until browned. Blend in the flour, then add the broth and soy sauce, stirring steadily to the boiling point. Cook over low heat 10 minutes, stirring occasionally.

To carve the chickens, cut into slices, starting at either the neck or tail.

Serves 8 to 10.

LECHE FLAN
Coconut Custard

    1 cup packaged flaked coconut   3 tablespoons water
    1½ cups light cream   12 egg yolks
    2 cups milk   1 cup sugar
    ¾ cup brown sugar

Bring the coconut, cream and milk to a boil; remove from the heat and let stand 30 minutes. Run in an electric blender for a few seconds, or strain, pressing through all the liquid.

Combine the brown sugar and water in a saucepan. Cook, stirring steadily, until the sugar dissolves, then cook over low heat until mixture caramelizes. Pour into a 1½-quart mold and turn quickly to coat the pan evenly.

Reheat the coconut milk. Beat the egg yolks and sugar together. Gradually add the hot coconut milk, stirring steadily to prevent curdling. Strain into the mold. Place mold in another pan and pour in enough hot water around the mold to reach halfway up the sides. Place on the bottom rack of a preheated 325° oven and bake 50 minutes, or until a knife inserted in the center comes out clean. Cool, then chill. To unmold, run a spatula around the edge of the mold. Place a serving dish upside down over the mold and quickly turn over, dish side down. Lift off the mold.

Serves 8 to 10.

SABAW ALMONDIGAS
Meat Ball Soup

1 cup rice noodles	1 tablespoon vegetable oil
½ pound ground pork	¼ cup sliced onions
¼ cup chopped onions	2 cloves garlic, minced
1 teaspoon salt	8 cups beef or chicken broth
¼ teaspoon black pepper	1 tablespoon soy sauce
2 tablespoons flour	Dash cayenne pepper
2 eggs	½ cup thinly sliced green onions

Rice noodles are available in Oriental food stores. When cooked, they are translucent. Soak the rice noodles in warm water for 1 hour.

Mix together the pork, chopped onions, salt, pepper, flour and eggs. Shape into walnut-sized balls.

Heat the oil in a large saucepan; sauté the sliced onions and garlic

5 minutes. Add the broth and bring to a boil. Drop in the meat balls one by one. Cook over low heat 20 minutes. Add the drained rice noodles and cook 5 minutes longer, or until the noodles are tender. Stir in the soy sauce and cayenne pepper. Serve sprinkled with the green onions.

Serves 8 to 10.

ESCABECHE
Sweet and Sour Fish

1 4-pound pompano, snapper or bass	1 cup julienne-cut sweet red or green peppers
2 teaspoons salt	2 cloves garlic, thinly sliced
Fat for deep frying	2 tablespoons cornstarch
3 tablespoons lard or vegetable oil	¼ cup cider vinegar
1 cup sliced onions	3 tablespoons soy sauce
	¼ cup sugar
	2 cups water

Have the fish scored and the head left on or not, as you prefer. Wash the fish, sprinkle with the salt and let stand 10 minutes. Drain off any liquid, and dry the fish thoroughly.

Put fat in a wide deep pan; use enough to cover the fish. Heat to 365°. Fry the fish in it until browned. Drain fish. Pour off fat and clean pan with paper towels. Return the fish.

Heat the lard or oil in a skillet; sauté the onions, peppers and garlic 10 minutes. Add to the fish.

Mix the cornstarch and vinegar to a smooth paste. Stir in the soy sauce, sugar and water. Cook over low heat 5 minutes. Pour over the fish and cook over low heat 5 minutes. Transfer the fish to a serving dish and pour the sauce over it.

Serves 4 to 6.

MORCÓN
Stuffed Meat Roll

2½ pounds round steak, in one piece
4 tablespoons soy sauce
2 tablespoons lemon juice
3 teaspoons salt
¾ teaspoon black pepper
½ pound ground pork
¼ pound ham, ground
¼ cup chopped sweet pickles
1 raw egg

2 tablespoons grated Edam or cheddar cheese
2 tablespoons seedless raisins
2 hard-cooked eggs, quartered
2 cups water
¼ cup cider vinegar
½ cup tomato sauce
1 bay leaf
1 large onion, sliced
2 cloves garlic, minced

Have the steak pounded very thin. Spread the meat flat and season with 1 tablespoon soy sauce, the lemon juice, 1 teaspoon salt and ¼ teaspoon pepper. Mix together the pork, ham, pickles, raw egg, cheese, raisins, ½ teaspoon salt and ¼ teaspoon pepper. Spread on the meat. Arrange the hard-cooked eggs in the center. Roll up like a jelly roll. Tie with string in several places.

Put the meat in a Dutch oven and add the water, vinegar, tomato sauce, bay leaf, onion, garlic, and the remaining soy sauce, salt and pepper. Bring to a boil, cover and cook over low heat 2½ hours. Transfer the meat to a platter, remove the strings and slice crosswise. Serve the gravy in a sauceboat.

Serves 4 to 6.

BUCO PASTELITOS
Coconut Pastries

Filling:

1 cup packaged flaked coconut
½ cup sugar
½ cup milk

1 tablespoon flour
1 tablespoon butter
1 egg yolk, beaten

Combine the coconut, sugar and milk in a saucepan. Bring to a boil and cook, stirring constantly, until very thick and fairly dry. Mix in the flour, butter and egg yolk. Cook, stirring frequently, for 5 minutes. Cool.

Pastry:

2 cups sifted flour	4 tablespoons ice water
½ teaspoon salt	1 egg yolk
½ teaspoon baking powder	2 tablespoons milk
¾ cup shortening	

Sift the flour, salt and baking powder into a bowl. Cut in the shortening until mixture looks like coarse cornmeal. Sprinkle with the water and toss with a fork until a ball of dough is formed.

Roll out the dough very thin on a lightly floured surface. Cut into 2-inch squares. Place about 1 teaspoon filling on each of half the squares and cover with the remaining squares, pressing the edges together firmly. Brush the tops with the egg yolk beaten with the milk. Arrange on a baking sheet. Bake in a preheated 375° oven 15 minutes or until browned.

Makes about 24.

Portugal

ALTHOUGH this nation's embassy building is a fine structure, with many attractive, handsome rooms, the dining room and its accessories warrant detailed attention.

The imposing dining room is decorated essentially in eighteenth-century Portuguese style, a somewhat novel manner, and one of exceptional interest because of its unique nationalistic qualities. The floor is laid with white Estremoz marble, having light pink markings; the window and door trim are of deep pink marble. The walls are beautifully decorated with blue and white Portuguese tiles. At one end of the room is a marble fountain with a dolphin spouting water. The table

and chairs, made from a Brazilian wood called jacaranda, were specially ordered from Lisbon's Art Museum. On the walls are two famous still
life paintings by Josefa d'Obidos, a seventeenth-century Portuguese
artist. Lighting for the room is furnished by large hurricane lamps
which provide a flickering candlelit atmosphere.

The china, created by Portugal's renowned Vista Alegre factory,
features a special pattern with government seal markings. The glassware, clear and pink crystal, was made by the Marinha Grande. The
elaborate silverware consists of extraordinary eighteenth-century Portuguese pieces of flatware, plates, platters and other table accessories.

Embaixada de Portugal

FORMAL MENU

Caldo Verde

Peixe á Moda do Alentejo
MATEUS ROSÉ

Arroz de Pato
DÃO

Toucinho do Ceu

INFORMAL MENU

Caldeirada á Fragateira
VINHO VERDE

Bifes de Cebolada
Arroz Dôce

CALDO VERDE
Green Soup

2 pounds potatoes, peeled and
   sliced
1½ cups sliced green onions
1 bunch parsley
2½ teaspoons salt

½ teaspoon white pepper
2½ quarts water
4 tablespoons olive oil
2 pounds kale, finely shredded

Combine the potatoes, green onions, parsley, salt, pepper and water
in a saucepan. Bring to a boil and cook over medium heat 30 minutes.
Put the mixture through a sieve and return to the pan. Add the oil
and kale. Bring to a boil and cook 5 minutes. Serve very hot.

Serves 8 to 10.

PEIXE A MODA DO ALENTEJO
Fish and Potato Casserole

2 pounds fish fillets
¼ cup olive oil
2 cups sliced onions
2 cloves garlic, minced
½ cup chopped parley
Salt

Black pepper
½ teaspoon crushed coriander
1½ pounds potatoes, peeled and
   sliced
1 pound tomatoes, sliced
1 bay leaf

Wash and dry the fillets, and cut each in four pieces, crosswise.

Heat the oil in a casserole; spread the onions on the bottom, then
sprinkle with the garlic, parsley, salt, pepper and coriander. Arrange
the fish over this; sprinkle with salt and pepper. Spread the potatoes
over the fish; sprinkle with salt and pepper. Cover with the tomatoes
and sprinkle with salt and pepper. Add the bay leaf. Cover the casserole and cook over low heat 45 minutes, or until the potatoes are
tender. Shake the casserole frequently.

Serves 6 to 8.

ARROZ DE PATO
Duck with Rice

2 5-pound ducks, disjointed	½ teaspoon pepper
2 quarts water	6 tablespoons butter
2½ cups chopped onions	3 cups rice
1 carrot, grated	¾ pound Portuguese or Italian
3 sprigs parsley	sausages
3 teaspoons salt	

Clean and wash the ducks. Combine the duck giblets and necks with the water, 1 cup of the onions, the carrot, parsley, 2 teaspoons salt and the pepper. Bring to a boil and cook 45 minutes. Add the duck pieces; cook 25 minutes. Drain and dry the duck pieces and arrange in a shallow roasting pan. Bake in a 375° oven 30 minutes, or until the duck is browned and tender. Strain the broth; cut the giblets in small pieces.

Melt 3 tablespoons of the butter in a large skillet; sauté the remaining onions 5 minutes. Mix in the rice and cook, stirring frequently, until browned. Add 4 cups of the broth and the remaining salt. Cover and cook 15 minutes or until the liquid is absorbed.

Slice and brown the sausages; drain.

Spread the rice in a greased casserole; arrange the duck pieces over it, then the giblets and sliced sausages. Dot with the remaining butter and place in a 375° oven for 15 minutes.

Serves 8.

TOUCINHO DO CEU
Almond Cups

¼ pound almonds	3 whole eggs
2 cups sugar	9 egg yolks
¼ cup water	1 tablespoon grated lemon rind

Blanch the almonds and grind very fine, using a Mouli grater or electric blender.

Combine the sugar and water in a saucepan. Bring to a boil, stirring until the sugar dissolves, then cook over low heat without stirring until syrupy. Cool.

Beat the eggs and egg yolks, then beat in the syrup until thickened. Mix in the rind and nuts.

Butter 16 cupcake pans and half fill with the mixture. Bake in a preheated 300° oven 25 minutes, or until delicately browned and a cake tester comes out clean. Cool.

Makes 16.

CALADEIRADA Á FRAGATEIRA
Fish Stew

4 pounds assorted sliced fish	½ cup chopped parsley
12 mussels	3 teaspoons salt
½ cup olive oil	¾ teaspoon black pepper
2 pounds onions, peeled and sliced	2 pounds potatoes, peeled and sliced
2 pounds tomatoes, peeled and sliced	

Buy a variety of fish: bass, flounder, whiting and eel. Wash and dry the fish. Scrub the mussels and put in a covered pan over low heat until they open. Remove from the shells.

Heat the oil in a casserole; add the onions and cook 10 minutes. Put the tomatoes and parsley in the casserole and sprinkle with some of the salt and pepper. Bring to a boil and cook 10 minutes. Arrange the potatoes in the casserole; sprinkle with some salt and pepper. Arrange the fish over the potatoes starting with the thicker pieces; sprinkle with remaining salt and pepper. Cover and cook over low heat 30 minutes, shaking the casserole frequently. Arrange the mussels on top and cook 5 minutes longer.

Serves 8 to 10.

BIFES DE CEBOLADA
Steak and Onions

5 pounds sirloin of beef
3 tablespoons olive oil
3 tablespoons butter
3 cloves garlic, minced
1½ pounds onions, peeled and sliced

1½ pounds tomatoes, quartered
2½ teaspoons salt
½ teaspoon black pepper
3 tablespoons minced parsley

Have the meat cut about 1½ inches thick.

Heat the oil and butter in a Dutch oven or casserole. Add the garlic, onions, tomatoes, salt, pepper and parsley; sauté 15 minutes, stirring frequently. Add the meat. Cover and bake in a 350° oven 1 hour, or until the meat is tender. Watch carefully and add a little water from time to time if necessary. Serve with mashed potatoes.

Serves 8 to 10.

ARROZ DÔCE
Sweet Rice

2 cups rice
5 cups milk
1 vanilla bean

12 egg yolks
2 cups sugar
Cinnamon

Combine the rice, milk and vanilla bean in a heavy saucepan. Bring to a boil, cover and cook over low heat 25 minutes, or until the rice is very soft. Discard the vanilla bean.

Beat the egg yolks and sugar; add a little hot rice, stirring steadily to prevent curdling. Return to balance of rice and cook, stirring steadily, for 3 minutes, but do not let the mixture boil.

Pour onto a flat serving dish and sprinkle with cinnamon.

Serves 8 to 10.

Russia

THE Russian Embassy building is an extremely modest one, occupying the former Pullman house, built by the developer of the individual chairs and sleeping cars on American railroads. Originally a showplace, it remains a fine house of its period, but it is quite small by Washington embassy standards. Because of the size of the Russian staff, the building itself has been completely outgrown and its facilities taxed to the utmost. The Russian government's attempt to arrange for larger quarters in the Washington suburbs was recently opposed on zoning grounds.

The embassy has several small rooms on its main floor which surround a rather attractive courtyard. Most of the important rooms are

on the second floor, reached by a broad staircase. The chief reception room is only medium in size, attractively decorated in Old World style; many smaller countries have far larger and more pretentious reception rooms. Adjacent may be found the dining room, which can be combined with the main reception room on special occasions. When the diplomats of other nations are expected for a large gathering, caviar, vodka, sturgeon, and other delicacies are served to the crowded guests. There is also a small, friendly library where the Ambassador and his family entertain their friends. Sometimes motion pictures are shown in the library to the embassy staff.

Embassy of the Union of Soviet Socialist Republics

Zakuski

Borsch   Pirozhki

Shashlik à la Karsky

Kasha   Po Derevenski

Kisel

ZAKUSKI
Hors d'Oeuvres

Pickled Mushrooms:

1 quart cider vinegar
1½ teaspoons salt
1 lemon, sliced
2 teaspoons sugar

2 tablespoons tomato paste
¼ cup allspice
2 pounds button mushrooms, cleaned

Combine and bring to a boil the vinegar, salt, lemon, sugar, tomato paste and allspice. Add the mushrooms and bring to a boil. Remove from heat immediately. Pack into jars and refrigerate for at least 24 hours before serving. Drain before serving.

Makes about 6 cups.

Marinated Fish:

4 pounds pike, salmon, sturgeon, perch
2 cups water
3 teaspoons salt
½ teaspoon black pepper
Flour
6 tablespoons vegetable oil
1½ cups thinly sliced onions

¾ cup thinly sliced carrots
1 6-ounce can tomato paste
2 bay leaves, crushed
6 peppercorns
2 cloves
¾ cup cider vinegar
1 tablespoon sugar
Chopped dill or parsley

Have the fish cut in serving-sized pieces. When buying the fish, ask for a fish head and some trimmings. Wash the head and trimmings and combine with the water. Bring to a boil and cook over low heat 30 minutes. Strain and reserve the stock.

While the stock is cooking, sprinkle the fish with 2 teaspoons of the salt and all the pepper; let stand 30 minutes. Dip in flour. Heat half the oil in a skillet, fry the fish in it until browned on both sides and flakes easily when tested with a fork. Drain and cool.

Heat the remaining oil in a saucepan; add the onions and carrots. Cook over low heat 10 minutes, stirring frequently. Mix in the tomato paste, bay leaves, peppercorns, cloves and remaining salt. Cover and cook over low heat 10 minutes, stirring frequently. Add the vinegar, sugar and fish stock. Cook 10 minutes longer. Cool 15 minutes and pour over the fish; marinate in the refrigerator 4 hours. Serve sprinkled with the dill.

Serves 12.

Ikra Baklazhan — (Eggplant Caviar):

1 3-pound eggplant	2 teaspoons salt
½ cup vegetable oil	½ teaspoon black pepper
1½ cups minced onions	1 teaspoon sugar
¾ cup minced green peppers	2 teaspoons vinegar
1½ cups peeled chopped	
tomatoes	

Wash the eggplant, wrap loosely in aluminum foil and bake in a 375° oven 45 minutes. Cool, peel and chop the eggplant.

Heat half the oil in a large skillet; sauté the onions and green peppers 5 minutes. Add the tomatoes; cook over medium heat 5 minutes. Mix in the salt, pepper, sugar, vinegar, eggplant and remaining oil. Cook over low heat 20 minutes, stirring frequently. Watch carefully, and add a little more oil if necessary to prevent burning. Taste for seasoning and chill. Serve with thinly sliced black bread buttered with sweet butter. *Makes about 4 cups.*

BORSCH
Beet Soup

3 pounds brisket of beef	½ cup sliced celery
Marrow bone	1 tablespoon salt
3½ quarts boiling water	10 beets, peeled and cut in
4 cups shredded cabbage	julienne strips, or 2 cans
2 bay leaves	julienne beets, drained
6 peppercorns	1 tablespoon vinegar
6 tablespoons butter	1 tablespoon flour
1½ cups sliced onions	2 cups peeled diced tomatoes
1 cup sliced carrots	

Wash the beef and bone and combine with 3 quarts of the boiling water, the cabbage, bay leaves and peppercorns in a large saucepan. Bring to a boil and cook over low heat while preparing the vegetables.

Melt 2 tablespoons of the butter in a skillet; add the onions, carrots and celery; cook until lightly browned, stirring frequently. Add to the soup with the salt.

Melt the remaining butter in a skillet; add the beets, vinegar and ½ cup of the remaining water. Cook over low heat 20 minutes. Blend in the flour and add to the soup with the remaining 1½ cups water. Cook 1½ hours. Add the tomatoes and cook 15 minutes longer. Taste for seasoning. Bite-sized pieces of meat can be served in the soup. Serve in soup plates with a heaping tablespoon of sour cream in each.

Serves 12.

PIROZHKI
Meat Pastries

2 cups sifted flour	¾ cup chopped onions
½ teaspoon baking powder	½ pound ground beef
1½ teaspoons salt	¼ teaspoon black pepper
¾ cup shortening	1 tablespoon chopped dill or
1 egg yolk	parsley
4 tablespoons ice water	1 hard-cooked egg, chopped
4 tablespoons butter	

Sift together the flour, baking powder and ½ teaspoon of the salt. Cut in the shortening. Beat the yolk and water together and add to the flour mixture tossing until a ball of dough is formed.

Melt the butter in a skillet; sauté the onions 5 minutes, stirring frequently. Add the meat and cook, stirring almost constantly, until meat browns. Season with the pepper and remaining salt. Cool and mix in the dill and egg.

Roll out the dough on a lightly floured surface ⅛ inch thick; cut into 3-inch circles. Place a tablespoon of the filling on each round.

Fold over into a half-moon and press the edges together with a little water. Arrange on a greased baking sheet.

Bake in a 400° oven 15 minutes or until browned.

Makes about 24.

SHASHLIK À LA KARSKY
Broiled Lamb and Kidneys on Skewers

3 whole loins of lamb	¼ pound butter
12 lamb kidneys	6 tablespoons flour
3 cups chopped green onions	3 cups beef broth
½ cup chopped celery leaves	2 tablespoons tomato paste
2½ teaspoons salt	1 cup thinly sliced onions
¾ teaspoon black pepper	1 cup sliced carrots
½ cup cider vinegar	⅓ cup Madeira or dry sherry
¼ cup lemon juice	12 very thin slices of lemon

Have the meat boned and each loin cut into four pieces. Wash the kidneys thoroughly, cut in half lengthwise and wash again; drain and dry. Put the lamb in one bowl and the kidneys in another. To each bowl, add half the green onions, celery leaves, salt, pepper, vinegar and lemon juice. Cover the bowls and let marinate for 4 hours.

Melt 6 tablespoons of the butter in a saucepan; blend in the flour until browned. Add the broth, stirring steadily to the boiling point. Mix in the tomato paste and cook over low heat while preparing the vegetables.

Melt the remaining butter in a skillet; sauté the onions and carrots 10 minutes. Add to the sauce and cook 30 minutes longer. Mix in the wine, and salt and pepper to taste. Strain.

Drain the lamb and kidneys. Using twelve skewers, put one piece of kidney on a skewer, then a piece of lamb and another piece of kidney. Broil in a hot broiler 15 minutes, turning the skewers to brown all sides. Garnish each piece of lamb with a lemon slice and serve the hot sauce in a sauceboat. *Serves 12.*

KASHA
Buckwheat Groats

2 cups medium buckwheat groats	1½ teaspoons salt
1 egg	6 tablespoons butter
4 cups boiling water	1 cup finely chopped onions
	¼ teaspoon black pepper

Put the groats in a heavy saucepan. Break the egg into it and mix well. Place over low heat and cook, stirring steadily, until grains separate. Carefully add the boiling water, then the salt. Cover and cook over low heat 20 minutes. If all the water isn't absorbed, drain.

Melt the butter in a skillet; sauté the onions 10 minutes. Mix into the kasha with the pepper.

Serves 12.

PO DEREVENSKI
Radish Salad

2 hard-cooked egg yolks	¼ teaspoon pepper
1¼ cups sour cream	4 cups thinly sliced radishes
¾ teaspoons salt	

Mash the egg yolks smooth. Mix into the sour cream with the salt and pepper. Add the radishes and mix well. Serve in lettuce cups.

Serves 12.

KISEL
Cranberry Dessert

3 pounds cranberries	2½ cups sugar
Water	Potato starch or cornstarch

Wash and pick over the cranberries. Put in a saucepan and add enough water to just cover the berries. Bring to a boil and cook over low heat 15 minutes. Force through a sieve. Return to the saucepan and stir in the sugar. Bring to a boil, stirring until the sugar dissolves. Measure the liquid. For each two cups you will need 1 tablespoon starch. Mix the starch until smooth with a little water, then add 1 cup of the berry juice, mixing again. Stir into all the juice and cook over low heat until thickened and clear. Cool and pour into twelve glass or other dessert dishes. Chill until set and serve with heavy or whipped cream.

Serves 12.

South Africa

THE Embassy of South Africa is housed in a fine building, and there are lovely reception rooms which make this a very much admired structure. However, the embassy's dining room and table service are so extraordinary that they warrant special discussion.

The stinkwood-paneled dining room of this embassy is regarded as one of the finest places in all of Washington for a dinner party. Twenty-four guests may be comfortably seated at a formal dinner in this large and gracious room. Stinkwood, also called stinkhout, is a rare South African wood from the Cape region which outwardly resembles walnut; it is so called because it emits a pungent odor when first cut. It loses the

odor shortly thereafter, and when dried takes on a magnificent surface. No other South African embassy anywhere in the world is paneled in stinkwood, and in fact, it is even quite rare in South Africa, because the tree takes hundreds of years to mature.

The embassy's formal dinner service is of white china with gold embossed bands and features a gold protea design, the protea being South Africa's national flower. The stemware is of a tulip shape, and this also has the protea design. The flatware has handles with beveled edges and decorations of the country's coat of arms.

Embassy of South Africa

FORMAL MENU

Mixed Fruit Cup with Mint Syrup
Clear Tomato Consommé
LIGHT DRY WHITE WINE

Curried Fish
DRY WHITE WINE

Chicken Pie
DRY WHITE WINE

Mock Venison
Rice   Green Peas   Carrots with Parsley
FULL-BODIED RED WINE

Wine Jelly
Coffee   Liqueurs

INFORMAL MENU

Sasaties   Boerewors
Putupap
Vetkoek   Green Fig Preserves
Corn on the Cob
Fresh Fruits in Season
Melktert
Coffee

MIXED FRUIT CUP WITH MINT SYRUP

3 cups sugar
3 cups water
⅓ cup lemon juice
3 sprigs of mint, minced
⅛ teaspoon salt
2 cups orange segments

2 cups grapefruit segments
2 cups tangerine segments
2 cups pineapple cubes
Maraschino cherries
Mint sprigs

Combine the sugar and water in a saucepan, bring to a boil, stirring constantly until sugar dissolves, then cook over high heat 2 minutes. Cool, then stir in the lemon juice, mint and salt. Let stand 30 minutes.

Mix oranges, grapefruit, tangerines and pineapples together, and pour the syrup over them. Chill at least 1 hour. Serve in individual fruit cups garnished with a cherry and a mint sprig.

Serves 10 to 12.

CLEAR TOMATO CONSOMMÉ

6 tablespoons butter
½ cup chopped onions
½ cup grated carrots
3 cups tomato purée
3 peppercorns
1 bay leaf

4 cloves
½ teaspoon thyme
4 sprigs parsley
6 cups beef broth
½ teaspoon black pepper
Croutons

Melt the butter in a saucepan; sauté the onions and carrots 5 minutes. Add the tomato purée, peppercorns, bay leaf, cloves, thyme and parsley. Cover, bring to a boil, and cook over low heat 1 hour. Strain mixture into a clean pan. Add the broth and pepper; heat and taste for seasoning. Serve in cups, with croutons.

Serves 10 to 12.

CURRIED FISH

5 pounds swordfish, kingfish or other firm-fleshed white fish	10 peppercorns
1 tablespoon salt	3 tablespoons slivered lemon rind
½ teaspoon black pepper	2 tablespoons minced ginger root
3 tablespoons vegetable oil	3 cups white vinegar
3 cups sliced onions	2 tablespoons sugar
2 tablespoons curry powder	

Wash the fish and cut in thin serving-sized pieces. Sprinkle with the salt and pepper and let stand 15 minutes. Rub a baking dish with 1 tablespoon oil and arrange the fish in it. Cover and bake in a 350° oven 20 minutes, or until fish flakes easily when tested with a fork. This will depend on the type of fish used—swordfish requires a longer time.

Heat the remaining oil in a saucepan; brown the onions in it. Blend in the curry powder and cook, stirring, for 2 minutes. Add the peppercorns, lemon rind, ginger, vinegar and sugar. Bring to a boil and cook over low heat 10 minutes.

In a covered dish, arrange layers of the fish and the spice mixture. Cover and let marinate in the refrigerate for at least 2 days before serving.

Serves 10 to 12.

CHICKEN PIE

Pastry:

3 cups flour	2 egg yolks
1 teaspoon salt	⅓ cup ice water
1 cup shortening	

Sift the flour and salt into a bowl; cut in the shortening with a pastry blender or two knives. Beat the egg yolks with the water and add, tossing until a ball of dough is formed. Wrap in foil or waxed paper and chill while preparing the chicken.

Chicken:

2 3-pound chickens, disjointed	4 cloves ⎫ tied in
½ cup flour	4 peppercorns ⎭ cheesecloth
4 teaspoons salt	Dash cayenne pepper
¾ teaspoon black pepper	¼ teaspoon mace
4 tablespoons butter	½ pound ham, cubed
1½ quarts water	3 hard-cooked eggs, sliced
4 tablespoons tapioca	2 raw egg yolks, beaten

Wash and dry the chicken pieces, then roll in a mixture of the flour, 3 teaspoons of the salt and ½ teaspoon pepper. Melt the butter in a large deep skillet; brown the chicken in it. Add the water and bring to a boil. Mix in the tapioca and remaining salt and pepper, then add the spice bag, cayenne and mace. Cook over low heat 45 minutes, or until chicken is tender. Remove the chicken and cut meat from the bones. Discard the spice bag. Taste the broth and season, if necessary. Mix the cut-up chicken with the ham and sliced eggs. Cool. Stir the broth into the beaten egg yolks, then cook, stirring steadily, until thickened, but do not let boil. Cool.

Divide the pastry into two pieces, one larger than the other. Roll out the larger piece and line a shallow 2-quart casserole with it. Put the chicken mixture in it, and pour the thickened broth over it. Cover with the remaining rolled-out pastry, sealing the edges. Make a few slits in the top to allow the steam to escape. Bake in a preheated 450° oven 10 minutes. Reduce heat to 350° and bake 30 minutes longer, or until browned. Serve directly from the pie plate.

Serves 10 to 12.

MOCK VENISON

1 6-pound leg of lamb	2 tablespoons vegetable oil
½ pound salt pork	6 cloves
1½ cups cider vinegar	1 cup boiling water
1 tablespoon sugar	3 tablespoons apricot jam
¾ teaspoon pepper	2 tablespoons flour
½ cup seedless raisins	1 cup cold water
2 cloves garlic, cut in thin slivers	1 can peach halves
1 tablespoon salt	2 tablespoons melted butter
½ teaspoon ground ginger	Currant jelly
¾ cup sliced onions	Parsley sprigs

Have the shank cut off the lamb. Cover the salt pork with water, bring to a boil and cook 5 minutes. Drain, dry and cut into ½-inch squares. Mix together the vinegar, sugar and ¼ teaspoon of the pepper. Marinate the pork squares in it for 1 hour. Remove the pork squares; reserve the marinade.

Cut slits in the leg of lamb, and into each insert a pork square, a raisin and a sliver of garlic. Rub the lamb all over with the salt, ginger and remaining pepper. Spread the onions over the lamb and pour the marinade over it. Let marinate in the refrigerator 48 hours, turning the meat frequently. Drain lamb well.

Heat the oil in a deep large skillet or Dutch oven. Brown the lamb in it well. Add the cloves and boiling water. Cover and cook over low heat 2 hours, or until the lamb is tender.

Mix together the jam, flour and cold water. Pour over the lamb. Bake, uncovered, in a 425° oven until browned and crisp, about 20 minutes. Transfer to a heated serving dish.

While the lamb is cooking, drain the peaches and arrange on a baking sheet. Brush with the melted butter. Bake in a 400° oven until delicately browned. Fill cavities with currant jelly. Arrange around the leg, and garnish platter with parsley sprigs.

Serves 10 to 12.

WINE JELLY

4 envelopes (4 tablespoons)
    gelatin
4 cups water
1½ cups sugar
12 cloves
3 cinnamon sticks
2 teaspoons lemon juice

2 teaspoons grated orange rind
1½ cups port or sweet red wine
Red and white grapes
1 egg white
Powdered sugar
Heavy cream

Sprinkle the gelatin into ½ cup of the water and let stand while making the syrup. Combine the remaining water with the sugar, cloves and cinnamon sticks. Bring to a boil, stirring until sugar dissolves, then cook over medium heat 5 minutes. Strain and stir in the gelatin until dissolved. Cool. Mix in the lemon juice, orange rind and wine. Pour into a wet or lightly oiled 1½-quart mold and chill until set. Unmold onto a chilled serving dish.

Dip the grapes in the well beaten egg white, and then roll in powdered sugar. Chill. Garnish the wine jelly with them and with some leaves, if possible. Serve with a pitcher of cream.

Serves 10 to 12.

SASATIES
Lamb Skewers

Meat:

3 pounds lamb, cut from leg or
    loin
1 clove garlic
2 teaspoons salt
½ teaspoon black pepper

1 tablespoon ground coriander
½ teaspoon ground ginger
2 tablespoons grated orange
    rind
½ cup milk

Cut the meat into ¾-inch squares. Rub a bowl with the garlic, and add the meat, salt, pepper, coriander, ginger, rind and milk. Cover and let marinate in the refrigerator for 48 hours, turning the meat several times. Drain. Put 4 to 6 pieces of meat on each skewer and broil over a charcoal fire or in the broiler 20 minutes, turning the skewers to brown all sides.

Sauce:

6 dried apricots	2 tablespoons sugar
2 cups sliced onions	2 tablespoons apricot jam
2 tablespoons curry powder	¾ cup cider vinegar
½ teaspoon salt	½ cup water
1 teaspoon turmeric	

Soak the apricots in water to cover overnight. Drain and chop, then combine with all the remaining ingredients. Bring to a boil and cook over low heat 10 minutes. Cool. Serve in a bowl.

Serves 10 to 12.

BOEREWORS
Spiced Sausages

3 pounds sirloin steak	2 teaspoons black pepper
2 pounds boneless pork	3 tablespoons crushed coriander
¼ pound pork fat	¼ cup vinegar
4 teaspoons salt	4 yards sausage casing

Cut the beef, pork and pork fat into small cubes and mix with the spices and vinegar. Let stand at room temperature for 3 hours, turning the mixture several times. Grind the mixture through the medium blade of a food chopper.

You'll need a sausage stuffer attachment for the food chopper. Cut the casing into 1-yard lengths and tie one end securely with thread. Put the meat mixture through the chopper again and into the casing. Twist at two- or three-inch intervals. Refrigerate overnight.

If you don't have a sausage stuffer, form the meat into sausage shapes and roll lightly in flour. Refrigerate overnight. Broil either over charcoal or in the broiler until cooked through, about 20 minutes. Turn to brown all sides.

Serves 10 to 12.

PUTUPAP
Cornmeal

2¼ cups water   3 cups cornmeal
1½ teaspoons salt

Bring the water and salt to a boil in a saucepan. Pour the corn-meal into the center of the water in a pyramid slowly enough so that the water never stops boiling. Don't stir. Cover and cook over low heat 10 minutes. Stir lightly with a fork; re-cover and let stand over very low heat, or on an asbestos pad, for 30 minutes.

Serves 10 to 12.

VETKOEK
Fried Bread

1½ cups flour   2 eggs, beaten
½ teaspoon salt   ½ cup water
2 teaspoons baking powder   Vegetable oil for deep frying
1 tablespoon sugar

Sift the flour, salt, baking powder and sugar into a bowl. Mix the eggs with the water and work into the flour mixture until a fairly firm dough is formed.

Heat the oil to 365°. Drop teaspoons of the mixture into it and fry until browned on all sides. Drain on paper towels. Serve hot.

Serves 10 to 12.

GREEN FIG PRESERVES

3 pounds firm green figs   2 pounds sugar
3 tablespoons baking soda   2 tablespoons lemon juice

Try to get two or three fig leaves, if possible. Wash the figs and remove a very thin layer of skin, leaving the stems.

Mix the baking soda with 1 gallon water and soak the figs in it overnight. Drain and rinse thoroughly. Cook the figs and leaves in boiling water to cover until tender but firm, about 10 minutes. Drain.

Mix the sugar with 3½ cups water and the lemon juice. Bring to a boil, and cook 10 minutes. Add the figs one by one and cook over medium heat 30 minutes. Cool in the syrup overnight.

Makes about 3 pints.

MELKTERT
Milk Pie

1½ cups flour	½ tangerine or orange, cut in
¼ teaspoon salt	pieces
½ cup shortening	5 tablespoons sugar
3 tablespoons ice water	2 tablespoons butter
2 cups milk	2 eggs
1 cinnamon stick	½ teaspoon cinnamon

Sift 1¼ cups of the flour and the salt into a bowl; cut in the shortening with a pastry blender or two knives. Toss in the water until a ball of dough is formed. Roll out and fit into a 9-inch pie plate, fluting the edges. Chill while preparing the filling.

Combine the milk, cinnamon stick and tangerine in a saucepan; bring to a boil. Cool to lukewarm, and discard the cinnamon stick and tangerine.

Mix 4 tablespoons sugar with the remaining flour. Gradually stir in the milk. Cook, stirring steadily, until thickened. Remove from the heat and stir in the butter. Cool and beat in the eggs. Pour into the pie shell. Sprinkle with remaining sugar. Bake in a 450° oven for 20 minutes. Reduce heat to 350° and bake 10 minutes longer. Sprinkle with the cinnamon and serve warm.

Serves 6.

Spain

THE Spanish Embassy is an attractive building externally, and its interior is exquisitely detailed. Few foreign embassies in the Washington area have such a wealth of fine detail, executed almost to a point of perfection.

In the entranceway, there is the original emblem given to the first diplomatic mission sent to the United States in 1789 by the King of Spain. On the opposite wall are several small religious paintings.

An interesting reception room is the Yellow Salon, a delightful place which is renowned in diplomatic circles for its fine proportions and cheerful hues. There is a fine portrait of Charles III, well placed opposite the mantel.

Perhaps the outstanding single room in the embassy is the Red Salon, decorated in dramatic and resplendent fashion. The walls at the end are covered with remarkable tapestries woven during the early seventeenth century by Raes, a master craftsman; the other walls feature excellent paintings. The furniture is richly upholstered in silks, velvets and damasks, all in handsome colors.

Luncheons tend to be simply served for the Ambassador, his family and friends. Evening dinner parties, although rarely large, tend to be somewhat formal. The dining room itself is handsomely decorated, and the table appointments are quite interesting.

Embajada de Espagna

INFORMAL MENU

Gazpacho Andaluz

Pescado a la Andalucia
MONTILLA

Paella Valenciana
VALDEPEÑAS

Tocino de Cielo
Café

GAZPACHO ANDALUZ
Cold Vegetable Soup

2 tomatoes, peeled
1 cucumber, peeled and sliced
2 green peppers, seeded and
    sliced
1 small onion, peeled
1 clove garlic
3 tablespoons olive oil

3 tablespoons wine vinegar
6 slices white bread, trimmed
    and cubed
4 cups water
1½ teaspoons salt
½ teaspoon black pepper

Garnish:

1 cup croutons
½ cup chopped green onions

1 cup diced cucumbers

Combine all the ingredients (except the garnish) in an electric blender bowl. Purée until very smooth. Chill very well. Just before serving, check consistency. The soup should be thick, but not solid. Add a little ice water if necessary. Serve in cups, with the garnish in individual bowls.

Serves 8.

୦⊂▭⊃୦

PESCADO A LA ANDALUCIA
Fish with Walnut Sauce

4 fillets of sole or 8 slices
    snapper or sea bass
2 teaspoons salt
½ teaspoon pepper
3 tablespoons olive oil

¾ cup ground walnuts
1 clove garlic, minced
1 cup minced onions
2 tablespoons minced parsley
½ cup tomato juice

If fillets are used, cut each in half crosswise. Rinse and dry the fish; season with the salt and pepper. Brush a shallow baking dish with half the oil. Mix together the remaining oil, the walnuts, garlic, onions, parsley, and tomato juice. Spread half the mixture in the dish. Arrange the fish in it in a single layer and cover with the remaining nut mixture. Cover the dish and bake in a 350° oven 40 minutes, removing the cover for the last 10 minutes.

Serves 8.

PAELLA VALENCIANA
Chicken, Rice and Seafood

2 dozen clams	4 cups long grain rice
2 1½-pound live lobsters	½ teaspoon powdered saffron
1 3-pound chicken, disjointed	8 cups boiling chicken broth or
½ cup lard or olive oil	water
2 chorizos (Spanish sausages) cut in 1-inch pieces	1 clove garlic, minced
3 tomatoes, peeled and diced	2½ teaspoons salt
2 sweet red peppers, cut julienne	½ teaspoon black pepper
½ pound scallops	1 cup canned green peas
	8 cooked or canned artichoke hearts

Wash and scrub the clams. Cut the live lobsters into small pieces, in the shell. Wash and dry the chicken.

Heat the lard or oil in a skillet; brown the chicken pieces in it. A "paellera" — a shallow, large, two-handled metal pan — is customarily used for making paella. Any large shallow pan can be used.

Arrange the chicken in the pan, then over it the clams, lobster, chorizos, tomatoes, peppers and scallops. Spread the rice over all. Mix together the saffron, broth, garlic, salt and pepper; pour the mixture into the pan. Cover, bring to a boil and cook over high heat 10 minutes. Arrange the peas and artichokes on top of the rice. Re-cover and cook over low heat 10 minutes longer, or until the rice is tender. Serve directly from the pan.

Serves 8.

TOCINO DE CIELO
Heavenly Custard

3¼ cups sugar   24 egg yolks
1¾ cups water

Combine 6 tablespoons of the sugar and 2 teaspoons of the water in a saucepan. Cook over low heat, stirring steadily, until mixture is clear. Pour into 8 custard cups.

Cook the remaining sugar and water until a thread is formed when a fork is lifted from it.

Beat the egg yolks until light in color. Drop by drop, beat in the hot syrup until eggs warm slightly, then add the syrup faster, still beating steadily. Strain into the custard cups. Cover tightly with foil and place cups in a pan of hot water. Bake in a preheated 350° oven 50 minutes, or until a knife inserted in the center comes out clear.

Serves 8.

Sweden

MANY diplomats regard the Swedish Embassy as one of the most attractive in Washington, a city of handsome embassy buildings. Although of good size, it is far from being as large as that of many other countries. The embassy, however, seems to create a perfect compromise between size and distinction.

The entrance hall features a wide marble staircase, partially covered by carpeting. Along the walls of the stairwell, numerous paintings are arranged, mostly seascapes. The Ambassador and his family particularly enjoy the comfort of the library, a fair-sized room, which has a rather modern-looking fireplace along one side. Much of the furniture has an ornate Italianate appearance, with light-colored upholstery. The

wooden furniture is sometimes elaborately carved, also remniscent of Italy. As a contrast, many of the decorative articles are from other parts of the world, notably a carved wooden plaque dating back to the fourteenth century, found in an old church in Trebizond, Turkey.

The embassy's drawing room is more than merely large, it is almost enormous in scale. The walls are painted a pale color, and the wall-to-wall carpeting is also a light shade. Tall French windows have white curtains and off-white drapes. The furniture, looking quite small in relation to the room's size, is basically French, and covered in fine, pale colors. Several medium-dark tapestries are used on the walls to offer contrast to the room's delicate coloring.

[309]

Royal Swedish Embassy

FORMAL MENU

Kaviarlåda

Buljong med Klimp

Lammstek

Potatismos

Helstekt Lök

Stekt Svamp

Tusenbladstårt

KAVIARLÅDA
Caviar Custard

1⅓ cups heavy cream
1⅓ cups fresh bread crumbs
12 eggs

1 cup minced chives
8 ounces black caviar
6 tablespoons butter

Scald the cream, then pour it over the bread crumbs. Let stand 10 minutes. Beat the eggs and mix in the undrained bread crumbs. Stir in the chives and caviar. Spoon into ten buttered custard cups or other individual baking dishes. Dot with the butter. Bake in a preheated 325° oven 20 minutes, or until a knife inserted in the center comes out clean. Serve hot.

Serves 10.

BULJONG MED KLIMP
Consommé with Dumplings

Consommé:

2 pounds soup meat
1 pound beef bones, cracked
3 quarts water
1½ tablespoons salt
4 carrots
2 leeks
2 stalks celery and leaves

2 parsnips
2 onions
4 sprigs parsley
1 bay leaf
1 clove
12 peppercorns
4 egg whites, lightly beaten

Wash the meat and bones and cut the meat into cubes. Combine the meat, bones and water in a saucepan. Bring to a boil and skim the top. Add the salt, vegetables and spices. Bring to a boil again, cover and cook over low heat 3 hours. Strain and chill. Remove all the fat.

Put the egg whites in a saucepan. Add the soup and bring to a boil, stirring constantly. Boil 2 minutes, cover and let stand off the heat for 30 minutes. Strain through cheesecloth.

Dumplings:

2 tablespoons butter	1 teaspoon sugar
5 tablespoons flour	¼ teaspoon ground cardamon
1½ cups milk	Ground blanched toasted
½ teaspoon salt	almonds
2 egg yolks	

Melt the butter in a saucepan; blend in the flour, add the milk, stirring steadily to the boiling point, then cook over low heat 10 minutes, stirring occasionally.

Beat the salt and egg yolks in a bowl. Gradually add the hot sauce, stirring steadily to prevent curdling. Return to the saucepan and cook, stirring steadily, for 2 minutes. Mix in the sugar and cardamon. Rinse a small bowl with cold water, then turn the paste into it. Let stand 1½ hours.

Bring the soup to a boil, and drop the dumpling mixture into it by the scant teaspoon. Serve in consommé cups, sprinkled with almonds.

Serves 10.

LAMMSTEK
Roast Leg of Lamb

5-pound leg of lamb	2 cups beef broth
1 tablespoon salt	1 cup strong-brewed coffee.
½ teaspoon white pepper	¼ cup heavy cream
2 carrots, sliced	½ teaspoon sugar
2 onions, sliced	3 tablespoons flour

Rinse, trim and dry the lamb; rub with the salt and pepper. Place the leg in a roasting pan and roast in a 450° oven 20 minutes, turning the leg to brown all sides. Pour off the fat. Add the carrots, onions and 1 cup of the broth. Reduce heat to 350° and roast 45 minutes, basting occasionally. Add the mixture of coffee, cream and sugar; roast 45 minutes longer, basting occasionally.

Transfer the leg to a heated platter. Strain the pan juices and skim the fat. Mix the flour with a little of the remaining broth and stir into the pan juices, cooking and stirring over low heat until mixture boils. Add the remaining broth and cook 5 minutes longer. Taste for seasoning. Serve the gravy in a sauceboat.

Serves 10.

POTATISMOS
Duchess Potatoes

3 pounds potatoes	2 teaspoons salt
6 tablespoons butter	½ teaspoon white pepper
5 egg yolks	

Peel the potatoes and cook until tender. Drain and mash very smooth. Beat in the butter, egg yolks, salt and pepper. Heap in a heatproof serving dish and place under the broiler until delicately browned.

Serves 10.

HELSTEKT LÖK
Glazed Onions

1½ pounds small white onions	6 tablespoons butter
1 quart water	2 teaspoons brown sugar
2 teaspoons salt	½ cup beef broth

Peel the onions. Bring the water and 1 teaspoon of the salt to a boil. Add the onions and cook 5 minutes. Drain and dry the onions.

Melt the butter in a skillet; add the onions, brown sugar and remaining salt. Cook over medium heat, shaking the pan frequently, until onions brown. Add the broth; cover and cook over low heat 10 minutes, or until onions are tender but still firm.

Serves 10.

STEKT SVAMP
Sautéed Mushrooms

3 pounds mushrooms	½ teaspoon white pepper
¼ pound butter	½ teaspoon lemon juice
1¼ teaspoons salt	

Trim the stem ends of the mushrooms; wash and dry. Melt the butter in a large skillet. Add the mushrooms; sauté 10 minutes, shaking the pan frequently. Season with the salt, pepper and lemon juice.

Serves 10.

TUSENBLADSTÅRT
Puff Paste Cream Tart

Pastry:

1⅔ cups flour	¼ cup ice water
½ pound sweet butter	3 tablespoons sugar

Sift the flour into a bowl; cut in the butter with a pastry blender or two knives until small particles are formed. With a wooden spoon, gradually mix in the ice water until a ball of dough is formed. Wrap in a damp towel and chill 30 minutes.

Divide the dough into six equal pieces, and roll out each piece into a 9-inch circle. Place each circle on wax paper-lined baking sheets. Prick the tops all over with a fork, and sprinkle with sugar. Bake in a preheated 450° oven 7 minutes, or until tops are golden brown. Cool, then remove carefully from the paper.

Filling:

3 egg yolks	5 tablespoons butter
1 tablespoon cornstarch	1 teaspoon vanilla extract
6 tablespoons sugar	2 cups applesauce
1⅓ cups heavy cream	

Beat the egg yolks in the top of a double boiler. Stir in the cornstarch and sugar until smooth, then mix in the cream and the butter. Place over hot water and cook, stirring steadily, until thickened and smooth. Remove from the heat and add the vanilla. Cool, stirring occasionally.

Spread the pastry layers alternately with applesauce and cream filling, sandwiching them together. Leave the top layer plain.

Topping:

1 cup confectioners' sugar	1 teaspoon sugar
2 teaspoons lemon juice	½ cup crushed toasted almonds
2 tablespoons water	Candied fruits
1 cup heavy cream	

Sift the confectioners' sugar into a bowl; stir in the lemon juice and water until it is a spreadable consistency. If too dry, add a little more water. Spread the mixture evenly over the top.

Whip the cream with the sugar and pipe around the sides of the tart. Sprinkle the almonds around the top edge of the tart and decorate with candied fruits.

Switzerland

AN impressive driveway leads from the streets of Washington to the extensive grounds of the Swiss Embassy. The physical setting of the embassy, surrounded by trees and rolling greens, and landscaped with shrubs and plants, is most attractive.

The entrance hall has a marble-enclosed fireplace, and there is a good-sized stairway which leads to the upper floors.

The formal drawing room, at its east end, consists entirely of casement windows, slightly bowed outward, offering a lovely view of the terrace and rolling lawns. On the north side of the house, the library may be found, a pleasant, friendly room, lined with books. Although the

embassy has a main dining room, there is a sort of intimate "family" dining room available when large numbers of diplomats are not expected. The second floor also features a small sitting room, intended for the use of the Ambassador's family, which has a view of the Potomac River.

The Swiss Embassy's dining room has indirect lighting; it is otherwise a quite formal room in its decor and furnishings. Built into one portion of the room is a silver closet with tray-like drawers suitable for storing an enormous quantity of silver and flatware.

Ambassade de Suisse

FORMAL MENU

Ramequins
DEZALAY CLOS DES PHILOSOPHES

Tournedos aux Truffes
Endives Braisées
PINOT NOIR LE NOTABLE

Salade Verte

Salade de Fruit   *Sablés*
CHAMPAGNE

Café

RAMEQUINS
Swiss Cheese Custard Tarts

3¼ cups sifted flour	4 egg yolks
1⅛ teaspoons salt	1 cup milk
½ pound sweet butter	1 cup grated Swiss cheese
¼ cup ice water	3 egg whites, beaten stiff
¼ cup heavy cream	

Sift 3 cups of the flour and 1 teaspoon of the salt into a bowl. Cut in the butter until very small particles are formed. Add just enough of the water to hold the particles together, tossing with a fork. Chill 2 hours.

On a lightly floured surface, roll out the dough into a rectangle; fold over into thirds. Repeat the rolling and folding three more times. Roll out the dough very thin, cut into circles large enough to fit muffin tins, and lightly press the dough into them. Chill while preparing the filling.

Mix the remaining flour and salt with the cream until smooth. Mix in the egg yolks, then the milk and finally the cheese. Fold in the beaten egg whites. Half fill the lined tins with the mixture. Bake in a preheated 375° oven 20 minutes, or until puffed and browned. Serve hot.

Makes about 20 tarts.

TOURNEDOS AUX TRUFFES
Fillet of Beef with Truffles

8 fillets of beef, cut 1 inch thick	Salt and pepper
3 tablespoons vegetable oil	⅓ cup beef broth
6 tablespoons butter	⅓ cup dry white wine
	2 truffles, cut in julienne strips

Have each fillet tied into a nice shape. Heat the oil and 2 tablespoons of the butter in a large skillet until it sizzles. Add the fillets and sauté over medium heat 3 minutes. Turn fillets over and sauté 3 minutes, or to desired degree of rareness. Transfer the fillets to a heated platter, sprinkle with salt and pepper and keep warm while preparing the sauce.

Pour the cooking fat out of the skillet and return skillet to high heat. Add the broth and wine and, with a wooden spoon, scrape the bottom of browned particles. Cook until liquid is reduced to half, then add the truffles. Remove from the heat and mix in the remaining butter until absorbed. Pour over the fillets.

Serves 8.

ENDIVES BRAISÉES
Braised Endive

16 firm endive	1½ tablespoons lemon juice
¼ pound butter	⅓ cup water
½ teaspoon salt	Parsley

Trim off the stem ends of the endive and discard discolored leaves. Wash each endive under cold running water and drain well.

Use a heatproof enamel, pottery or glass baking dish. Rub the dish heavily with butter, then arrange the endive in two layers, sprinkling each layer with salt and lemon juice, and dot with butter (reserve and melt 2 tablespoons). Add the water; cover, bring to a boil and cook over medium heat 10 minutes.

Remove the cover, and place a piece of buttered parchment or brown or wax paper over the endive. Replace the cover and bake in a preheated 325° oven 30 minutes. Remove the cover, but leave paper on the endive. Bake 15 minutes longer. Remove the paper. Pour the melted butter over the top and place under the broiler until delicately browned. Sprinkle with parsley.

Serves 8.

SALADE DE FRUIT

Any combination of fresh fruits, according to the season, may be used. Cut them into bite-sized pieces and sprinkle them with a little sugar and kirsch (cherry liqueur). Chill for an hour or so, then serve topped with whipped cream.

SABLÉS
Butter Cookies

1¾ cups sifted flour
½ cup sugar

¼ pound plus 2 tablespoons
butter
1 teaspoon vanilla extract

Sift the flour and sugar into a bowl. Cut in the butter until a smooth dough is formed, adding the vanilla when particles begin adhering.

Roll out the dough thin and cut with a round cookie cutter. Transfer to a baking sheet and bake in a preheated 375° oven 8 minutes, or until delicately browned.

Makes about 36 cookies.

Thailand

THE Royal Thai Embassy is decorated with lustrous handwoven Thai silks and numerous artifacts. Embassy guests find much to intrigue the eye and mind, for the many carvings and figures are unique art forms.

The dining room has painted brick walls, with an open fireplace on one long wall. Huge Thai designs are on either side of the low windows, and three crystal chandeliers hang from the ceiling.

There is a horseshoe table which is usually covered with a fitted Thai silk cloth. Four tall silver candelabra are placed around the table at suitable intervals. The china and flatware bear the Royal Thai crest, an imposing design. Guests are seated on both sides of the horseshoe table, making the gathering more intimate, and conversation easier.

Royal Thai Embassy

FORMAL MENU

Kaeng Chüd

Hor-Mok

Kaeng Masaman

Fried Rice

'Tossed Green Salad

Tako Saku

KAENG CHÜD
Chicken-Mushroom Soup

4-pound chicken
3½ quarts water
2 teaspoons salt
4 peppercorns
2 cloves garlic
8 coriander seeds

2 tablespoons chopped Chinese
    parsley (or minced
    coriander leaves)
1 teaspoon anchovy paste
1 12-ounce can sliced mush-
    rooms

Wash the chicken and giblets and put in a saucepan with the water. Bring to a boil and add the salt. Cover loosely and cook over low heat 1½ hours. Remove the chicken and giblets. Remove the skin of the chicken and cut the meat and giblets into small pieces. Place the pieces between two plates weighing them down.

Return the skin and bones to the stock, and cook over low heat 2 hours. Strain. Skim the fat and reserve.

Pound together the peppercorns, garlic, coriander and parsley until fine. Heat 2 tablespoons of the reserved fat in a skillet. Add the pounded ingredients and fry 3 minutes, stirring frequently. Blend in the anchovy paste, then add the chicken pieces and giblets. Cook 2 minutes, stirring. Add to the stock and bring to a boil. Add the mushrooms, cover and cook 5 minutes. Serve very hot in Chinese soup cups or bouillon cups.

Serves 10.

HOR-MOK
Steamed Fish Curry

3 pounds fish fillets
2 tablespoons anchovy paste
2 teapoons minced garlic
1½ cups shredded packaged
    coconut
3 cups milk
1 tablespoon salt
¾ teaspoon dried ground chili
    peppers
8 peppercorns

6 coriander seeds
1 teaspoon grated lemon rind
3 tablespoons chopped shallots
    or onions
1 egg, beaten
10 large cabbage leaves
½ cup thinly sliced green
    onions
4 tablespoons minced Chinese
    parsley

Wash the fish and cut into paper-thin julienne strips. Add the anchovy paste and garlic. Mix well and refrigerate while preparing the coconut milk.

Rinse the coconut under cold running water, then combine in a saucepan with the milk. Bring to a boil, remove from the heat and let stand 30 minutes. Run the coconut and milk in an electric blender or strain. Add the milk to the fish, mixing well.

Pound together the salt, chili peppers, peppercorns, coriander seeds, lemon rind and shallots until a paste is formed. Add to the fish and mix well. Mix in the egg, stirring with a wooden spoon until thickened.

Cut ten pieces of aluminum foil or parchment paper about 8 inches long. On each, place a cabbage leaf. Divide the fish mixture among them, pouring any excess liquid on top. Sprinkle the tops with the green onions and parsley. Fold over the leaves, then make envelope-type packages with the foil. (In Thailand, banana leaves are used in place of the foil.)

Put a rack in a deep pan, and add hot water to reach the rack. Arrange the packages on the rack. Cover the pan, and cook over medium heat 45 minutes, adding boiling water from time to time to maintain the water level. Unwrap the packages and serve the fish in the cabbage leaves. *Serves 10.*

⊶⊷

KAENG MASAMAN
Beef Curry

4 pounds sirloin steak	2 tablespoons minced ginger
1½ cups shredded packaged	root
coconut	1 tablespoon caraway seeds
3 cups milk	4 cloves
2 tablespoons soy sauce	1 teaspoon salt
¾ cup ground peanuts	Seeds of 3 cardamons
5 cloves garlic	¼ teaspoon mace
8 shallots or 2 white onions	1 bay leaf
1 tablespoon coriander seeds	1 teaspoon cinnamon
1 teaspoon dried ground chili	1 teaspoon anchovy paste
peppers	3 tablespoons grenadine
	3 tablespoons lemon juice

Cut the meat into shoestring pieces. Rinse the coconut under cold running water, then combine in a saucepan with the milk. Bring to a boil, and let stand 30 minutes. Run the coconut and milk in an electric blender or strain. Combine the coconut milk, soy sauce, peanuts and meat in a saucepan. Bring to a boil and cook 25 minutes. Remove the meat and cook the liquid over high heat 5 minutes.

While the meat is cooking, peel the garlic and shallots or onions. Place in a small oiled skillet and brown the garlic and shallots or onions in it on all sides. Chop fine, then add the coriander, chili peppers, ginger, caraway, cloves, salt, cardamon, mace, bay leaf and cinnamon. Pound to a paste, then blend in the anchovy paste.

Stir this paste into the coconut cream and cook over low heat 5 minutes. Return the meat to the sauce. Cover tightly and cook over low heat 15 minutes. Blend in the grenadine and lemon juice. Serve hot. *Serves 10.*

FRIED RICE

¼ pound butter
2 teaspoons minced garlic
1 cup diced onions
1 pound ground beef
2 tablespoons curry powder

4 cups cold cooked drained
   rice
½ cup sliced green onions
3 tablespoons minced parsley

Melt the butter in a large skillet; add the garlic, onions, meat and curry powder. Cook, stirring steadily, until meat browns. Add the rice and cook, stirring frequently, for 5 minutes. Serve sprinkled with the green onions and parsley, and, if desired, a one-egg omelet, cut into julienne pieces.

Serves 10.

TAKO SAKU
Tapioca-Coconut Pudding

3 cups shredded packaged
   coconut
6 cups milk
1½ cups tapioca

1½ cups brown sugar, packed
¾ cup rice flour
1½ teaspoons salt

Combine the coconut and milk in a saucepan. Bring to a boil and let stand 30 minutes. Run the coconut and milk in an electric blender or strain.

Combine 3 cups of the coconut milk and the tapioca in a saucepan. Bring to a boil and cook over low heat 20 minutes. Dissolve the brown sugar in 1½ cups of the coconut milk and add to the tapioca. Cook over low heat, stirring very frequently, for 10 minutes, or until thickened. Cool slightly and pour into a serving dish.

Blend the rice flour and salt with the remaining coconut milk. Cook, stirring steadily, to the boiling point, then cook 5 minutes longer. Pour over the tapioca. Serve hot or cold.

Serves 10.

Trinidad and Tobago

THE embassy is used mainly as an office. The Ambassador entertains on official occasions in his own home.

Embassy of Trinidad and Tobago

FORMAL MENU

Trinidad Rum Punch
Cream of Cucumber Soup
Baked Stuffed Fish
Salmi of Duck
Eggplant au Gratin   Rice
Mixed Salad
Coconut Jelly
Coffee
Guava Liqueur

TRINIDAD RUM PUNCH

¾ cup water
½ cup sugar
½ cup lime or lemon juice

1½ cups light rum
2 teaspoons Angostura bitters

Bring the water and sugar to a boil, stirring constantly until the sugar dissolves, then cook 5 minutes without stirring. Chill. Mix the chilled syrup with all the remaining ingredients. It is customary for this punch to be prepared a few days before serving. Serve very cold.
Serves 6.

CREAM OF CUCUMBER SOUP

3 large cucumbers
4 tablespoons butter
3 tablespoons flour
1 cup milk
3 cups chicken broth

1 teaspoon salt
¼ teaspoon white pepper
½ cup heavy cream
1 teaspoon Angostura bitters

Peel and thinly slice the cucumbers. Melt 2 tablespoons of the butter in a skillet; add the cucumbers, and cook over low heat 5 minutes, stirring frequently. Don't let the cucumbers brown.

Melt the remaining butter in a saucepan; blend in the flour until smooth. Gradually add the milk and broth, stirring steadily to the boiling point. Add the cucumbers; cook over low heat 15 minutes, or until the cucumbers are soft. Purée the mixture in an electric blender or force through a sieve. Return to the saucepan and add the salt and pepper. Reheat, and, just before serving, stir in the cream and bitters.
Serves 6.

BAKED STUFFED FISH

2 2-pound red snappers or mackerels	½ cup fresh bread crumbs
2½ teaspoons salt	¼ cup chopped dill pickles
¾ teaspoon pepper	1 tablespoon capers
4 tablespoons butter	3 tablespoons minced parsley
½ cup chopped onions	3 hard-cooked eggs, chopped
½ cup chopped green peppers	⅓ cup olive oil
	¼ cup dry bread crumbs

Have the fish split for stuffing, and the head removed or not, as you prefer. Wash and dry the fish. Rub the skin with 2 teaspoons of the salt and ½ teaspoon pepper.

Melt the butter in a skillet; sauté the onions and green peppers 10 minutes, stirring frequently. Mix in the fresh bread crumbs, pickles, capers, parsley, chopped eggs and the remaining salt and pepper. Divide the stuffing between the fish, and skewer or sew the openings.

In a shallow pan heat the oil until it bubbles. Place the fish in it and sprinkle the tops with the dry bread crumbs. Bake in a 350° oven 45 minutes, or until the fish flakes easily when tested with a fork. Baste frequently.

Serves 6.

SALMI OF DUCK

2 5-pound ducks, disjointed	1½ tablespoons vinegar
2½ teaspoons salt	1 tablespoon sugar
½ teaspoon black pepper	½ teaspoon thyme
⅛ teaspoon powdered cloves	¼ cup dry red wine
2 cloves garlic, minced	1 tablespoon flour
4 tablespoons vegetable oil	½ cup sliced green olives
1 cup sliced onions	1 teaspoon capers
2 cups boiling water	1 tablespoon Angostura bitters
1½ cups peeled diced tomatoes	

Wash and dry the duck pieces; rub with a mixture of the salt, pepper, cloves and garlic. Let stand 30 minutes.

Heat the oil in a Dutch oven or casserole; brown the duck in it. Pour off the fat. Add the onions; cook 5 minutes. Add 1 cup of the water. Cover and cook over low heat 30 minutes, adding the remaining water from time to time. Add the tomatoes, vinegar, sugar and thyme. Re-cover and cook 30 minutes.

Mix the wine and flour until smooth, then stir into the gravy. Cook 5 minutes. Add the olives, capers and bitters.

Serves 6 to 8.

EGGPLANT AU GRATIN

2 eggplants	1½ teaspoons salt
6 tablespoons butter	½ teaspoon black pepper
1 cup chopped onions	3 tablespoons dry bread crumbs
1 cup peeled chopped tomatoes	

Wash the eggplants, wrap loosely in aluminum foil and bake in a 375° oven 1 hour. Let stand until cool enough to handle, then peel and chop the eggplant.

Melt 4 tablespoons of the butter in a skillet; sauté the onions 5 minutes. Add the tomatoes, salt and pepper; cook over low heat 10 minutes. Mix in the eggplant; cook 5 minutes, stirring frequently. Turn the mixture into a greased 9-inch pie plate. Sprinkle the top with the bread crumbs and dot with the remaining butter. Place on the upper level of a 450° oven for 10 minutes, or until the tip is browned.

Serves 6.

MIXED SALAD

1 head lettuce	¼ cup lime or lemon juice
2 tomatoes	½ teaspoon salt
3 avocados	¼ teaspoon black pepper
¾ cup olive oil	

[333]

Wash and dry the lettuce; tear into serving-sized pieces. Peel the tomatoes and cut them into eighths. Peel and slice the avocados. Arrange the prepared ingredients on salad plates. Make a dressing of the oil, fruit juice, salt and pepper; pour over the salads.

Serves 6.

COCONUT JELLY

2 cups grated coconut	¼ cup sugar
4 cups milk	Candied cherries
2 envelopes (2 tablespoons) gelatin	

Combine the coconut and 3 cups of the milk in a saucepan. Bring to a boil, remove from the heat and let stand 30 minutes. Strain the milk, pressing the coconut to extract all the liquid.

Sprinkle the gelatin into the remaining milk. Add the sugar, place over hot water and stir until gelatin and sugar dissolve. Add to the coconut milk. Pour into a lightly oiled 1-quart mold, or into six individual serving dishes. Chill until set. Serve garnished with candied cherries, or a mixture of candied fruits.

Serves 6.

Turkey

ONCE *an elaboarate private mansion, the Turkish Embassy gives an overall impression remniscent of the Italian Renaissance. Although the house was remodeled for embassy usage, many of its original features have been retained. The four-story building has an enormous entrance gallery of black and white marble which is very striking in appearance. On the right-hand side, where the former owner had a billiard room, there is now the private study of the Ambassador, a room paneled in dark woods, hung with oil paintings.*

The center stairway is positioned in the middle of the foyer. Halfway up the flight of stairs there is a large music gallery. From here, by means of a double staircase, the various reception rooms may be reached.

The main reception room is renowned for its remarkable Chinese teak-wood floors, burnished to a high degree of luster, and partly covered with fine rugs. The drawing room has a French theme, with curved arched windows, recessed drapes, double marble fireplaces and brilliantly lit chandeliers.

On the opposite side of the drawing room, the embassy has its richly furnished dining room. The walls are paneled in mahogany, intricately carved in the Old World style. The table service is elegant, and the embassy is well known in diplomatic circles for its elaborate repasts and skillful formal service.

Embassy of Turkey

FORMAL DINNER MENU

Shishti Bosphorus
MERSAULT

Bildircinli
Pilaf Ali Pasha
BUZBAG, TURKISH RED WINE

Yer Elmasi
Tchoubouk Baklava
CHAMPAGNE

Café Turc

DINNER MENU

Tarama   Beurek
Yaprak Dolmasi
Cerkes Tavugu
Taze Fasulya Zeytinyağli
Serail Mahallebi
Café Turc

FAMILY DINNER

Yoğurt Çorbasi
Tas Kebab   Beyendi
Portakal Kompostosu

SHISHTI BOSPHORUS
Lobster on Skewers

12 lobsters or 24 lobster tails	1 tablespoon salt
3 cups dry white wine	1½ teaspoons white pepper
½ cup lemon juice	Mushroom caps
½ cup vegetable oil	½ cup heated brandy
¼ cup grated onion	

Remove the meat of the raw lobsters and cut into 2-inch pieces. In a glass or pottery bowl, mix together the wine, lemon juice, oil, onion, salt and pepper. Marinate the lobster pieces in the mixture overnight in the refrigerator, basting and turning a few times. Drain.

Put the mushroom caps in the marinade, and let stand 10 minutes. Using 12 oiled skewers, alternately thread the lobster pieces and mushroom caps, starting and ending with the lobster. Arrange the skewers on a broiling pan, and broil in a hot broiler 10 minutes, turning the skewers to cook all sides.

Arrange the skewers on a serving dish. Pour the warm brandy over them, set aflame and serve flaming.

Serves 12.

BILDIRCINLI
Broiled Quail

24 quail	2 cups chopped mushrooms
½ pound butter	½ cup dry red wine
4 teaspoons salt	24 sautéed bread rounds
1½ teaspoons pepper	3 inches across
2 cups fine bread crumbs	

Have the quail split. Chop or grind the livers and giblets. Wash and dry the quail. Melt all but 4 tablespoons butter and brush the quail with the melted butter inside and out, then season with the salt and pepper. Sprinkle the quail inside and out with the bread crumbs. Arrange on broiling pan and broil 10 minutes on each side, basting frequently with melted butter.

While the quail are broiling, melt the remaining butter. Sauté the chopped liver mixture and mushrooms 5 minutes. Add the wine and salt and pepper to taste. Cook over low heat 10 minutes. Spread the mixture on the sautéed bread and put a broiled quail on each.

Serves 12.

PILAF ALI PASHA
Rice and Nuts

1½ cups dried black currants	1½ teaspoons pepper
6 cups converted rice	½ teaspoon ground allspice
½ pound butter	1 tablespoon sugar
1½ cups chopped onions	3 tablespoons tomato paste
¾ cup pine nuts	2 cups sliced scallions
12 cups boiling chicken broth	Chopped fresh dill
1 tablespoon salt	

Wash the currants thoroughly, then soak in hot water for 30 minutes. Drain and dry. Put the rice in a bowl and wash in cold water until the water runs clear. Drain well and dry in a towel.

In a large heavy pan, melt the butter; sauté the onions until golden. Add the rice and nuts; cook, stirring steadily, for 3 minutes. Add the broth, stir well and remove from the heat. Mix in the salt, pepper, allspice, sugar, tomato paste and scallions. Cover tightly and cook over low heat until the liquid is absorbed, about 20 minutes. Sprinkle the currants on top. Re-cover, place pan on an asbestos pad over very low heat for 1 hour. Stir with two forks. Sprinkle with dill before serving. *Serves 12.*

YER ELMASI
Braised Artichokes

24 artichokes	3 tablespoons sugar
10 lemons	1 tablespoon salt
⅔ cup olive oil	5 cups boiling water
3 cups chopped onions	Chopped fresh dill

Select tightly formed, even-sized artichokes. To help open the leaves, shake and press two together. Gently remove all the leaves of artichokes, leaving the stem and bottom. Peel off the outer rough skin of the stem. With a vegetable scraper, carefully round the bottom, starting at the stem. Rub all exposed surfaces with a cut lemon to keep it from darkening. Fill a bowl with ice water, add the juice and peel of 5 lemons, and, as each artichoke is prepared, put it into the bowl. With a small spoon, scoop out the fuzzy centers, and rub the inside with lemon.

Heat the oil in a large pan; add the onions and cook over low heat until soft but do not let brown. Drain the artichokes and arrange in the pan in layers. Add the sugar, salt and juice of the remaining lemons. Cover, and cook over low heat until artichokes begin to turn golden, shaking the pan occasionally. Add the water; cover with waxed paper, and a heavy plate to weigh the artichokes down. The water should reach the level of the plate. Cover the pan and cook over low heat 1½ hours. Let cool; cover to prevent artichokes from changing color. Serve sprinkled with dill.

Serves 8 to 12.

TCHOUBOUK BAKLAVA
Walnut Pastries

1 pound yufka, philo leaves or strudel leaves	1½ cups ground walnuts
2 cups sugar	Egg white
½ cup water	Vegetable oil for deep frying
2 teaspoons lemon juice	1½ cups whipped cream
3 tablespoons rum	1 cup chopped green pistachio nuts

Yufka, philo leaves and strudel leaves are paper-thin sheets of pastry, available in Middle East or specialty food shops. They must be kept covered with a wet cloth when working with them, to keep them from drying out.

Cook the sugar and water until syrupy, stirring only until the sugar dissolves. Cool and mix in the lemon juice and half the rum.

Cut a strip of pastry lengthwise about 4 inches wide. (Cover unused portions with wet cloth.) Put a teaspoonful of walnuts on one end and roll up, sealing the edges with egg white. Continue making the pastries. Heat the oil to 375° and fry four or five at a time until golden brown. Drain, and place in the cold syrup.

Arrange the pastries on an oval serving dish and pour any extra syrup over them. Mix the remaining rum into the whipped cream, and heap it in the center. Sprinkle the pistachio nuts over all.

Makes about 60.

CAFÉ TURC
Turkish Coffee

Turkish-style coffee is best made in individual portions, but it may be made for not more than four people with moderate, although not complete, success. For perfect coffee, buy a long-handled brass *çezve*, a Turkish utensil specifically designed for the purpose. If you are making only one cup at a time, place 2 rounded teaspoons of finely ground Turkish coffee (American coffee is not satisfactory) in the *çezve*, add 1 or 2 teaspoons of sugar, and 1 demitasse cup of cold water. Bring to a boil over very low heat, and stir only once to dissolve the sugar. Remove from heat, let froth subside, and bring to the boil again; repeat a third time. Pour immediately into the demitasse cup. There will be a certain amount of sediment at the bottom of the cup, which need not be drunk.

For four people, use a small saucepan, and add 4 demitasse cups of cold water, 4 to 8 teaspoons of sugar, and 8 rounded teaspoons of finely ground Turkish coffee. Bring to the boil 3 times, as described above.

TARAMA
Caviar Spread

½ pound tarama	½ cup lemon juice
½ cup sesame or vegetable oil	2 tablespoons mayonnaise
1 tablespoon fresh bread crumbs	

Tarama, salted fish roe, is available in jars in Near Eastern or other specialty food shops.

Put the tarama in the bowl of an electric mixer. Press the grains down firmly with a wooden spoon, adding a little of the oil drop by drop. Turn mixer on, and continue adding the oil in a very slow steady stream. Add the bread crumbs, then gradually add the lemon juice. Taste the mixture after half is added. You may not need all the lemon juice, or, if you like it tart, use more. Beat until smooth, fluffy and a pale pink. Mix in the mayonnaise. Chill.

Serve in a mound, surrounded with thin slices of rye or pumpernickel.

Makes about 3 cups.

BEUREK
Cocktail Cheese Pastries

1 pound yufka, philo leaves or strudel leaves

1 pound Beyez cheese or ½ pound Feta and cottage cheese

½ pound butter, melted

3 eggs

2 cups chopped parsley

Yufka, philo or strudel leaves are paper-thin pieces of pastry, about 11 inches wide by 17 inches long. They are available in Middle East or specialty food shops. So is the cheese.

Mash the cheese smooth, and beat in 1 tablespoon of the melted butter, the eggs and parsley.

Brush a pastry sheet heavily with butter.

It is important to keep the pastry sheets you are not working with covered with a damp towel to keep them from drying out. Cut one sheet in half crosswise, making a piece about 11 inches by 8½ inches. Fold into thirds lengthwise, and brush the top layer with butter. Place a teaspoon of the filling on one corner of the long side, and fold over into a triangle, folding from one side to another until the other end is reached. Place on the baking sheet and cover with Saran, while preparing the balance. When all are made, brush the tops with butter, then bake in a preheated 325° oven 30 minutes, or until golden in color. Serve warm. The beureks may be reheated, if desired.

Makes about 45.

YAPRAK DOLMASI
Stuffed Grape Leaves

1 quart jar grape leaves

½ cup raw rice

1 pound onions

4 tablespoons butter

¼ cup lemon juice
2 teaspoons salt
1½ teaspoons black pepper
2 teaspoons sugar
1 tablespoon tomato paste

1 tablespoon chopped fresh dill
    or 1 teaspoon, dried
4 drops rose water
2 pounds ground beef

Grape leaves are available in Middle East or specialty food shops. Wash the leaves in cold water several times to remove the salt, then let them drain thoroughly in a colander. Soak the rice in boiling water for 15 minutes, then drain well.

Grate the onions on a fine grater. Melt the butter in a skillet; add the onions and cook, stirring with a wooden spoon, until golden. Mix in the lemon juice, salt, pepper, sugar, tomato paste, dill, rose water and rice. Cook over low heat, stirring frequently, until all the liquid is absorbed. Remove from heat and let cool 15 minutes. Mix in the meat very well.

Put a leaf on a plate, smooth side down. Cut off the stem. In the center of the leaf, put some filling, shaping it into a rectangle 2 inches long and 1 inch wide. Fold over the piece opposite the stem end, then the stem end, then the other corners. The completed dolma should look like a cigar. Continue making the dolma one by one.

Use a heavy stainless steel Dutch oven. Cover the bottom of the pan with aluminum foil. Starting at the outer edge, arrange the dolma in a circle, working towards the center, wrapped sides down so they will not unwrap while cooking. Make as many layers as necessary. Put a plate on top of the last layer and weigh it down. Add enough boiling water to reach the top of the plate. Cook over very low heat for 2 hours. Cool.

When ready to serve, heat, then pour off the liquid and reserve. Place a large plate over the pan, turn pan over and unmold the dolma. They should come out in a compact cake. Pour the liquid over the top, and serve with a bowl of yogurt or sour cream.

Makes about 60.

◦⟨⟩⟩

CERKES TAVUGU
Circassian Chicken

2 4-pound pullets
2 quarts water
1 onion
2 stalks celery
1 carrot
1 bay leaf

2 cloves garlic
1 tablespoon salt
1 pound shelled walnuts
3 slices white bread, trimmed
1 tablespoon paprika
⅛ teaspoon cayenne pepper

Clean and wash the chickens. Combine in a kettle with the water, onion, celery, carrot, bay leaf and garlic. Bring to a boil, cover loosely and cook over low heat 1½ hours, or until chickens are tender. Add the salt after half the cooking time. Let the chickens cool in the broth, then remove the skin and bones and cut chicken into small pieces. Strain the broth.

Put the nuts through a Mouli grater or twice through a food chopper. The nuts must be ground very fine. Soak the bread in a little broth, mash smooth and squeeze dry. Add to the walnuts with the paprika and cayenne. Put in a large bowl and, with an electric mixer or rotary beater, gradually beat in 3½ cups of the chicken broth. Beat until mixture looks like mayonnaise. Taste for seasoning. Mix 1 cup of the sauce with the chicken pieces, then arrange on a serving dish. Cover evenly with the remaining sauce. Sprinkle with paprika. Chill.
Serves 12.

◦⟨⟩⟩

TAZE FASULYA ZEYTINYAĞLI
Cold Green Beans

4 packages frozen French-cut
    green beans
¾ cup chopped onions
2 teaspoons salt

2 20-ounce cans stewed
    tomatoes
1 tablespoon sugar
¼ cup olive oil
½ cup boiling water

Thaw the beans, drain well and dry on paper towels. Combine the beans, onions and salt in a heavy saucepan. Mix very well. Mix in the tomatoes, sugar, oil and water. Put a plate over the mixture to weigh it down. If liquid doesn't reach the edges of the plate, add a little more boiling water. Cover the pan, bring to a boil and cook over low heat 1 hour. Shake the pan occasionally. Let cool covered, to prevent beans from turning yellow, then chill.

Serves 12.

SERAIL MAHALLEBI
Palace Rice Pudding

1 cup rice flour	1 cup sugar
6 cups milk	1 cup shredded coconut

Rice flour *must* be used; it is available in health food or specialty food shops.

Mix the rice flour with a little of the milk until very smooth and free of lumps. Combine the remaining milk, sugar, half the coconut and the rice flour in a heavy saucepan. Cook over very low heat, stirring steadily with a wooden spoon until it begins to thicken, then cook until very thick. Pour into 12 serving dishes. Serve chilled, sprinkled with the remaining coconut.

Serves 12.

YOĞURT ÇORBASI
Anatolian Soup

6 cups beef broth	3 egg yolks
4 tablespoons rice	½ cup yogurt
2 tablespoons flour	Chopped fresh mint
1 cup cold water	Melted butter

Bring the broth to a boil. Break up the rice with a rolling pin and add to the broth; cook over low heat 15 minutes.

In a small pan, mix the flour with a little water until smooth, then add all the water. Beat the egg yolks with the yogurt and a little hot broth. Add to the flour mixture. Cook, stirring steadily, until mixture boils. Add to the rice mixture, stirring well. Taste for seasoning. Serve sprinkled with mint and a little melted butter.

Serves 6 to 8.

TAS KEBAB
Lamb Stew

3 pounds boneless lamb	4 tablespoons butter
2 teaspoons salt	¾ cup chopped onions
½ teaspoon black pepper	1 20-ounce can tomatoes
3 tablespoons lemon juice	

Cut the lamb into 2-inch cubes. Sprinkle with the salt, pepper and lemon juice. Toss well, then let stand 1 hour at room temperature, mixing a few times. Drain the meat, reserving any liquid.

Melt the butter in a Dutch oven or deep skillet. Brown the lamb and onions in it very well. Add the tomatoes and reserved liquid. Bring to a boil, cover and cook over low heat 2 hours, or until the lamb is tender.

Serves 6 to 8.

BEYENDI
Puréed Eggplant

3 medium-sized eggplants	½ teaspoon white pepper
6 tablespoons butter	2 cups hot milk
4 tablespoons flour	¼ cup grated Parmesan cheese
2 teaspoons salt	1 tablespoon lemon juice

Wash and dry the eggplants. Broil them as close to the heat as possible until tender and skins turn black. Peel off the skin and mash the pulp smooth.

Melt 4 tablespoons of the butter in a saucepan; blend in the flour, salt and pepper. Add the milk, stirring steadily to the boiling point. Cook over low heat 5 minutes. Mix in the cheese, and lemon juice. Gradually add the eggplant purée. Taste for seasoning, and add more cheese if desired.

Serves 6 to 8.

PORTAKAL KOMPOSTOSU
Orange Compote

6 navel oranges	2 cups water
2 cups sugar	1 teaspoon lemon juice

Remove the peel of the oranges carefully, then cut away any white part that adheres to the peel. Cut the peel in julienne strips; cover the strips with cold water; bring to a boil and cook 10 minutes, or until tender. Drain well, and return to the pan. Add the sugar, the 2 cups water and the lemon juice. Cook, stirring steadily, until sugar dissolves, then cook over low heat 20 minutes longer.

Slice the oranges and arrange in a heatproof bowl. Pour the syrup and peel over them. Cover and cool, then chill. Serve with curaçao-flavored whipped cream, if desired.

Serves 6 to 8.

Index

Poultry. *See* Chicken; Duck; Quail; Squabs; Turkey

Prawns, Dublin Bay, IRELAND, 163

Preserves, Green Fig, SOUTH AFRICA, 299-300

Psari me Shordalia (fish with walnut sauce), GREECE, 138-139

Puddings
    Almond-Rice (Risengrød med Mandeldejg), DENMARK, 91
    Coconut (Pudim de Côco), BRAZIL, 36-37
    Corn (Pudín de Maíz), ECUADOR, 104
    Dutch Apple (Appelschoteltje), NETHERLANDS, 235
    Fruit-Nut (Roompudding), NETHERLANDS, 232-233
    Liver (Maksalaatikko), FINLAND, 109-110
    Potato (Imellytetty Perunavuoka), FINLAND, 112-113
    Rice
        Flour (Firni), PAKISTAN, 250
        Palace (Serail Mahallebi), TURKEY, 347
        Tapioca-Coconut (Tako Saku), THAILAND, 328

Pulao Yakhni (fried rice curry), INDIA, 145-146

Pumpkin Soup (Sopa de Abobora), BRAZIL, 35

Punch, Trinidad Rum, TRINIDAD AND TOBAGO, 331

Putupap (cornmeal), SOUTH AFRICA, 299

QUAIL, BROILED, 339-340

RABBIT, MARINATED (Hazepeper), NETHERLANDS, 232

Radish Salad (Po Derevenski), RUSSIA, 287

Raita (cucumbers in yogurt), INDIA, 146

Ramequins (Swiss cheese custard tarts), SWITZERLAND, 319

Raspberry
    Sauce (Himbeersauce), AUSTRIA, 13-14
    Soufflé (Soufflé aux Framboises), FRANCE, 119

Red Cabbage (Rødkaal), DENMARK, 90

Relishes. *See* Pickles and relishes

Rice
    Eight Jewel, CHINA, 76-77
    Festive, ISRAEL, 177
    Flour Pudding (Firni), PAKISTAN, 250
    Fried, THAILAND, 328

Rice (*continued*)
    Curry (Pulao Yakhni), INDIA, 145-146
    Yangchow Style, CHINA, 70-71
  and Nuts (Pilaf Ali Pasha), TURKEY, 340-341
  Pudding
    Almond (Risengrød med Mandeldejg), DENMARK, 91
    Palace (Serail Mahallebi), TURKEY, 347
    Sweet (Arroz Dôce), PORTUGAL, 278
    Wild (Riz Sauvage), BRAZIL, 33-34

Rigo Torte (chocolate torte), AUSTRIA, 17-18

Rinderroulade (beef rolls), GERMANY, 131

Risengrød med Mandeldejg (almond-rice pudding), DENMARK, 91

Rødkaal (red cabbage), DENMARK, 90

Rogan Josh (lamb curry), INDIA, 147

Roompudding (fruit-nut pudding), NETHERLANDS, 232-233

Roughan Josh (lamb stew), PAKISTAN, 247

Rum Punch, Trinidad, TRINIDAD AND TOBAGO, 331

SABAW ALMONDIGAS (meatball soup), PHILIPPINES, 268-269

Sablés (butter cookies), SWITZERLAND, 321

Salads
  Avocado
    Ensalada de Aguacates, COLOMBIA, 83
    Vinaigrette, BRITAIN, 45
  Cabbage (Krautsalad), AUSTRIA, 17
  Cucumber
    Abalone and Seaweed, JAPAN, 194-195
    Agurkesalat, DENMARK, 95
    Hors d'Oeuvre (Kurkkusalaati), FINLAND, 110
    in Yogurt (Raita), INDIA, 146
  Endive, CANADA, 53
  Heart of Palm (Salada de Palmito), BRAZIL, 34
  Hearts of Lettuce, MOROCCO, 226
  Mixed, TRINIDAD AND TOBAGO, 333-334
    Salade Sabzi, IRAN; 158
  Radish (Po Derevenski), RUSSIA, 287
  Tomato and Onion (Tomates y Cebollas), CHILE, 61
  Tara, IRELAND, 168

Salmi of Duck, TRINIDAD AND TOBAGO, 332-333

Salmon
  Broiled, with Béarnaise Sauce (Darne de

FRANCE

TRINIDAD

JAPAN

ITALY

MEXICO

AUSTRIA

GREECE

BRITAIN

GERMANY

CHILE

SOUTH AFRICA

INDIA

PERU

PAKISTAN

BELGIUM

CHINA

BRAZIL

TURKEY

THAILAND

AUSTRALIA